Dictionary of
Rational Emotive
Behaviour Therapy

Dictionary of Rational Emotive Behaviour Therapy

Windy Dryden and Michael Neenan

Whurr Publishers
London

© 1996 Whurr Publishers
First published 1996 by
Whurr Publishers Ltd
19b Compton Terrace, London N1 2UN, England

Reprinted 1997

British Library Cataloguing in Publication Data
A catalogue record for this book is available from the
British Library.

ISBN 1-897635-71-0

Photoset by Stephen Cary
Printed and bound in the UK by Athenaeum Press Ltd,
Gateshead, Tyne & Wear

Contents

Preface

As in the other books in the Whurr Dictionary Series, this dictionary is intended to provide definitions of key terms, concepts and the major treatment techniques associated with a particular school of therapy, in this case Rational Emotive Behaviour Therapy. As such we anticipate that this volume will be of use and interest to practising REBT therapists, cognitive-behavioural therapists, and trainees in REBT and CBT as well as a more general readership.

In this dictionary, we have tried to be both comprehensive and concise in explaining the theory and practice of REBT, and, hence, the dictionary is used best as an essential adjunct to more general texts on REBT. However, we do see this book as an encapsulated form of current REBT wisdom. We use the word 'current' here because we recognise that REBT concepts are continually under review and are subject to revision and refinement. As such, we invite comment from readers about any entry in this dictionary. This feedback will enable us to refine and improve the next edition. Please send any feedback to us c/o Whurr Publishers.

In conclusion, we hope that readers will find much that is interesting, stimulating and even provoking in this book. If not, this would be disappointing to us, but hardly awful!

Windy Dryden
Michael Neenan
London, July 1994

Conventions Used in the Dictionary

Entries are arranged in alphabetical order. The entry word or term is shown in **bold**. Cross-references are marked in SMALL CAPITAL LETTERS and occasionally vary from the actual entry (e.g. PSYCHOEDUCATIONAL instead of **psychoeducation**). The cross-referencing is not exhaustive, but aims to highlight certain entries for futher explanation or clarification. Italicised words and phrases represent Latin terms; or emphasis; or subheadings within an entry (e.g. *shame-attacking exercises* within **shame**); or the titles of books, journals and films. We have avoided the linguistic encumbrance and stylistic inelegance of the terms 'he/she' and 'his/her', and instead have striven for gender balance within and across the entries.

Training Facilities in the UK and USA for Rational Emotive Behaviour Therapy (REBT)

Centre for REBT
156 Westcombe Hill
Blackheath
London SE3 7DH

Tel: 0181 293 4114

Institute for Rational-Emotive Therapy
45 East 65th Street
New York, NY 10021
USA

Tel: 0101 212 535 0822

ABC a model of emotional disturbance. Also known as the ABC's of REBT. This model is the centrepiece of REBT practice and sets out a primarily cognitively-oriented theory of emotions. A stands for ACTIVATING EVENTS (including interpretations and inferences of A) which are mediated by evaluative BELIEFS (B) which, in turn, largely determine emotional and behavioural CONSEQUENCES (C). Clients are shown that B not A is at the core of their emotional reactions at C. By expanding the model, clients are taught DISPUTING (D) of their dysfunctional evaluative beliefs in order to achieve new EFFECTS (E) – a rational philosophy of living. In time, clients learn to apply the model in order to become their own counsellors. Within the model, A's, B's and C's are not discrete categories but are continually interacting processes, e.g. a man who believes (B) 'I must always be approved of by others' turns a friend's mild rebuke at A into outright rejection and thereby experiences DEPRESSION rather than SADNESS at C (see Ellis, 1991).

absolutist thinking rigid and unqualified attitudes, e.g. 'Everyone is totally selfish'. Absolutist thinking is couched in the form of MUSTS, SHOULDS, HAVE TOS, GOT TOS, and OUGHTS, e.g. 'I must always be successful.' REBT hypothesises (Ellis & Dryden, 1987) that such thinking is at the heart of human emotional disturbance and will usually block or prevent individuals from achieving their goals in life. REBT therapists do not dogmatically insist that clients' absolutist thinking always leads to emotional disturbance but clients who follow a philosophy of RELATIVISM are more likely to reduce its occurrence than those who do not (see PREFERENCES).

acceptance unqualified and nonjudgmental attitude to self and others as well as an acknowledgement that what exists is bound to exist given the conditions that are present at that moment. Individuals accept themselves and others as FALLIBLE human beings who do not have to act other than they do and are too complex to be legitimately given a single global RATING such as 'worthless' or 'perfect', and have importance in the world simply because they exist (REBT used to aver that humans had intrinsic worth not linked to any extrinsic achievement; however, the word 'worth' was eventually dropped because it implied a measurement or rating of the person). Self-acceptance is more likely to stimulate constructive change than is self-condemnation, e.g. striving to change those aspects of ourselves which we dislike without damning ourselves for having them in the first place (see SERENITY PRAYER). Individuals also accept empirical reality or LIFE CONDITIONS as they actually are but this does not preclude them from not liking these conditions. Acceptance of empirical reality does not imply passivity or resignation – individuals atempt to alter those aspects of reality which they discern can be changed or modified. The theory of acceptance is one of the most important features of REBT (see DAMNATION; HIGH FRUSTRATION TOLERANCE).

accounting cognition the irrational belief that is primarily responsible for the presence of a client's disturbed negative emotion, e.g. the anger-producing belief 'You absolutely should not talk to me like that. I hate your guts!' Such methods as INFERENCE CHAINING are used to reveal the client's accounting cognition before DISPUTING commences.

acquisition of disturbance how psychological problems are acquired. REBT does not dwell on the acquisition of human disturbance, mainly because of ELLIS's (1976) views on the biological basis of human irrationality. Environmental conditions can certainly contribute to reinforcing individuals' innate ability to disturb themselves over life events but the primary responsibility for such disturbance rests with individuals. REBT's major focus is on the PERPETUATION OF PSYCHOLOGICAL DISTURBANCE (see BIOLOGICALLY-BASED TENDENCIES).

A-C thinking thinking engaged in by individuals who believe that others or life events directly cause their emotional problems, e.g. 'My boss's behaviour makes me so angry.' Probably the majority of clients who enter REBT are A-C thinkers and therefore the therapist's task is to teach clients that as people have different emotional reactions to the same event it is our attitudes and BELIEFS about the event that largely determine the emotional outcome, e.g. 'You've agreed that most people in the office are not upset by his behaviour, so what are

you telling yourself to make yourself angry about it?' Such questions encourage clients to understand the B-C CONNECTION of emotional causation and thereby move away from A-C thinking. Such a philosophical shift does not usually happen quickly, so therapists are continually alert for clients reverting to A-C language (see Walen, DiGiuseppe & Dryden, 1992).

action tendencies an orientation towards action when one experiences an emotion. In emotional disturbance, action tendencies have short-term advantages but long-term disadvantages, e.g. avoiding a fearful situation rather than facing it in anxiety. As Dryden (1987a) notes, action tendencies 'can be seen as general categories of behaviour rather than as specific responses. . .' (p.24). In depression, withdrawal would be the general category of behaviour and a specific response might be going to bed for an indefinite period (see RESPONSE OPTIONS).

activating events (A's) external and internal events which individuals emotionally respond to. Such events can refer to past, present or future occurrences, e.g. losing one's job; the prospect of marriage. Certain goals, purposes or values are brought to A's by individuals and when these are blocked or thwarted in some way, A's can trigger EVALUATIVE BELIEFS (B) which, in turn, largely determine emotional reactions at C in the ABC framework. Activating events are not discrete entities but interact with and partly include COGNITIONS and EMOTIONS. Some REBT therapists include INFERENCES under A while others group all cognitive processes under B.

active-directive style an often vigorous, forceful approach that guides clients to the salient issues of their presenting problems and is deemed to be more effective in helping clients change than a passive or non-directive style of intervention. REBT therapists are active in, among other things, asking questions, gathering information, limiting extraneous material, problem defining, goal setting, DISPUTING, negotiating HOMEWORK assignments – all with the express purpose of directing clients to the cognitive core of their emotional and behavioural problems. However, it is important to adjust an active-directive approach to the requirements and interactional functioning of individual clients otherwise a monolithic style may well have an adverse effect on the counselling relationship (see ALLIANCE; 'AUTHENTIC CHAMELEON').

addiction compulsive need for or dependence on usually drugs or alcohol. Ellis *et al.* (1988 p.25) suggest that the 'primary cognitive dynamic that creates and maintains addiction is what we call the abstinence LFT [LOW FRUSTRATION TOLERANCE] pattern', i.e. individuals who are deprived or deprive themselves of a substance they believe they MUST have convince themselves, for example, that 'I can't stand my life without a drink.' Such irrational beliefs lead to DISCOMFORT ANXIETY. Working with addicts is doubly difficult as their 'I-CAN'T-STAND-IT-ITIS' beliefs not only ensure a quick return to substance abuse to ease their discomfort anxiety but also militates against the hard work required to change addictive behaviour. However, vigorous DISPUTING of clients' LFT beliefs and employing behavioural methods such as STIMULUS CONTROL can effect a significant reduction in or eventual elimination of substance abuse. The abstinence LFT pattern can be applied to other addictions such as sex, gambling or food (see RATIONAL RECOVERY).

adventuring seeking or undertaking exciting, pleasurable, risky, etc. adventures. Adventuring can help individuals to widen their opportunities, free themselves from many self-imposed restrictions and lead more fulfilling and SELF-ACTUALISED lives, e.g. sexual adventuring involves experimenting with a variety of partners and practices to max-imise one's sexual enjoyment. If a client's goal is to be more adventurous in life, REBT therapists uncover and DISPUTE their goal-blocking beliefs, e.g. 'I must know in advance if I will be successful'; 'I can't stand being rejected'. Adventuring or RISK-TAKING in REBT is seen as a criterion of PSYCHOLOGICAL HEALTH.

agenda setting drawing up a list of items to be discussed and thereby establishing a procedure to follow. Agenda setting is seen as an effective way of structuring therapy sessions. Client and therapist agree on which items to put down on the agenda for discussion. The usual format would be: FEEDBACK from the previous session; discussion of the last session's HOMEWORK tasks; problems to be discussed in the present session; negotiating further homework assignments; feedback from the present session. Agendas can be viewed as keeping both therapist and client on track, i.e. how to quickly and efficiently realise the client's goals for change. Agenda setting can be suspended if a crisis supervenes, e.g. with a suicidal client.

ahistorical approach focusing on the here and now of a client's problems rather than trawling through the past to understand how they developed. The problems' antecedents are not seen as helpful in the present as a guide to overcoming the problems, e.g. 'Your anxiety at work may have started three years ago when you were promoted but what are you telling yourself today in order to maintain your anxiety?' However, REBT therapists are not absolutely against exploring the past particularly if not to do so will threaten the therapeutic ALLIANCE. Dryden (1991a) has suggested that for some clients exploring the past can actually promote therapeutic movement because they can DISPUTE their currently held irrational ideas which they received and accepted from significant others in the past, e.g. parents. Additionally, clients can examine whether such figures really were infallible guides to constructing personal rules of living, e.g. 'My parents always taught me to believe that "weakness equals failure"'.

alliance an association or union, usually made by formal agreement. The therapeutic or working alliance refers to the relationship developed and the milieu created by the therapist and client in order for the former to help the latter overcome her emotional problems. Bordin (1979) has identified three major components of the therapeutic alliance. (1) BONDS – along with the CORE CONDITIONS of therapy, forging an appropriate relationship with clients based on their interpersonal style to encourage them to carry out their goal-directed tasks. (2) GOALS – both client and therapist agree on the client's outcome goals for change. (3) TASKS – at different stages of the therapeutic process, client and therapist have various tasks to execute, e.g. at the beginning stage, the client generates a PROBLEM LIST while the therapist attempts to link the problems to realistic goals. Greater therapeutic benefits are likely to be achieved if a successful alliance is created (see Dryden, 1987b).

all-or-nothing thinking attitude of placing events in black or white categories with no middle gound. An inferential distortion stemming from underlying MUSTS, e.g. 'If I don't get this job, as I must, then I am a complete failure'. Such thinking forms the foundation of PERFECTIONISM and leads to self-downing and DEPRESSION when mistakes are made, imperfections found or goals not achieved. Therefore a goal in REBT is to encourage clients to see things on a continuum (shades of grey) and not in black and white categories.

alternative thinking considering other choices as possibilities in problem-solving. REBT therapists teach clients to look for alternative solutions to their problems on both the philosophical and prac-

tical level. Clients are encouraged to surrender their rigid philosophies (e.g. 'I must always be in a relationship otherwise my life will be awful') and develop open-ended, flexible ones which are adaptable when goals are not reached (e.g. 'I would prefer to be in a relationship but as I'm not, too bad. I can still be happy and get on with my life'). Ellis (quoted in Dryden, 1991b) states that being 'determined to find alternative roads to happiness when the one you most want is not open is one of the main essences of non-disturbance' (p.48). On the practical level, clients can learn to generate alternative solutions to their problems, e.g. looking at other careers when the one the client most wants is closed to him. Usually in REBT, clients develop flexible philosophies before focusing on practical problem-solving.

always and never thinking the attitude that negative events (e.g. rejection, failure) will eternally be present in one's life and will not change. An inferential distortion stemming from underlying MUSTS, e.g. 'Things in my life are going poorly as they must not do. Therefore things will always go poorly and they'll never get any better.' Such predictions reveal clients' rigid outlook towards negative events in their lives. By introducing flexibility into their thinking, clients can realistically estimate how frequently negative events will continue to occur and re-evaluate the idea that things will never change.

ambivalence having opposite and conflicting feelings or ideas about something, e.g. 'I very much want the promotion but not the greater pressure that goes with it.' REBT therapists elicit the irrational ideas underlying clients' ambivalence about change in their lives, e.g. 'I really want to stop being a doormat for my husband but if I stand up for myself he'll leave me. I couldn't stand living alone.' Clients are encouraged to challenge and change the self-defeating ideas implicit in their ambivalence and thereby make a firm commitment to constructive change (see 'YES, BUT' STATEMENTS).

analogy partial similarity between like features of two things on which a comparison may be based. Analogies are used to make therapeutic points, e.g. a client is asked to imagine learning to play tennis incorrectly and then later being taught by a professional coach the correct strokes; at first the new strokes would seem unnatural and therefore it would take HARD WORK AND PRACTICE to improve his tennis performance until it became natural. Similarly, the client's newly acquired RATIONAL BELIEFS seem strange and unnatural yet through vigorous challenging of his familiar self-defeating ideas and continually acting on his new beliefs he will eventually internalise a rational philosophy of living. The analogy of change in tennis is designed to show clients that they will usually experience similar difficulties in therapeutic change (see 'HEAD-GUT' ISSUE).

anger strong feeling of condemnation and often hostility. Anger is an UNHEALTHY NEGATIVE EMOTION. Anger, stemming from DEMANDS, can fall into three main categories: when one's personal rules have been violated; when one's goals or actions have been blocked or thwarted in some way; and ego-defensive anger – lashing out at others because one's self-perceived weaknesses or failings have been revealed (unwittingly or not). Anger can often lead to DAMNATION of self, others or the world. Behavioural responses can be retaliatory: overtly physical and/or verbal; indirectly through passive-aggressiveness. Leading REBT practitioners have written extensively on the subject of anger: Dryden (1990a), Ellis (1977a) and Hauck (1980a) (see ANNOYANCE; BLAME).

annoyance displeasure or irritation. Annoyance is seen as a HEALTHY NEGATIVE EMOTION. The themes in annoyance are

the same as in ANGER (experience of rule-breaking or frustration, threats to ego) but are evaluated in terms of PREFERENCES and the actions or traits of others are deemed to be bad or criticised rather than the individuals themselves. Behavioural responses include assertion of rights and confronting obnoxious behaviour.

anti-awfulising an evaluation of the relative badness of an event that can be placed on a 0–99.9 scale of badness. REBT therapists point out to clients that no matter what the negative event is, it could always be worse, e.g. learning that one has terminal cancer leaves time for making the most of one's remaining life rather than dying suddenly and unexpectedly from a heart attack. Such methods encourage clients to evaluate more realistically the badness of negative events, to accept the empirical reality of such events and to adapt constructively to them (see AWFULISING).

antiprocrastination exercises activities carried out by clients to encourage them to undertake tasks they have been avoiding or putting off. Such exercises include making lists of the short- and long-term advantages and disadvantages of procrastination; diary keeping to see how individuals spend their time; imaginal rehearsal before tackling the avoided tasks. Choice of exercises will be guided by the underlying IRRATIONAL BELIEFS which are maintaining the procrastination, e.g. SHAME-ATTACKING EXERCISES for clients who believe 'I must not make a fool of myself in public' and thereby avoid public speaking engagements (see PROCRASTINATION).

anxiety state of worry or overconcern. An UNHEALTHY NEGATIVE EMOTION. Anxiety stems from DEMANDS that a threat MUST not occur and it would be AWFUL if it did. Typically, individuals with anxiety problems overestimate the probability of the feared event occurring and underestimate their ability to cope with it if it did occur. REBT distinguishes between ego and discomfort anxiety: the former involves threats to one's SELF-ESTEEM and the latter involves threats to one's personal COMFORT. Both forms of anxiety frequently interact. Behavioural responses in anxiety are usually to avoid or withdraw from the perceived threat; also to seek reassurance from others. These tactics may bring short-term relief but perpetuate the anxiety in the long-term (see CONCERN).

aphorism short, pithy saying which expresses a generally recognised truth. Aphorisms can be used to help promote client change, e.g. 'No gain without pain'. Aphorisms are used as adjuncts to cognitive DISPUTING techniques.

appraisal act of evaluating the worth, importance, significance, of someone or something. According to REBT, the appraisal of ACTIVATING EVENTS will largely determine our emotional reaction to them, e.g. the anxiety-provoking belief 'I must not be left at home on my own because something terrible will happen if I am.' Such a self-defeating appraisal is challenged through DISPUTING to produce a self-helping appraisal, e.g. the concern-producing belief 'I would greatly prefer not to be left at home on my own but there is no reason why I must not be. If something unpleasant does occur, it will be bad but not awful'. REBT therapists encourage clients to avoid appraisals of indifference (e.g. 'I really don't care one way or another') as this will not help them to adapt constructively to adverse events and may indicate that they are attempting to suppress their rational desires for such events not to occur (see EVALUATIVE BELIEFS).

approaches avoided in REBT techniques usually omitted from REBT practice. REBT does not favour approaches with iatrogenic features (client problems inadvertently induced or exacerbated by therapy or the therapist) which actually reinforce clients' IRRATIONAL BELIEFS (Ellis, 1982). Some of these approaches include: giving undue WARMTH and love may foster dependency on the therapist thereby strengthening clients' dire needs for APPROVAL; cathartic and abreactive techniques which give vent to suppressed feelings (e.g. anger) may well prolong such feelings because underlying beliefs may be unwittingly strengthened; maintaining instead of tackling LOW FRUSTRATION TOLERANCE by gradual desensitisation rather than IMPLOSIVE methods; placing the locus of control for change outside of the individual, e.g. Narcotics and Alcoholics Anonymous; distraction techniques such as relaxation or meditation when not used in conjunction with DISPUTING dysfunctional beliefs.

appropriate negative emotions see HEALTHY NEGATIVE EMOTIONS.

approval favourable opinion or judgement; considered worthy or satisfactory. Dire NEEDS for approval are key IRRATIONAL BELIEFS underpinning much emotional disturbance, e.g. 'I must have your approval; without it, I'm nothing'. REBT therapists remain alert to exuding too much WARMTH and thereby unwittingly reinforcing clients' approval needs. If this occurs, clients can FEEL BETTER but not actually GET BETTER because their self-acceptance is still conditional; in this case, on the approval of the therapist. A healthy alternative is for therapists to offer clients unconditional acceptance and thereby encourage them not to rate themselves in any way and prefer but not demand the approval of others.

arbitrary inference jumping to conclusions that are not justified by the facts of the situation. An inferential distortion stemming from underlying MUSTS, e.g. 'Because my train was late, as it should (must) not have been, the whole day will be ruined.'

arguing giving reasons for or against something; quarrelling or disagreeing. Clients may state, for example, that therapy will not be able to help them, they will never change or the therapist does not understand 'real life' problems. REBT therapists are advised not to engage in arguing with clients over such issues because it may help to create a power struggle which results in an impasse in therapy. Dryden (lecture, 1992) suggests the following possible resolution to this problem: 'If you win the argument you also lose it because you will remain emotionally disturbed. If I win the argument you will also win because I can help you to overcome your emotional disturbance. Now whom do you want to win the argument?' Clients usually suggest the therapist and therapy can then constructively proceed. If some clients state that they want to win they are likely to find it is a Pyrrhic victory (won at great emotional cost to themselves) they have achieved (see WILFULLY RESISTANT CLIENTS).

assertion Hauck (1991) defines it as 'standing up for one's rights without anger' (p.207). Clients who are unassertive allow others to violate their rights, take advantage and generally behave badly towards them. Blocks to learning assertiveness include individuals damning others for frustrating them; fearing rejection or disapproval; feeling guilty for acting in a 'selfish' way in order to fulfil their wishes. In order to tackle unassertiveness clients challenge their self-blocking beliefs, e.g. 'If I stand up to my partner he will dump me. It would be awful if that happened'; 'If I tell my boss how well he runs the department, everyone will think I'm a sycophant. I couldn't stand that'. Clients are taught to distinguish between assertion based on negative reasons (e.g. criticising another's obnoxious behaviour) and assertion based on positive reasons (e.g. praising a work colleague's skill at meeting deadlines). In addition, clients can learn new skills in assertion through such activities as role play and *in vivo* HOMEWORK tasks. Assertion does not mean individuals always get their own way 'but merely that they express their desires and try to have them fulfilled' (Ellis & Abrahms, 1978, p.56).

assessment determining the nature and extent of a client's problems. Using the ABC framework, a problem is described at A, focusing on that part of the problem which the client is most upset or disturbed about. At C, a disturbed negative emotion (as defined in the REBT TAXONOMY OF NEGATIVE EMOTIONS) relating to the problem is clearly pinpointed. Intervening IRRATIONAL BELIEFS at B are elicited in order to understand how the disturbed emotion is being maintained. It is important for the therapist and client to arrive at a shared understanding of the client's problem as well as agreeing on what accounts for the existence of it, before the therapist moves on to employ a range of techniques and strategies to challenge the client's self-defeating beliefs. Assessment also includes agreement on the client's goals for change, what tasks will be needed to get there, and what is the most effective BOND in forging a therapeutic ALLIANCE.

assuming temporarily that A is true therapists, for the purpose of assessment, take for granted that clients' accounts and interpretations or inferences of negative activating events (A's) are factual. Assuming temporarily that A is true assists the therapist to find, through such methods as INFERENCE CHAINING, the client's most clinically relevant aspect of A, i.e. what the client is most disturbed about which triggers her irrational belief which, in turn, largely determines her UNHEALTHY NEGATIVE EMOTION (e.g. guilt). Once this has been achieved, then the therapist can DISPUTE the client's distortions of and DEMANDS about A.

assuming the worst encouraging clients to suppose that their ultimate fears have been realised, e.g. dying young; being unloved. As part of the ELEGANT SOLUTION to emotional problem-solving, clients are asked to assume that the worst has occurred and to see themselves adapting constructively to the grim reality of negative events – this is achieved through removing the 'horror' (emotional disturbance) from such events. By imagining themselves coping with the worst, clients are more likely to have less trouble tackling actual events (see AWFULISING).

attribution implying that something originates with a definite person or from a definite cause, e.g. he attributed her loneliness to being an only child. A key responsibility of REBT therapists is to change clients' attributions about their emotional problems from external causation, e.g. 'He makes me angry with his behaviour' to internal causation, e.g. 'What is anger-provoking in your mind about his behaviour?' without neglecting the important point that external events contribute to but do not cause clients' emotional problems. External attributions which reflect client hopelessness, e.g. 'The whole world's against me. There's nothing I can do about it' can be restructured by therapists into self-attributions of internal causation coupled with attributions that engender hope and change, e.g. 'You make life more difficult for yourself than it has to be. If you get down to some hard work you should see a marked improvement in your present situation' (see Wessler & Wessler, 1980).

audience participation see FRIDAY NIGHT WORKSHOP.

audiotape supervision by mail therapists who send through the post their tape-recordings of therapy sessions in order to have their work overseen by an experienced and suitably qualified counsellor.

Dryden (1984a) suggests there are three main ways of 'supervising audiotapes by mail. Supervisors can (1) listen to an entire session and then either write or tape their comments; (2) give ongoing written or taped comments while listening to the session; and (3) listen to the entire session first, give general comments and then listen to the session again giving ongoing supervision' (p.140). One disadvantage of this form of supervision is that face-to-face discussion of the session is missing; while an advantage of this approach is that therapists from anywhere in the world can have their tapes supervised.

'authentic chameleon' therapist as described by Kwee and Lazarus (1986, p.333) as 'the therapist mak[ing] use of the most helpful facets of his or her personality in order to establish rapport with a particular client' while remaining genuine in the process. REBT therapists as 'authentic chameleons' modulate their INTERACTIVE STYLE in order to meet, at least initially, clients' preferences for a particular BOND, e.g. informal and humorous for some clients; serious and formal for others. REBT therapists are wary of meeting clients' expectations which may reinforce their existing problems, e.g. avoiding excessive WARMTH with clients who believe they need the APPROVAL of others. Flexibility is the hallmark of the 'authentic chameleon' as he adapts himself to and blends in with the requirements of the therapeutic ALLIANCE at any given time.

avoidance behaviour action which allows or enables individuals to keep away from actual or potentially threatening situations. Therapists encourage clients to act forcefully against their ACTION TENDENCIES to avoid or withdraw from fearful situations, e.g. sitting at the front of a class and putting up one's hand to answer questions rather than 'hiding' at the back. In order to effect such constructive behaviour clients need to DISPUTE their disturbance-producing ideas, e.g. 'I must not reveal my ignorance to the rest of the class. It would be awful to give the wrong answer.' Avoidance behaviour may also be underpinned by LOW FRUSTRATION TOLERANCE, i.e. clients' demands for comfort while carrying out their behavioural tasks. Such LFT ideas can be tackled by therapists encouraging clients to carry out, for example, 'STAY-IN-THERE' ASSIGNMENTS.

awfulising believing that unpleasant or negative events are the worst they could conceivably be. Awfulising is one of the three major DERIVATIVES in REBT and stems from the belief that such events must not occur or be as bad as they are, e.g. 'It's awful to be shown up as a fool, as I must not be'. As things in life can always be worse, awfulising is a greatly exaggerated response to negative life events and therefore clients are shown how to distinguish between evaluating the BADNESS of such events and awfulising about them (see ANTI-AWFULISING).

backsliding slipping back into self-defeating patterns of thinking, feeling and behaving. Clients' therapeutic gains are frequently sabotaged by their LOW FRUSTRATION TOLERANCE beliefs, e.g. 'Change is not only hard, it's too hard. I can't stand it'. When clients backslide, ELLIS (1984a) urges them to accept their FALLIBILITY and avoid RATING themselves, only their actions (e.g. 'I accept myself for slipping back but not my lazy behaviour'). By returning to the ABC model, clients can pin-point the cognitive causes of their backsliding, forcefully dispute these IRRATIONAL BELIEFS in order to strengthen their RATIONAL BELIEFS. Further occurrences of backsliding can be reduced if clients continue to work hard to think and act against their irrational beliefs.

badness negative evaluation given to a state of affairs that go against a person's preferences; morally objectionable; evil (when applied to a person). A rational alternative to AWFULISING and derived from primary PREFERENCES. Here the relative badness of a negative event is evaluated by the criterion that things could always be worse, e.g. 'What happened to me was very bad but not awful'. With this statement, clients legitimately rate negative events along a continuum of badness but refuse to awfulise about them thereby removing emotional disturbance from these events. When individuals vio-

late their MORAL CODE they condemn their actions as well as themselves, e.g. the guilt-inducing belief 'I did a bad thing and this makes me a bad person'. By challenging and changing such a belief, individuals can feel the healthy alternative of REMORSE, e.g. 'I don't like committing a bad act but there is no reason why I must not act that way. I am a fallible human being who acted badly rather than a bad person'.

bag lady/tramp scenario a feared outcome to a client's problem that could theoretically occur but is not usually the client's actual worry. For example, a client may say she is anxious about making mistakes in front of her work colleagues. In order for the therapist to find out what the client is most anxious about, he can initiate INFERENCE CHAINING by asking: 'Let's assume temporarily that you do make mistakes in front of your colleagues. Then what?' By asking 'THEN WHAT?' QUESTIONS, the therapist discovers that the client is anxious about a number of things: looking a fool, being laughed at, jeopardising her promotion chances, being sacked, losing her husband and home, ending up on the streets, living in a cardboard box. Some REBT therapists, particularly novices, may automatically assume that the client's greatest fear is becoming a bag lady and therefore DISPUTE her presumed belief that 'this must not happen'. Such an outcome to a client's problem is possible but it is much more probable that the client's actual worry is located earlier in the inference chain and the therapist's task is to review the chain with the client in order to find it, e.g. 'I couldn't bear being laughed at. I'd just want to curl up and die' (see CLINICALLY RELEVANT PART OF THE A).

B-C connection the hypothesis that individuals' evaluative beliefs not only precede but also largely determine their emotional states or consequences. REBT teaches clients that BELIEFS mediate emotional responses to events. Therefore if a client states: 'He makes me anxious' emphasising A-C THINKING, the statement is restructured thus: 'What are you telling yourself about him to make yourself anxious?' in order to reinforce the B-C connection and eventually tease out the client's underlying irrational beliefs, e.g. 'I must not appear weak in his eyes otherwise I will condemn myself as completely pathetic'. For many clients, the B-C connection represents a paradigmatic shift in their understanding of emotional causation. Client (and therapist) need to be mindful of employing B-C language and avoiding A-C language in their therapeutic interaction (see ABC; INFERENCE CHAINING).

beginning phase of individual therapy the concerns and problems encountered at the outset of REBT as well as the distinctive features of this particular stage. Clients' INDUCTION into REBT may include filling out a BIOGRAPHICAL INFORMATION FORM as part of the assessment process. REBT emphasises an early problem-solving focus (e.g. 'What problem would you like to start with?') as part of clients' SOCIALISATION into REBT. Clients generate and prioritise a PROBLEM LIST. Client problems are placed within the ABC paradigm and clients are taught the ABC model of emotional disturbance, i.e. the cognitive dynamics underpinning their emotional problems. Clients are informed that REBT is primarily concerned with emotional problem-solving, though practical problems can be addressed later in therapy (e.g. a client who is depressed about being in debt learns how to overcome his depression first before looking at practical ways of getting himself out of debt). During the assessment stage, therapists pay particular attention to SECONDARY EMOTIONAL PROBLEMS (e.g. ashamed of feeling anxious) which may, with clients' agreement, be tackled first. Once the problem-focus has been agreed upon, placed within the ABC framework, then DISPUTING can commence to show clients the illogical and unrealistic nature of their IRRATIONAL BELIEFS and the logical, realistic and goal-directed features of their rational alternatives. HOMEWORK assignments are negotiated which help clients to strengthen their newly acquired rational beliefs and weaken their irrational beliefs. Reading SELF-HELP MATERIAL can also assist the process of therapeutic change. ROAD-BLOCKS to therapeutic progress, which can occur at this stage of therapy, include therapists spending too much time on developing the therapeutic relationship as an end in itself rather than developing it through an early problem-focus; not adapting the pace of therapy to clients' LEARNING STYLES; not dealing with clients' misconceptions about and anticipations of the kind of therapy offered by REBT can lead to early TERMINATION of therapy or RESISTANCE; and clients believing that INSIGHT alone (instead of coupled with repeated hard work) is sufficient to bring about enduring change in their lives (see ENDING STAGE; MIDDLE PHASE).

behavioural consequences actions resulting from particular emotions. Disturbed negative emotions, stemming from IRRATIONAL BELIEFS, usually contain counter-productive behaviours (e.g. avoidance in anxiety; retaliation in anger) and block goal-attainment. Nondisturbed negative emotions, stemming from RATIONAL BELIEFS, usually contain constructive behaviours (e.g. facing one's fear in concern; assertion in annoyance) and aid goal-attainment (see NEGATIVE EMOTIONS). In the ABC model, C stands for emotional and behavioural consequences and when the emotional C is the focus for intervention dysfunctional behaviours can be viewed as hiding or masking disturbed emotions, e.g. a client would be encouraged to stop procrastinating in order to 'release' the hidden emotion(s) such as anxiety.

behavioural paradox asking clients to act in ways that are the opposite of what they normally do and thereby seem to fly in the face of commonly accepted wisdom, e.g. a client who is terrified of going insane would be encouraged to try and make herself go insane by acting in a 'mad' way. Behavioural paradox helps to reduce such fears by not only teaching clients that they cannot make themselves insane no matter how hard they try but also by weakening their underlying irrational beliefs, e.g. 'I must be certain that I will not go mad' (see COGNITIVE PARADOX).

behavioural rehearsal encouraging clients to practise the kinds of goal-directed actions they wish to execute, e.g. asking a work colleague not to keep on interrupting him every few minutes. In this exercise, the client may be acting against his dire need for APPROVAL. Behavioural rehearsal can be carried out in therapy sessions with the therapist acting as the work colleague or as part of HOMEWORK assignments with a friend acting as a therapeutic aide (see COGNITIVE REHEARSAL).

behavioural techniques methods which enable clients to act against their irrational beliefs, e.g. encouraging clients to stay in unpleasant situations in order to dispute behaviourally their belief 'I can't stand discomfort'. By powerfully acting against such beliefs, behavioural evidence is obtained to undermine their validity. Clients may not believe in the efficacy of their new rational beliefs unless they are put into action. REBT favours, but does not insist upon, behavioural techniques that use IMPLOSION (flooding) rather than gradual desensitisation. Implosive methods, according to REBT, can rapidly help to remove emotional disturbance and effect a deeper attitude change than more gradual methods which may actually prolong or reinforce LOW FRUSTRATION TOLERANCE beliefs (see RISK-TAKING; 'STAY-IN-THERE' EXERCISES).

behaviourally-based change a therapeutic outcome which involves clients replacing self-defeating actions with self-helping ones. Behaviourally based change is one of the therapeutic COMPROMISES IN REBT. If clients are unable to, for whatever reason, challenge and change their irrational beliefs, then the focus of therapy can be switched to replacing maladaptive behaviour with adaptive behaviour. For example, an anxious client who avoids disputing the belief 'I must not face this fear and it would be awful if I did' can be taught relaxation exercises, breathing retraining, distraction techniques, gradual desensitisation, etc. which may help her tackle her anxiety. Behaviourally-based change may bring a change in INFERENCES (e.g. 'My fear is nowhere as bad as I first thought') but generally leaves intact the underlying disturbance-producing MUST.

belief cognitive structure which is evaluative at its core; attitude. REBT hypothesises that at the heart of our emotional reactions to life events lie two types of EVALUATIVE BELIEFS: rational and irrational. The former are seen as flexible, adaptable, logical, realistic, practical, goal-oriented, and lead to healthy emotions and behaviours (a philosophy of PREFERENCES). The latter are seen as inflexible, unadaptable, illogical, unrealistic, impractical, goal-blocking, and lead to unhealthy emotions and behaviours (a philosophy of DEMANDS). Only irrational beliefs are targeted for DISPUTING. Frequently, both rational and irrational statements are found in the same sentence: 'I want a new car therefore I must have one'. The 'want' (preference) would be supported but the 'must' (demand) would be challenged. INFERENCES in REBT are not seen as beliefs but rather as non-evaluative cognitions stemming from underlying beliefs, e.g. a woman who is depressed because she believes that 'no one loves me' would be shown that her disturbance actually derives from the belief 'I must be loved in order to be happy'.

'best bet' hypothesis clients who make the most favourable inference(s) about themselves, others or the world based on the immediately available information, e.g. a man whose girlfriend does not turn up for a dinner date believes it is because she has simply forgotten rather than rejected him. Clients who do not wish, for whatever reason, to pursue an ELEGANT SOLUTION to their problems by surrendering their musturbatory thinking, e.g. 'I must not be rejected', are supported by therapists in making INFERENTIALLY-BASED CHANGE to achieve emotional stability (see 'WORST BET' HYPOTHESIS).

best rational arguments described by Hauck (1980b) as 'a series of logical arguments ... which are so reasonable, so irrefutably right, that an opposing idea cannot exist once the rational one has been grasped' (p.117). Examples of such arguments presented by Hauck include: anger – in nearly all cases it is self-defeating because someone else's misconduct against us is made much worse when we inflict anger upon ourselves over it – a clear case of double jeopardy. To suffer injustice without anger is to nullify the potentially destructive effects of anger; worry and fear – if individuals never believed that anything was horrendous then they would prevent themselves ever becoming emotionally upset and therefore 'catastrophising is the first step toward almost all other forms of emotional disturbance' (*ibid*. p.131). Hauck suggests that one's credibility and strength as an REBT therapist is partly due to having a wide range of rational arguments at one's fingertips in order to combat clients' irrational ideas.

bibliotherapy the use of reading material to assist the process of therapeutic change. Bibliotherapy is used in REBT as a COGNITIVE TECHNIQUE. REBT literature can be studied by clients before, during and after therapy in order to deepen their understanding of the REBT view of human disturbance, accelerate and deepen the process of change, and sustain their therapeutic gains. A considerable range of self-help books are available to the general public.

big I/little i diagram a means of showing clients the illogicality of rating themselves on the basis of their actions or traits. Devised by Lazarus (1977), this diagram consists of one big block 'I' and contained within it are many small 'i's' (see Figure 1). The big 'I' stands for the self or person; the little 'i's' represent a person's deeds, traits or actions. By circling one or more of the small 'i's' the therapist can ask the client whether she should be judged on the basis of certain actions or traits, e.g. 'Because you did some good (or bad) things does this make you a good (or bad) person?' Such questions attempt to break the connection between the big 'I' and little 'i's' and teach clients that the self is too complex and in a state of flux to be pinned down by a single global RATING. Individuals can make themselves vulnerable to emotional disturbance if they not only condemn their traits or actions but also themselves (see VISUAL MODELS; VIVID REBT).

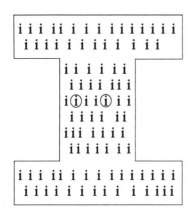

I = the person or self
i = an action or trait

Figure 1 Big I/Little i diagram (see entry)

big picture trap the insistence of some REBT therapists 'on obtaining a total picture of the client's past, present and future before beginning an intervention program' (Grieger and Boyd, 1980, p.77). Obtaining a total picture or life history of the client is not necessary in REBT as the client's presenting problems are placed within the ABC model of emotional disturbance. Additionally, without requiring much biographical information, therapists can quickly zero in on clients' disturbance-producing ideas by remembering the THEMES IN EMOTIONAL PROBLEMS, e.g. loss or failure in depression may suggest that a depressed client is telling herself 'Because I lost my job, as I shouldn't have done, this means I'm worthless'.

biographical information form a form used to obtain basic details of both a client's life history and presenting problems. By reading out aloud Item 23 on the form ('Briefly list (PRINT) your present main complaints, symptoms, and problems'), therapists can quickly teach clients about and SOCIALISE them into the early problem-solving focus of REBT by encouraging them to start with their most troubling problem on the list.

biologically-based tendencies the assertion by ELLIS (1976) that humans have two powerful innate inclinations to think both irrationally and rationally. This theory of biological predisposition to disturbance and the ability to minimise or counteract its effects sets REBT apart from other therapies including other cognitive-behavioural approaches. Evidence to support the REBT view of the biological basis of human irrationality (reinforced by environmental factors) includes: human disturbance appears to transcend all cultures; no human seems to be immune from irrationality (including REBT therapists); acknowledging that dysfunctional thoughts and behaviours are self-defeating does not necessarily mean that people will give them up; individuals returning to counterproductive or self-destructive behaviours after working hard to abandon them. With our biological tendency to think rationally – to critically examine our irrational thinking – we can choose to dispute our irrationalities forcefully and energetically and thereby limit their influences on our lives.

black and white thinking oversimplified ideas which are usually expressed in absolute terms e.g. 'Either you are for me or against me'. An inferential distortion stemming from underlying MUSTS, e.g. 'If she doesn't go out with me, as she must do, this means I am completely unlikeable'. Such rigid ideas frequently lead to emotional disturbance (e.g. depression) but clients can reduce its occurrence by allowing shades of grey into their thinking, i.e. flexibility (see ALL-OR-NOTHING THINKING).

blame to find fault with or hold responsible for something reprehensible. According to Hauck (1980a), blame 'is the central issue of anger' (p.76). Blame occurs when one individual not only finds fault with another's behaviour but also damns him for the behaviour, e.g. 'You pushed in front of me, as you shouldn't have done, and are a complete bastard for doing so!' Blaming others can help to make their obnoxious behaviour worse or teach them to hate themselves. In order to avoid this, REBT suggests separating people from their actions and thereby replacing anger with ANNOYANCE or non-damning anger, e.g. 'I'm angry at your rude behaviour but not with you'. With annoyance, individuals are more likely to be assertive rather than retaliate and thereby point out, with regard to the above examples, that queues are for waiting in and not jumping. Hauck asserts that without blame 'hate, cruelty, and needless pain of all kinds would be unthinkable' (*ibid*. p.76).

'blow up' procedure clients are encouraged through imagery to exaggerate their fears greatly in order to diffuse them by seeing how unrealistic they are. For example, a client who believes that a mistake at work will have dire consequences is presented with a picture of the company closing down, hundreds unemployed, whole industries disappearing and the country grinding to a halt. The humorous intention is to place the mistake in a realistic rather than a grandiose context, e.g. the therapist may warn the client not to make a mistake because the country's balance of payments situation will grievously suffer (see IMAGERY TECHNIQUES).

bond something which binds or holds things together, e.g. the bond of friendship. Bonds are one of the three major components of the therapeutic ALLIANCE. A client-therapist bonded relationship is established on the basis of the client's interpersonal and learning style in order to promote change and realise his/her goals. Different clients require different bonds. One client may want a 'no nonsense' approach while another favours a 'proceed with caution' style from the therapist. Clients' preferences for particular bonds are respected unless the therapist considers that in some cases bond

preferences will reinforce rather than help overcome clients' disturbances, e.g. a too gentle style from the therapist may strengthen a client's need for COMFORT in facing her problems (see 'AUTHENTIC CHAMELEON').

booster session a counselling session designed to give help and encouragement to clients to maintain their therapeutic gains. Booster sessions occur after the formal end of therapy and are a good way of monitoring clients' progress as self-therapists.

brainwashing systematic indoctrination to change a person's beliefs or attitudes. Clients frequently say they have been brainwashed by others into believing certain things about themselves, e.g. 'I've been told so many times by my husband that I'm a failure; what else can I do but accept it'. REBT therapists teach clients that they are primarily responsible for believing such ideas because they have been insufficiently critical of them or the ideas were already in their mind which is why they agreed with their partners or others' accusations. If there has been any brainwashing, clients have been doing it to themselves (see INSIGHT). Clients are encouraged to subject their 'brainwashed beliefs' to logical, empirical and pragmatic examination in order to DE-INDOCTRINATE themselves and then construct self-helping beliefs, e.g. 'It is true I've had my share of failures in my life but this does not make me a failure as a person. I shall certainly analyse from now on not only what others say about me but also what I believe about myself'. Clients who say that society has brainwashed them (e.g. 'You have to be thin in this culture to be happy and successful and valued') are also shown that as they accepted the brainwashing they are responsible for believing such ideas.

brevity shortness of duration. Brevity in REBT is considered to be a hallmark of EFFICIENCY in psychotherapy. REBT therapists quickly direct clients to the cognitive determinants of their emotional problems and through DISPUTING, help them to realise a goal-oriented and rational philosophy of living within a relatively brief timescale (with RESISTANT clients this process usually takes considerably longer). ELLIS (1985a) suggests that 'if it is possible to achieve effective treatment in a short period of time, more clients will tend to come, stay in it, and benefit from it in various ways' (p.126).

but-rebuttal method a technique for challenging clients' statements of hesitation, indecision, ambivalence, etc. which prevent or block them from carrying out goal-directed tasks. For example, client: 'I want to do my homework assignments but I simply haven't got the time'; therapist: 'The time is there if you wish to find it – the real question is: do you want to overcome your problems or prolong them?' Every 'but' statement from the client is met by a rebuttal from the therapist until the client's 'buts' are exhausted and a commitment is obtained to carry out the agreed tasks. The but-rebuttal method helps to mobilise clients to tackle the disturbance-producing ideas usually underpinning their 'but' statements, e.g. 'I must feel comfortable in order to do my homework tasks'. The but-rebuttal method can be used by clients as part of their developing role as a self-therapist (see Burns, 1980).

catastrophising greatly exaggerating the negative consequences of actual or potential adverse or unpleasant events. REBT distinguishes between catastrophising and AWFULISING: in the former, catastrophes do occur, e.g. failing to secure a contract will sometimes lead to the collapse of a business and the loss of many jobs; earth tremors do often presage a major earthquake; while in awfulising, the DEMAND exists that such catastrophes must not be as bad as they are or must not occur. Not awfulising about catastrophes or the possibility of them occurring can help individuals to avoid emotional disturbance, accept the grim reality of such events and thereby learn how to adapt constructively to them. Therapists should be very careful not to minimise the adverse impact of catastrophes while teaching clients the pitfalls of awfulising about them (see TRAGEDY).

catch-22 of low frustration tolerance (LFT) the apparently inescapable dilemma derived from Joseph Heller's eponymous novel applied to the problems of discomfort disturbance. Overcoming one's problems usually requires hard work but individuals with LFT believe they cannot tolerate the discomfort associated with such effort (e.g. 'I shouldn't have to work hard to get ahead in life') and thereby block themselves from achieving important life goals. A seemingly irresolvable problem. However, ELLIS (1988, p.120) urges clients not to 'forget that Catch-22 stems from an idea in your head and doesn't really exist in itself. And if it is mainly a thought – RE[B]T clearly says – you can overcome it by debating and Disputing it!' Challenging and changing one's LFT beliefs can lead to HIGH FRUSTRATION TOLERANCE and a philosophy of LONG-RANGE HEDONISM.

catharsis expressing suppressed emotions (e.g. anger) in an often dramatic way. This technique is usually eschewed in REBT because it provides respite from but not removal of disturbed negative emotions and may actually reinforce some clients' disturbance-producing ideas, e.g. the anger-provoking belief 'I shouldn't have so much bloody hassle at work!' However, catharsis may be used in some cases to release (via ventilation) a variety of cognitions as part of a wider analysis in determining a client's underlying beliefs or identify UNHEALTHY NEGATIVE EMOTIONS (e.g. hurt).

causal attributions see ATTRIBUTIONS.

chaining the process of linking cognitions and/or emotions and sometimes behaviours in order to represent the interconnectedness and frequent complexity of clients' presenting problems. Dryden

(1989) has listed four types of chains: COMPLEX CHAINS, DISTURBANCE ABOUT DISTURBANCE, INFERENCE and INFERENCE-EVALUATIVE. Unravelling these various chains by using the ABC model can be an exceedingly difficult task.

challenging, but not overwhelming assignments that are sufficiently stimulating to promote therapeutic change but not so daunting as to possibly inhibit clients from carrying them out. The term was coined by Dryden (1987b) in negotiating HOMEWORK tasks. Despite ELLIS's (1983a) emphasis on employing flooding or total exposure methods to tackle clients' DISCOMFORT ANXIETY, not all, or even most clients, will agree to this approach. A middle way is negotiated between total and minimal exposure: challenging assignments increase clients' tolerance to uncomfortable situations but do not overwhelm them so that they are unable to do what they have agreed to do. If the latter happens, clients run the risk of becoming discouraged from trying again. A therapist's insistence on flooding methods may well jeopardise the therapeutic alliance and reveal the therapist's rigid attitudes to homework tasks (see COMPROMISES IN REBT).

change calculus a technique which helps clients to determine the pace of therapeutic change and the commensurate amount of work required to sustain it, e.g. quick change = hard work. However, problems arise when some clients want the quick change but are not prepared to do the hard work that this involves. When such discrepancies are apparent to the therapist, she may target for disputing the possible LOW FRUSTRATION TOLERANCE beliefs underpinning them, e.g. 'I want to lose weight but I shouldn't have to work hard by sticking to my diet and exercising in order to achieve it'.

change in REBT the various therapeutic outcomes which can be achieved through this particular approach.

Change can occur at various levels. REBT encourages individuals to strive for a profound philosophical change (see ELEGANT SOLUTION): uprooting irrational beliefs based on demands and replacing them with rational beliefs based on preferences. Philosophical change can occur within a specific situation(s) or occur at a general level towards all life events. To bring about philosophical change, individuals are required to understand: that they largely disturb themselves; that they have the ability to undisturb themselves; that emotional problems largely stem from irrational beliefs; how to detect their irrational beliefs and discriminate them from their rational ones; how to dispute their irrational beliefs on logical, empirical, pragmatic grounds; how to internalise their new rational philosophies through multimodal methods of change and realise that disputing irrational beliefs is a life-long process; how to cope with lapses and RELAPSES as part of the NON-LINEAR MODEL OF CHANGE. Non-philosophical change (see INELEGANT SOLUTION) is also a goal of REBT though philosophical change is preferred (see COMPROMISES IN REBT).

changing the A making modifications in or avoiding unpleasant or negative activating events. Changing the A is a therapeutic compromise in REBT. Instead of facing an unpleasant ACTIVATING EVENT (e.g. waiting in long queues) and challenging the associated irrational beliefs, e.g. 'I can't stand the boredom of long queues. I shouldn't have to put up with it', a client may make subtle changes in the A by wearing headphones in queues as a form of distraction, or blatant ones by always looking for the smallest queues. The client's anger, in this example, may be alleviated by such means while leaving intact the philosophical underpinnings of his anger. Clients may also change their INFERENCES about A (since inferences are A's) in order to effect change, e.g. 'I'm not going to lose my job after all. That's a relief!' However, the underlying MUST, e.g. 'I must not lose my job', remains undetected and/or unchallenged.

child therapy the therapeutic arena in which children are counselled. Bernard and Joyce (1991, p.322) describe 'a four-stage RE[B]T model for working with young clients and their significant others: relationship building, assessment, treatment, and evaluation (RATE)'. Relationship building is carried out within the context of the therapeutic ALLIANCE and includes arranging the first meeting in an environment familiar to the child and finding out a child's hobbies and interests in order to use these for explaining REBT concepts. Assessment involves identifying the problem and self-defeating cognitions, emotions and behaviours associated with it. Treatment aims at eliciting the disturbance-producing ideas which can be challenged, depending on the cognitive sophistication of the child, at an inferential level (e.g. 'Is it really true that no one at school likes you?') or at the philosophical level within a specific context (e.g. 'Why must everyone at school like you?') in order to modify emotional upsets and construct rational messages or coping self-statements (e.g. 'Not everyone at school dislikes me so I can put up with some people not liking me'). Evaluation involves two forms: a global appraisal which compares the child's present behaviour with the goal for change (e.g. no longer truanting from school); a monitoring process which involves changing the treatment plan or deciding when COPING CRITERION has been reached with one problem before moving on to the next one. Parents may also be counselled because of, among other things, the emotional upsets (e.g. guilt, anxiety) that they develop in relation to their child's problems and which usually make them less effective as problem-solvers and may exacerbate their child's behavioural difficulties (see Hauck, 1980b).

client resistance an individual's opposition to, obstruction of, or action against a counsellor's therapeutic interventions. Client resistance can be seen as a general form of anti-therapeutic behaviour resulting in specific types of client resistance, e.g. stemming from feelings of hopelessness – 'I can't change'; discomfort anxiety – 'It's much too hard to change and I can't stand the discomfort involved'; fear of disclosure and shame – 'If I tell the therapist I am a peeping tom, he will be disgusted and reject me'. ELLIS (1985a, p.1) states that 'overcoming clients' resistance to therapeutic change is in some ways the most important problem of psychotherapy' and advocates the use of force and energy in applying multimodal techniques to challenge and modify the irrational beliefs which underpin clients' resistance (see RESISTANCE).

clinically relevant part of the A the part or aspect of an activating event which triggers a client's irrational beliefs. Some REBT therapists refer to this part of the A as the CRITICAL A. If a client is anxious about giving a presentation to his work colleagues, the therapist, through INFERENCE CHAINING, can tease out the client's most relevant inference (e.g. 'I will bore my colleagues') which triggers the irrational belief (e.g. 'I must not bore my colleagues') which, in turn, largely creates his anxiety. In order to establish that the clinically relevant part of the A has been located, the therapist reviews the inference chain with the client. Another technique is to manipulate the A by asking the client if he was assured that he would not bore his colleagues, whether or not he would still be anxious? If the answer is 'yes', then further investigation of the A is required.

cognition refers to various mental activities including descriptions, attributions, predictions, images, expectations, meanings. Even though these activities are interconnected, REBT pays particular attention to two types of cognitions: INFERENCES and BELIEFS. Inferences are personally significant interpretations of clients' ACTIVATING EVENTS, while beliefs are evaluations of actual or perceived events. As irrational beliefs are instrumental in creating disturbed emotional reactions, they are the main focus of intervention; distorted inferences are tackled later in therapy if they remain in place once irrational beliefs have been replaced by rational ones.

cognitive deficits a lack of or deficiency in certain mental skills, e.g. attention, memory, information processing, thought organisation, problem-solving. As REBT therapists hope to teach clients to think about their thinking in more critical and self-helping ways 'it is to the therapist's advantage to briefly assess the cognitive functioning of the client' (Walen, DiGiuseppe & Dryden, 1992, p.47) in order to determine if cognitive deficits are present and what accounts for them, e.g. do they have a neurological basis or are they the result of chronic substance misuse? Clients with cognitive deficits can be taught cognitive skills-training (e.g. problem-solving training) in an attempt to improve both their cognitive function and therapeutic outcome. ELLIS suggests that by determining the level of cognitive competence of clients with borderline personality disorder he can estimate the degree of difficulty in helping them to think rationally and, therefore, may at times encourage them to adopt POLLYANNISH THINKING. However, 'I do find that the majority of borderlines [personalities] really hate themselves for their deficiencies – especially for their disturbances – so I work very hard to convince them that they can fully accept themselves no matter what!' (quoted in Dryden, 1991b, p.80).

cognitive dissonance theory proposition that conflict arises when an individual's beliefs either contradict each other or their behaviour. According to Festinger (1957) individuals strive to maintain an equilibrium between their attitudes and behaviour. When information is presented which disturbs this equilibrium, cognitive dissonance or disharmony is created in individuals and they may try either to incorporate this new information or ignore it in some way in order to re-establish this equilibrium. REBT uses cognitive dissonance-inducing methods by asking clients to examine such beliefs as 'I can't stand panic attacks' and then point out that they have been 'standing them' for a long time – the behaviour is in conflict with the beliefs. Collecting such evidence helps to restore the equilibrium between rational beliefs and adaptive behaviour (see DISSONANCE-INDUCING INTERVENTION).

cognitive distortions illogical and anti-empirical (unrealistic) inferences or interpretations stemming from MUSTURBATORY thinking in emotional disturbance. Examples include JUMPING TO CONCLUSIONS, EMOTIONAL REASONING and PERSONALISATION.

cognitive-emotive dissonance clients' complaints of feeling 'strange' or 'unnatural' as they work towards strengthening their newly acquired rational beliefs and weakening or removing their long-held irrational beliefs. This occurs when clients recognise their irrational beliefs and how to replace them with rational ones, yet continue to think and feel in the same self-defeating ways. As Grieger and Boyd (1980, p.161) observe: 'They see a better way, but cannot yet actualise it, so they conclude that they cannot possibly overcome their disturbance'. Ways to tackle this form of dissonance include warning clients in advance of this potential block; setting coping rather than mastery goals in order to reduce clients' discouragement; challenging the irrational ideas behind cognitive-emotive dissonance, e.g. 'Change shouldn't be this hard' and encouraging clients to keep acting in accord with their rational beliefs until they have strengthened these beliefs sufficiently.

cognitive interactionism see INTERACTIONISM.

cognitive levels hierarchial arrangement of thought processes. Walen, DiGiuseppe and Dryden (1992) postulate three different levels of cognition and the associated degree of difficulty in making clients aware of them. Easiest to access are inferences about events by asking, for example, 'What was going through your mind when your friend didn't show up?' Harder to discover are evaluative cognitions implicitly found in inferences: e.g. 'What demand were you making about your friend not showing up?' Core irrational beliefs are at the deepest level of awareness and may lie dormant until activated in some way, e.g. a man who is rejected by his friends believes 'I absolutely must have the approval of important people in my life otherwise I will be worthless'. Profound philosophical change in REBT consists of uprooting these core irrational ideas and replacing them with core rational ones.

cognitive paradox therapists deliberately exaggerating rather than attempting to modify clients' irrational ideas, e.g. a therapist telling her client that he has to work much harder if he wants to fulfil his demand that he 'must please everyone'. By feeding back his irrational ideas in an exaggerated form, the therapist hopes to encourage the client to reappraise such ideas and introduce some flexibility into them e.g. 'I would like to please everyone but I don't have to' (see BEHAVIOURAL PARADOX; COGNITIVE RESTRUCTURING).

cognitive rehearsal preparing rational beliefs or coping self statements for use within an avoided situation, e.g 'I very

much hope I don't panic in the supermarket but if I do it will only be bad, certainly not awful'. This technique helps clients visualise themselves entering rather than withdrawing from unpleasant situations.

cognitive restructuring refers to the process of removing, through disputing, irrational beliefs and replacing them with rational beliefs – a change from a philosophy of demands to a philosophy of preferences. This philosophical restructuring can take place within specific situations or generally towards all life events and is viewed by REBT as enduring and the ELEGANT SOLUTION to tackling emotional disturbance. Restructuring (non-philosophical) can occur at an inferential level, the INELEGANT SOLUTION, where cognitive distortions can be shown to be incorrect, e.g. 'My wife isn't going to leave me after all'; but the philosophical implications, e.g. 'She must never leave me otherwise it would be too terrible to bear', remain unexamined and therefore not disputed. REBT hypothesises that the potential for emotional disturbance is greatly increased if change only takes place at the inferential level.

cognitive slippage thinking disorder or distortion. The most self-defeating form of cognitive slippage is expressed in rigid and unqualified musts and shoulds, e.g. the guilt-inducing belief 'I absolutely should not have done such a bad thing but as I did this makes me a bad person'. REBT hypothesises that such CROOKED THINKING is biologically-based and occurs when individuals transmute their PREFERENCES into DEMANDS.

cognitive techniques defined by Wessler and Wessler (1980, p.113) as 'techniques that rely solely on verbal interchange between therapist and client (within sessions), between the client and himself (written or thinking homework), and between author and client (reading and

21

listening to tapes as homework)'. The verbal interchange is to assess irrational beliefs, discover their self-defeating nature and replace them with rational and self-enhancing beliefs. Dryden (1987a) distinguishes between techniques used to acquire INTELLECTUAL INSIGHT and those to achieve EMOTIONAL INSIGHT. The former include disputing irrational ideas and discriminating them from rational ideas; the latter include devil's advocate disputing and writing rational essays.

cognitive therapy an approach 'based on an underlying theoretical rationale that an individual's affect and behaviour are largely determined by the way in which he structures the world' (Beck *et al.*, 1979, p.3). Developed by Aaron T. Beck during the 1960s, cognitive therapy (CT) is one of the major approaches within the field of cognitive-behavioural therapy. It shares many of the COGNITIVE RESTRUCTURING methods and behavioural tasks used in REBT to effect attitudinal change: REBT stresses evaluations that individuals make about events in their lives while CT emphasises meanings that individuals assigns to events. Important differences include the nature and priority given to working at various COGNITIVE LEVELS. Working deductively, REBT therapists 'plunge' into deeper cognitive levels in the early stages of therapy because they use REBT theory to focus on the clients' irrational beliefs (musturbatory thinking and its derivatives); distorted inferences are tackled later. In contrast, cognitive therapists work inductively: examining more superficial levels of thought first (automatic thoughts and inferential distortions) because they have no a priori idea of the precise form of clients' underlying cognitions (silent assumptions) – these are eventually clarified through a process called guided discovery (see Dryden, 1984a).

'cold cognitions' these are observations, descriptions and non-evaluative inferences and conclusions, e.g. 'My manager can be difficult to work with sometimes'. 'Cold cognitions' usually result in little or no emotional arousal as they do not rate or evaluate an event or a person's actions in terms of one's goals – in the above example, does the person prefer or demand that his manager should not be difficult to work with? A person's goals can be expressed in terms of 'WARM COGNITIONS' (preferences or desires) and/or 'HOT COGNITIONS' (commands and demands).

collaboration the notion of therapist and client working together as equal collaborators in looking for ways to overcome the client's problems (called collaborative empiricism in COGNITIVE THERAPY). This can be disadvantageous, according to ELLIS (quoted in Dryden, 1991b, p.120), because 'almost any good cognitive-behavioural therapist knows more, much more, than the client and does more direct teaching than "collaboration".' The idea of equality in a therapeutic relationship is a false one because, ELLIS continues, effective therapy is based on therapists knowing 'much more about therapeutic change than their clients do, and had better not be therapists unless they do!' (*ibid.*). REBT does take a collaborative stance but with the therapist in the role of authoritative (but not authoritarian) teacher.

comfort contented well-being; state of pleasant freedom from suffering. Clients' dire needs for comfort underpin DISCOMFORT DISTURBANCE. Demands are made on self, others and life conditions that clients have a trouble free and easy passage through life – these demands form a philosophy of LOW FRUSTRATION TOLERANCE such as when a client states: 'I can't stand it' not being liked, staying in a boring job, stuck in traffic jams, etc. In order to tackle their dire need for comfort, clients are encouraged to develop HIGH FRUSTRATION TOLERANCE, e.g. 'I can stand it but I don't like it' (see Dryden & Gordon, 1993a).

commitment to creative pursuits pledge to become involved in stimulating and constructive activities. Such a commitment is seen as a criterion of PSYCHOLOGI- CAL HEALTH (see Ellis & Dryden, 1987). Individuals who have vital and absorbing pursuits outside of themselves (rather than indulging in excessive introspection) tend to be happier and healthier than those who do not pursue such interests.

complex chains thoughts, feelings and behaviours which are intricately interwoven in an escalating pattern of emotional and behavioural disturbance. One of the four types of chains identified by Dryden (1989). For example, a 'reformed' drinker experiences boredom while on his own, becomes restless and anxious, seeks relief by having a drink, feels guilty for 'falling off the wagon', has another drink to cope with his guilty feelings, expresses disgust at his weakness, drinks more to stem his sense of shame, condemns himself as a 'hopeless drunk', feels depressed and becomes completely intoxicated. The therapist teaches the client not only how to disentangle a complex chain but also how to intervene early on in the chain to prevent escalation by identifying psychological triggers.

comprehensive cognitive disputing proposed by DiGiuseppe (1991a) as a model for covering all aspects of the verbal disputing process: the nature of the dispute; the style of disputing irrational beliefs; the level of abstraction of the irrational beliefs; and irrational belief processes. The nature of the dispute refers to the logical, empirical and practical arguments against irrational beliefs and the rational alternatives that are available in order to promote client change. Disputing styles are as important as the arguments presented: didactic (teaching); Socratic (asking questions in order to encourage the client to think for herself); metaphors and parables as a

way of crystallising therapists' arguments; humour directed at the client's behaviour, not the client; an additional style suggested by Dryden and Yankura (1993) is THERAPIST SELF-DISCLOSURE. The level of abstraction ranges from irrational beliefs held in specific situations (e.g. 'My boss must treat me fairly') to those held at more general or abstract levels (e.g. 'I should not have to work too hard in order to get what I want in life'). It is important for the therapist to tackle all irrational beliefs at all levels of abstraction. Irrational belief processes refers to disputing both the musts (demandingness) and the relevant derivatives from the musts. Disputing only one irrational belief does not automatically or necessarily lead to rational changes in other irrational beliefs. DiGiuseppe observes that comprehensive cognitive disputing is a powerful addition to the therapist's armamentarium.

compromises in REBT clients who are unable, for whatever reason, to achieve a profound philosophical change in their lives by replacing irrational beliefs with rational beliefs are shown other ways of achieving emotional stability by switching the therapeutic focus to a non-philosophical or more superficial level. This compromise, between philosophical change or little or no change if the focus is not switched, can still bring considerable benefits for clients. Such compromises include BEHAVIOURALLY-BASED CHANGE, CHANGING THE A and INFERENTIAL- LY-BASED CHANGE (see ELEGANT SOLUTION; INELEGANT SOLUTION).

concern to be of interest or importance; uneasy state of apprehension or uncertainty. A HEALTHY NEGATIVE EMOTION and a rational alternative to ANXIETY. Fears or threats are evaluated in terms of PREFER- ENCES, e.g. 'I hope I don't experience panic in a crowded restaurant but if I do it would be unfortunate and not terrible'. Behavioural responses in concern

23

include facing one's fears in order to learn how to cope with them.

concreteness refers to the level of specificity in addressing clients' problems. Clarity not vagueness is the rule of thumb for REBT therapists: for example, clear descriptions of activating events, precise labelling of emotional states, distinguishing between different types of cognitions. Explicit attention to detail reduces or removes ambiguity or uncertainty so that the therapist and client can keep in therapeutic step.

concrete thinking understanding based on specific instances or examples rather than abstractions. Concrete thinkers may be able to effect philosophical change in specific contexts (e.g. 'I want this job very much but I don't have to get what I want') but find considerable difficulty in tackling their IRRATIONAL BELIEFS at a general level (e.g. 'It's all above my head this "why must I always get what I want" stuff you keep asking me'). However, if such a belief is challenged and changed in a number of specific situations this may bring about a general philosophical change of a sort, but clients who are concrete thinkers remain vulnerable to emotional upsets in situations, where the belief would be present, that have not been identified for DISPUTING.

conditional self-acceptance the idea of accepting oneself on the basis of one's deeds, traits or actions, e.g. 'I've done some good things so I can accept myself'. However, the danger with this idea is that when things go wrong or when bad things happen individuals may condemn themselves on the basis of their actions or traits, e.g. 'As I can't seem to cope with problems in my life, this makes me totally pathetic' and therefore more likely to experience emotional disturbances such as depression. REBT's antidote to conditional self-acceptance is to encourage clients to strive energetically for UNCONDITIONAL SELF-ACCEPTANCE.

confrontation 'is not abrasive or aggressive, but rather assertive. Never should confrontation be used to subtly degrade or express anger toward the client' (Grieger & Boyd, 1980, p.102). Confrontation can be used to point out inconsistencies or contradictions between a client's thoughts, feelings and behaviours, e.g. 'You keep on telling me how keen you are to tackle your problem but every week you find some excuse not to carry out your homework tasks'; 'You say that you have resolved your anger regarding your husband's unfaithfulness but every time I mention his affair you flare-up'. The degree of vigour used by the therapist in confrontation can be adjusted to meet the requirements of the client's INTERACTIVE STYLE. It is important that after a confrontation the therapist seeks FEEDBACK from the client to determine the impact of his intervention as well as the consequences for the therapeutic ALLIANCE (see Walen, DiGiuseppe & Dryden, 1992).

conjunctive phrasing a technique used to help clients uncover their irrational ideas by helping them to complete the sentences containing them, e.g. an anxious client may say 'I might be rejected ...'; the therapist can reply 'and that would mean ...?' in order to elicit the disturbance-producing idea such as '... that I'm worthless'. Conjunctive phrasing can help to reveal to clients some of the self-defeating philosophies that underpin their problems.

consequences effects, results or outcomes of something that occurred earlier. The emotional and behavioural consequences at C in the ABC model. Unhealthy negative emotions and behaviours, e.g. depression and withdrawal, anger and retaliation, largely stem from irrational beliefs about negative life events. Healthy negative emotions and behaviours in response to these same events, and alternatives to those listed, are respectively, sadness and constructive engagement 'with life', annoyance and assertion.

These healthy emotions and behaviours are largely the product of rational beliefs which are arrived at after DISPUTING (see NEGATIVE EMOTIONS).

consequential thinking the ability to consider the consequences of one's actions. Clients with this COGNITIVE DEFICIT may require skills training. With illicit drug users who pursue short-range HEDONISM, drawing up lists of the likely consequences (e.g. going to jail, losing friends) if they continue to steal to finance their drug taking may modify or change present behaviour.

constructivism the theory that self-knowledge and identity, largely developed through relationships with major attachment figures (e.g. parents) are contained within deep and unconscious core cognitive structures (tacit knowing). Recent attempts have been made by some authors (Guidano, 1988; Mahoney, 1988) to divide cognitive-behavioural therapies into two groups: RATIONALIST and constructivist. REBT has been placed in the first group by these authors. Important differences include the constructivist view that reality is subjective and idiosyncratic in exploring clients' self-knowledge in emotional disturbance while rationalist approaches see reality as external and stable and clients' disturbance-producing cognitions can be confirmed or disconfirmed by collecting and examining evidence. Constructivism sees emotions, behaviours and feelings as inseparable and equal processes in acquiring and validating knowledge while rationalist approaches give primacy to cognitions in this process. Change in the constructivist framework takes place by introducing flexibility and adaptability into core cognitive structures while rationalists effect client change by focusing on more peripheral and conscious cognitive material (explicit knowing). ELLIS (1990, p.169) has strongly refuted this attempt to place REBT in the rationalist camp and claims that REBT 'is not only non-rationalist but that it is in several important respects more constructivist ... than just about all the other cognitive therapies, including those of Guidano (1988) and Mahoney (1988)'.

consumerism in psychotherapy the extent to which clients' interests are served by the profession of counselling. ELLIS (1989a, p.159) suggests 'I think I was always interested in effective consumerism in psychotherapy, especially in therapists providing their clients with efficient treatment'. However, as ELLIS shows, ineffective consumerism can manifest itself in various ways including: self-defeating consumerism of clients, e.g. they pick a therapy which will help them to FEEL BETTER but not to GET BETTER, i.e. their disturbance-producing ideas remain intact; ineffective consumerism of psychotherapists, e.g. clients may actually get worse in therapy because therapists, who believe they NEED the approval of their clients, will refuse or be reluctant to push clients to undertake the hard work usually associated with constructive change; ineffective consumerism in cognitive-behavioural therapies, e.g. unlike REBT such approaches usually involve only disputing clients' distorted INFERENCES rather than removing the philosophical core (absolute shoulds and musts) of their emotional disturbances. (Some REBT therapists regard these comparisons with REBT as both unfair and incorrect and appear to belittle the comprehensiveness of the CBT approach.) ELLIS suggests drawing up guidelines to tackle ineffective consumerism in psychotherapy which is generally overlooked in the profession's codes of ethics. Such guidelines would include therapists paying attention to research literature in order to be aware of which techniques are deemed effective and those which are not; and therapists being alert to and challenging clients' desires for therapeutic methods that will only bring relief from but not removal of their psychological problems. Effective consumerism can occur if, along with other changes, therapists 'aim for personal dedication to the consumers we are trying to help and a willingness to sacrifice some of our own desires to maximize our helpfulness' (*ibid.* p.172).

constructive negative emotions see HEALTHY NEGATIVE EMOTIONS.

contingency management clients whose pleasurable activities are made dependent upon them first carrying out avoided or difficult tasks, e.g. cleaning up one's room before watching television. Contingency management can help clients to reduce or remove such problems as procrastination and thereby instil or increase self-discipline (see OPERANT CONDITIONING).

coping criterion a method of assessing when clients have reached the stage of managing their problems but not always smoothly or easily. Coping criterion is used by therapists to determine the right time to switch from one client problem to another. COPING V. MASTERY MODELS offers two views on tackling clients' problems. A coping model reflects REBT'S stance on human fallibility and the consequent vicissitudes involved in the change process. A mastery model implies a 'perfect' resolution of problems and therefore out of reach of fallible clients. Such a model could discourage some clients and lead to early termination of therapy (see coping model used in THERAPIST SELF-DISCLOSURE).

coping self-statements declarations or assertions which help clients to tolerate or tackle problematic situations. These are used by clients who find it difficult to 'think about their thinking' and engage in verbal disputing. Short statements can be memorised or written down on cards in order to help clients cope with stressful or emotionally fraught situations.

REBT uses two different kinds of coping statements. The first kind counter unrealistic thoughts, e.g. 'Just because my present relationship has failed it certainly doesn't mean I'm never going to find another one'. The second kind are philosophical self-statements and challenge musturbatory thinking, e.g 'I would strongly prefer to get this job but there is no reason why I must get it. If I don't get the job, it will be bad but not awful'. A very brief coping statement for general use towards negative events might be 'Tough shit!' This statement encapsulates certain aspects of REBT: acceptance, anti-awfulising, vividness, force and the occasional use of profane or scatological language.

core conditions essential requirements for the effective practice of psychotherapy. These core conditions are usually seen as EMPATHY, GENUINENESS and unconditional positive regard. REBT endorses the first two qualities and replaces the last with offering clients unconditional acceptance as fallible human beings. Offering clients unconditional positive regard may actually make their self-acceptance conditional because they believe, for example, 'I'm okay because my therapist says so'. Unconditional acceptance, on the other hand, teaches clients that they can accept themselves no matter what others (including therapists) think of them. REBT therapists also avoid giving their clients undue WARMTH as this may strengthen their dire needs for love and approval and reinforce their LOW FRUSTRATION TOLERANCE beliefs.

core irrational beliefs basic or central disturbance-producing philosophies that largely create an individual's self-defeating emotions and actions. Common themes can be found in clients' irrational beliefs about their problems. Once these themes have been identified they usually coalesce in core irrational beliefs which link their problems. For example, a client may present with problems of anger at work ('My boss shouldn't give me so much work'), general frustration ('I shouldn't have to put up with this in my life') and experiencing rage at 'needless' delays ('I shouldn't have to wait so long in queues'). The core irrational belief here may be one of DISCOMFORT DISTURBANCE: 'Other people and life conditions should make things easy and trouble free for me and when they don't, I can't stand it.' Clients may well have more than one core irrational belief and these eventually become the focus of therapeutic attention in order to show clients that their problems are interconnected rather than discrete.

countertransference the feelings and attitudes of the therapist towards the client. These may be transferred on to the client from the therapist's reaction to significant others in her life (e.g. 'I can't stand people like my mother who endlessly whinge and whine') or her reaction to the client may provide useful information of the impact the client may have on other people (e.g. 'I wonder if my anger towards him is reflected in other people's attitude to him?'). With regard to the latter reaction, Walen, DiGiuseppe and Dryden (1992, p.246) observe that countertransference 'enables you [the therapist] to use yourself as a measuring device'. For example, the therapist may dread the appointment time because she will have to face the client's obnoxious behaviour (the client may have previously stated that everyone he has admired in his life, including the therapist, has always rejected him). If the therapist is angry towards the client her irrational belief might be: 'I shouldn't have to tolerate such behaviour. I can't stand him'. The therapist's irrational beliefs would be examined in SUPERVISION so that the therapist could undisturb herself before constructively tackling the client's behaviour and the dysfunctional beliefs underpinning it. If the therapist's irrational beliefs are strongly held then a period of personal therapy is advisable.

couples therapy the therapeutic arena in which couples are counselled. The approach in REBT to couples therapy is to view 'the individual partners as the clients – the relationship is important but secondary to their happiness as people. What is good for one or both of the individuals may not be good for their relationship, and vice versa' (ELLIS *et al.*, 1989, p.26). Therefore, REBT focuses on helping individuals to undisturb themselves emotionally about their dissatisfactions with the relationship or their partner's behaviour (e.g. 'She should want as much sex as I do') before looking at practical ways of improving the relationship or, if both partners cannot be reconciled, unangrily separating. Frequently, individual partners will be seen separately to reduce the emotional intensity of their problems before conjoint sessions are started or recommenced – this enables a more productive dialogue to take place rather than indulging in verbal abuse or acrimony. REBT therapists also help couples to examine some of the myths about loving relationships that they may subscribe to and which reinforce their existing problems, e.g. 'We were always told that when you're in love, sex takes care of itself'.

courtroom evidence technique a cognitive method for challenging irrational beliefs. The client presents the evidence for and against his irrational beliefs in two separate trials: in the first he plays the role of the prosecutor; in the second he plays the role of the defence counsel. The hope is that the client will have powerful evidence for his rational beliefs and will be able to discredit his irrational ones during the summing up when he acts as judge. If the 'verdict' goes in favour of the irrational beliefs, then the REBT counsellor will have more work to do and therefore will 'appeal' against the client's judgement (see Dryden, 1987a).

creativity in REBT imaginative and inventive use of this therapeutic approach.

Such creativity includes INFERENCE CHAINING to discover what clients are most upset about in regard to their problems; THERAPIST SELF-DISCLOSURE to challenge and help change clients' irrational beliefs; the THIRTEEN STEP COUNSELLING SEQUENCE which provides a systematic account of the causation, maintenance and eventual amelioration of emotional disturbance; vivid methods such as RATIONAL ROLE REVERSAL for disputing clients' self-defeating ideas. Creativity in REBT is only limited by the therapist's imagination and the ability to provide a clinically relevant explanation for a particular intervention or technique (see VIVID REBT).

credibility quality of being believable or trustworthy. The main goal of REBT therapists is to encourage clients to surrender their irrational philosophies of living and replace them with rational ones. One way of doing this is for the therapist to show credibility: that she is a trustworthy figure; that she can demonstrate her therapeutic expertise; that she displays confidence and an obvious sincerity in what the client is saying; that she expresses genuine concern for the client's predicament; and that she can blend in with the client's interactional style without seeming less than genuine. Wessler and Wessler (1980, p.15) suggest 'there will be more attitude change [from the client] in the desired direction if the therapist has high credibility rather than low credibility'.

criteria for disputing standards by which to challenge clients' irrational beliefs and examine the efficacy of their rational alternatives. Following a scientific paradigm, three major criteria are used to DISPUTE clients' self-defeating beliefs. (1) Logic, e.g. 'Just because you want your girlfriend to love you, how does it logically follow that therefore she must love you?' (2) Empiricism, e.g. 'Where is the law of the universe that says you must get what you want?' (3) Pragmatism, e.g.

'What are the likely consequences of holding on to the belief "she must love me"?' Dissecting the basis for such beliefs encourages clients to surrender their rigid musturbatory philosophies and construct self-helping, flexible and goal-oriented beliefs, e.g. 'I would greatly prefer my girlfriend to love me but she doesn't have to and I can still be happy without it', which are equally subjected to logical, empirical and pragmatic scrutiny.

critical A see CLINICALLY RELEVANT PART OF THE A.

critical incidents in therapy pivotal points or moments when the therapeutic relationship can be put in jeopardy and therefore requires tactful and sensitive handling by the therapist – such moments also create opportunities for client change. For example, if the therapist misses or cancels a session with the client, she might believe that she has been rejected and this means she is worthless; she might feel depressed and contemplate terminating therapy. Such critical incidents provide REBT therapists with further cognitive data to help clients uproot their disturbance-creating ideas.

critical rationality derived from Popper (1966), an attitude distinguished by its openness to criticism from self and others, its ability to learn from experience and its examination of the wider society and culture. As human knowledge is fallible, learning is based on trial and error – an evolutionary process to find solutions to problems. ELLIS employs critical rationality as a method of encouraging clients to subject their IRRATIONAL BELIEFS to the LOGICO-EMPIRICAL METHOD of science in order to FALSIFY them (e.g. a client who is rejected by a close friend and remains relatively calm about it is able to falsify her belief that 'I must be approved of by all my friends otherwise it will be terrible if I'm not'). With the same critical rigour,

RATIONAL BELIEFS are examined to determine if they will help clients to reduce or remove their emotional disturbances and thereby enable them to become more effective problem solvers. As we can never be certain that we have the right answers to our problems, the concept of critical rationality reminds individuals that their current self-helping beliefs may need to be modified or revised in the light of new information, evidence, changing circumstances, etc. (see SCEPTICISM).

crooked thinking thought disorder or distortion. ELLIS (1980a, p.5) suggests that 'the most profound and pervasive forms of crooked thinking ... that lead to self-defeating Consequences [C in the ABC model] are almost always forms of absolutistic evaluation of unqualified shoulds, oughts, musts, commands, and demands'. REBT hypothesises that crooked thinking mainly arises from humans' innate ability to disturb themselves (see BIOLOGICALLY-BASED TENDENCIES).

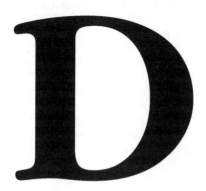

damnation state of being condemned or cursed. One of the three major DERIVATIVES from primary MUSTS. Damnation reflects the tendency for individuals to damn or condemn themselves, others and/or the world if their demands are not met e.g. 'You must not treat me in this way and you are an utter bastard for doing so'. The rational alternative to damnation is to teach individuals the concepts of (1) ACCEPTANCE of self and others as FALLIBLE human beings; and (2) acceptance of the world as it is (but not liking certain aspects of it).

death the end of life. The REBT approach to death teaches clients how to be healthily concerned about the inevitability of death rather than being unhealthily overconcerned or anxious about it. Healthy concern means that clients accept (though not necessarily like) the sometimes grim reality of death and are still able to enjoy their lives and pay due regard to those factors which will help them to maintain their health and wellbeing, e.g. driving carefully, giving up smoking. Unhealthy anxiety about death refers to clients' DEMANDS that they, *inter alia*, must not die, or must not die before their 'right time', or must not die in pain, and conclude that it would be terrible or awful if these events occurred. With these self-defeating ideas, clients can become obsessively preoccupied with the prospect of death, refuse to accept UNCERTAINTY in their lives (not knowing when, where and how they will die), restrict their lives in the hope that this will keep death at bay, and generally end up making their lives miserable. As ELLIS and Abrahms (1978, p.69) succinctly observe: 'The more people worry about dying, the less pleasure they have while living'.

de-awfulising see ANTI-AWFULISING.

decatastrophising encouraging clients to rate often highly unpleasant events along a continuum of relative badness rather than viewing these events as horrible or awful. This method enables clients to adapt constructively to negative life events, e.g. 'Losing both my house and job was very bad but not the end of the world. I can stand what happened to me and still get on with my life'. Barlow and Craske (1989) suggest that decatastrophising can be summed up in a single phrase – 'so what?' This phrase is not meant to suggest INDIFFERENCE to unpleasant events but an ACCEPTANCE that they have occurred. However, therapists should be mindful of when use of the phrase might be apt, e.g. if a person does not obtain the approval she believes she must have, and when it would be entirely inappropriate, e.g. death of a spouse. The term de-awfulising or anti-awfulising is preferred now in REBT because catastrophes do occur (see CATASTROPHISING).

decentring encouraging clients to stand back from their self-defeating ideas and realistically consider them, e.g. 'If your friend made the same mistakes as you did, would you condemn him as utterly worthless as you have done to yourself?' Such decentring techniques teach clients, as in the above example, that they have flexible and compassionate rules for others' behaviour but only rigid and unforgiving ones for themselves. Decentring enables clients to develop greater objectivity in their role as a PERSONAL SCIENTIST.

deduction form of logical reasoning which derives a conclusion from a specific set of assumptions - the conclusion must be true if the assumptions are. REBT therapists use a hypothetico-deductive model in assessing clients' problems i.e. derived deductively from REBT theory, therapists know the precise form of clients' disturbance-creating ideas (MUSTS and their associated DERIVATIVES) but not the specific content of these ideas (e.g. a demand for approval) and therefore develop hypotheses in order to pinpoint it. Therapists subject their hypotheses to logical and empirical examination and present their findings to clients, e.g. 'By what you've told me so far, could it be that you're demanding certainty of success before you undertake this important task?' Therapists' hypotheses can be confirmed, modified or rejected in the light of clients' comments. Therapists also develop hypotheses regarding clients' UNHEALTHY NEGATIVE EMOTIONS (e.g. guilt) if the latter are not able to identify them clearly. Hypothesis testing teaches clients how to develop SCIENTIFIC THINKING.

defence mechanisms unconscious processes which serve to protect individuals from becoming aware of painful or unpleasant realities in their lives. REBT hypothesises that if such individuals were to accept responsibility for their problems then they would also severely berate themselves for having these problems and thereby make themselves emotionally disturbed. To avoid such disturbance, defence mechanisms such as RATIONALIZATION are used, e.g. an individual might say 'I didn't like her anyway' to explain why a relationship failed. This may seem a plausible explanation but if he honestly admitted that he really did like her, he might damn himself as completely worthless because he was rejected. Therapists help clients uncover the ideas underpinning their defensiveness in order to bring them to clients' conscious attention (see PRECONSCIOUS). These self-defeating ideas are then challenged and changed to help clients achieve emotional stability and engage in constructive behaviour (see AVOIDANCE BEHAVIOUR).

deindoctrination process of removing the irrational ideas that individuals have uncritically accepted from others or imbued themselves with. REBT therapists carry out deindoctrination by asking clients to examine their irrational beliefs, e.g. 'I can never be happy without a woman in my life' in order to determine if they help or hinder the attainment of their goals. Therapists do not seek to reindoctrinate clients with RATIONAL BELIEFS as the panacea for all their problems: they encourage clients to subject their new self-helping beliefs to the same scrutiny as their irrational ones and revise or modify them in the light of new information, changing circumstances, etc. Deindoctrination teaches clients to practise open-minded thinking rather than the rigid and closed form associated with indoctrination (see BRAINWASHING).

demand rigid and dogmatic evaluative belief couched in the forms of an absolute must, should, ought, have to, got to, e.g. 'I must never make mistakes'. REBT views demandingness as the cornerstone of emotional disturbance (Ellis & Bernard, 1985). When individuals transmute their wishes, hopes, desires into devout demands they run the considerable risk of disturbing themselves emotionally, e.g. the depression-inducing belief 'Because I want your love therefore I must have it. Without your love I am completely worthless'. Demands form the basis of irrational beliefs: primary MUSTS and the irrational conclusions derived from them of AWFULISING, LOW FRUSTRATION TOLERANCE and DAMNATION (in the above example, the conclusion is damnation). Musts can be reduced to three basic demands: on ourselves, others or the world/life conditions. To reduce or remove emotional disturbance, demands are disputed in order to arrive at PREFERENCES and nondisturbed negative emotional reactions.

dependency refers to the overreliance on or undue attachment to the therapist by the client or vice versa. Some clients' dire needs for approval and/or comfort can be unwittingly reinforced in therapy by REBT counsellors exuding too much warmth towards clients rather than offering them unconditional acceptance. This approach can make some clients more, not less, dependent on the therapist, and may inhibit him from encouraging his clients to work hard and make themselves uncomfortable in order to overcome their problems. ELLIS (1985a) points out that therapists too can have approval needs, e.g. 'I have to be greatly respected and loved by all my clients'. With both the therapist and client, the irrational beliefs underlying their dependency problems are targeted for challenge and change.

depression psychological disorder marked by melancholy, lethargy, withdrawal, beliefs of hopelessness, helplessness, inadequacy and sometimes accompanied by suicidal ideas. An UNHEALTHY NEGATIVE EMOTION. Depression largely stems from DEMANDS that a loss (e.g. death of a spouse) absolutely should not have occurred and it is terrible that it did. Typically, depressed clients believe they are helpless to tackle their problems and see everything as hopeless in that they believe that nothing will change. Behavioural responses in depression are usually to withdraw from others and 'into oneself'. Depression can refer to a loss of self-esteem, e.g. 'I'm a complete failure' (ego depression) and/or to a loss in the realm of personal comfort, e.g. 'It is unbearable when life is too hard' (discomfort depression). Hauck (1974) lists three causes of depression: self-blame, self-pity and other-pity which he describes as making oneself depressed over the misfortunes of others, e.g. starving children (see SADNESS).

depth-centredness psychotherapeutic idea that clients' presenting problems have deeply-rooted causes and therefore the therapeutic focus should be at this level if productive and enduring change is to occur. REBT views depth-centredness as one of the main features of EFFICIENCY in psychotherapy (Ellis, 1985a). REBT therapists show clients how to uncover and dispute their core disturbance-producing musturbatory philosophies. The advantages of a depth-centred approach are, according to ELLIS, that clients will have a much clearer understanding of how they disturb themselves, be better placed because of this understanding to lead a more enjoyable life and generally increase their understanding of human behaviour.

derivatives irrational or rational conclusions stemming from irrational or rational premises, e.g. 'I must not lose my job and I am a complete failure for doing so'. Irrational derivatives or conclusions in REBT fall into three main groups: awfulising – more than 100% bad, the worst it could conceivably be; low frustration tolerance – difficulty and discomfort in life are too much to bear ('I can't stand it'); damnation – when demands are not realised people can damn or condemn themselves, others and/or the world. There has been some discussion within REBT as to whether or not 'musts' are primary processes and derivatives are secondary ones, or vice versa. Dryden (1987a, p.28) has offered a compromise by suggesting that they are 'in all probability, interdependent processes and often seem to be different sides of the same "cognitive coin".' Rational derivatives or conclusions drawn from rational beliefs are, respectively: anti-awfulising or evaluations of badness –negative or unpleasant events in life are 'bad but not awful'; high frustration tolerance -difficulty and discomfort can be tolerated even though not liked; acceptance of fallibility -people can accept themselves and others as fallible and complex human beings who therefore cannot legitimately be given a single global rating. This view of complexity is extended to the world which is also not given a single global rating.

descriptions straightforward and objective accounts of events if corroborated by impartial observers, e.g. 'I was made redundant from my job today'. Descriptions form part of external ACTIVATING EVENTS and stay within the bounds of fact. Accounts of events that go beyond the available information and are personally significant are called INFERENCES and are the subjective aspects of activating events.

desensitisation process of habituating clients to unpleasant or uncomfortable situations (e.g. fear of lifts) through behavioural or imaginal methods. REBT prefers *in vivo* methods of desensitisation, particularly FLOODING, because it hypothesises that if clients rapidly and fully expose themselves to unpleasant situations they will quickly confront and remove their disturbance-producing beliefs. Gradual desensitisation approaches may actually reinforce low frustration tolerance beliefs, e.g. 'I have to go slowly because I can't bear much discomfort'.

deservingness the idea that people deserve to have good or beneficial things in their lives, e.g. an interesting job, exciting sex life, lots of friends (however some people might believe they deserve an unhappy life because of the bad things they have done). Deservingness can lead to demandingness: 'Because I've gone through some bad times I deserve to be and must be happy, and life is no damn good because I'm still unhappy'. Such an attitude can lead to anger against others and/or the world and feelings of self-pity and hurt towards oneself. REBT argues that there is no inherent deservingness in life but hard work and determination as well as giving up one's demands may secure more desirable goals and fewer emotional problems. REBT therapists help clients to distinguish between deservingness and demandingness, e.g. 'Even though I deserve to be treated well, I don't have to be treated in the way I deserve'.

desires wishes, wants, preferences, hopes. A philosophy of desires is seen as one of the main features of PSYCHOLOGICAL HEALTH. The potential for psychological disturbance arises when individuals transmute their desires into dogmatic demands (MUSTS), e.g. 'Because I greatly desire you, and want you to desire me, therefore you must desire me'. Desires form the basis of rational beliefs from which are drawn rational DERIVATIVES. Desires lead to healthy negative emotions and constructive behaviours when goals are blocked or thwarted in some way.

detective work therapist-as-sleuth in attempting to discover what clients are most disturbed about in relation to their presenting problems and what accounts for them. Meichenbaum (1985) suggests that therapists 'might wish to emulate that fine clinician ... the television detective character, Columbo' (p.29) in the apparent perplexity he experienced with his cases but with dogged and skilful questioning eventually assembled the evidence that 'cracked the case'. Similarly REBT therapists can sift the evidence for and against their hunches, ask clients to help them with their doubts or queries (e.g. 'Can I just go over the details again because I'm not sure if I have understood what you're saying') or suggest hypotheses for clients to consider (e.g. 'By what you've been telling me, it seems that guilt is the main problem rather than the anger') in order to pinpoint the CLINICALLY RELEVANT PART OF THE A and the associated ACCOUNTING COGNITION which will then allow DISPUTING to commence.

devil's advocate disputing a cognitive technique whereby therapists challenge clients' newly acquired rational ideas in order to test the strength of them. Once a client has developed some proficiency in disputing her irrational beliefs and strengthening her rational ones, the therapist takes the contrary position of disputing the client's rational beliefs. This is done to test the client's skill in defending these beliefs as well as how competent she is in finding the weaknesses and errors in the arguments of the therapist-as-devil's advocate. Devil's advocate disputing can help to flush out the client's doubts about her newly acquired rational beliefs, as well as assess how strongly held are her implicit irrational beliefs whose existence make it difficult for her to embrace the new rational ideas (see RATIONAL ROLE REVERSAL).

diagnosis the process of identifying clients' disturbance-creating ideas and what treatment interventions will be required to tackle them. REBT does not spend an inordinate amount of time collecting diagnostic data or subjecting clients to batteries of tests before therapy proper can begin. As Grieger and Boyd (1980, p.52) observe: 'In RE[B]T, the diagnostic process begins with the first session of therapy, and, depending upon the therapist's expertise and the complexity of the client's problems, it can take from 10 minutes to several sessions'. Therapeutic interventions can proceed before a firm diagnosis has been established: an initial or tentative diagnosis can be confirmed, modified or rejected in the light of incoming information. Clients' problems are conceptualised within the ABC model in order to elicit the disturbance-producing irrational beliefs – the most important part of the REBT diagnostic procedure. In addition, clients' emotional problems rather than their practical problems are the diagnostic focus, e.g. depressed about living alone, angry about being in debt.

dialectics the practice of testing the truth of a theory or opinion by logical discussion. One of the major features of irrational beliefs is their illogicality, e.g. 'I would like people to respect me, therefore they must'. In emotional disturbance, clients' powers of logical thinking are absent and therefore they are taught to subject their irrational beliefs to logical scrutiny by the therapist asking, e.g. 'How does it logically follow that just because you would like other people's respect therefore you must have it?' Dialectics can show clients that their preferences are logical and reality-based ('I would like other people to respect me') but their demands ('therefore they must') are illogical and unrealistic and can often lead to emotional problems.

diary keeping recording entries in a book or journal on a daily or frequent basis. Clients can be encouraged to keep diaries during the course of therapy in order to provide information for both the therapist and client about the latter's emotional and behavioural problems and their associated cognitions e.g. anger about carrying out homework tasks: 'I absolutely shouldn't have to work this damn hard in order to overcome my problems!' Diary keeping can provide regular and reliable information as well as indicating clients' progress.

dichotomous thinking see BLACK-AND-WHITE THINKING.

didactic approach method intended to teach or instruct. REBT therapists are didactic when they act as authoritative teachers in providing explanations of the REBT theory of the causation, maintenance and eventual remediation of emotional and behavioural disturbance. When a didactic approach is used, as opposed to a SOCRATIC one, it is important for the therapist to obtain client feedback that she has understood the explanation, e.g. 'Could you put into your own words what I mean by "unconditional self-acceptance".' Too much didacticism from the therapist can inhibit the client's ability to think for herself, turn her into a passive rather than active collaborator in therapy and bring about only superficial changes in her problems.

difficult customers clients who usually present a formidable challenge to a therapist's ability to help them tackle their emotional problems. Also known as DCs or Tough Customers (TCs). ELLIS and Dryden (1987, p.136) describe DC's as 'individuals who are in the psychotic, borderline, organic or mental deficient category'. Such categories help ELLIS (quoted in Dryden, 1991b, p.71) to determine 'how difficult it will probably be to help these clients change'. REBT may work less well with more disturbed clients but it can still show them how to accept themselves with their disturbances and to reduce or avoid self-denigration. Young's (1988, p.132)

categories of TCs 'include individuals from lower socioeconomic classes, uncooperative adolescents, Fundamentalist Christians, and those with limited intelligence' and advocates teaching rational self-value to them, i.e. only to rate or judge a person's deeds or traits but not the person. Young presents a diagnostic framework to tackle TCs dysfunctional thinking which includes 'Less Me thinking': a person who believes he is worthless or inadequate because he has been rejected or failed in some way. Young distinguishes between 'less of a person', which the client believes and a 'person with less' – still the same person but with less (e.g. a failed relationship in his life).

disappointment state of not having one's hopes or desires met. A HEALTHY NEGATIVE EMOTION and a rational alternative to HURT. Disappointment occurs when an individual infers she has been betrayed or let down but evaluates this in terms PREFERENCES, e.g. 'I would strongly prefer to have been treated fairly and not let down but there is no reason why I must get what I prefer. What happened was pretty bad but not terrible'. Behavioural responses include acting assertively to communicate her sense of disappointment about another's behaviour towards her.

disclosure refers to clients' willingness to talk openly about their problems. Disclosure enables the therapist to plan various strategies to help clients tackle their problems more effectively. ELLIS (1985a) states that fear of disclosure usually stems from clients' feeling ashamed of their problems and therefore prevent themselves 'getting at the source of some of the things they find most bothersome' (p.12). Fear of disclosure is addressed by identifying, challenging and changing (a) the irrational beliefs underpinning the fear, e.g. demands that one must not have sexual feelings towards members of the same sex and (b) the distorted inferences associated with the fear, e.g. predicting that one would be condemned by the therapist if one disclosed one's 'shameful' feelings (see THERAPIST SELF-DISCLOSURE).

discomfort state of physical and psychological agitation individuals experience when faced with actual or potential adverse life events. Individuals who believe they cannot tolerate such discomfort in their lives run the risk of developing DISCOMFORT ANXIETY and/or DISCOMFORT DEPRESSION.

discomfort anxiety worry that individuals experience when anticipating pain, unpleasantness or agitation. Discomfort anxiety is created by individuals' irrational beliefs that such pain or unpleasantness must not be too great and it is unbearable if it is. REBT hypothesises that discomfort anxiety or LOW FRUSTRATION TOLERANCE is particularly prevalent among individuals who have ADDICTION problems, e.g. 'I can't stand not having a joint [cannabis] when I've had such hassle at the office'. To overcome their discomfort anxiety, clients are encouraged to experience the pain or unpleasantness they are attempting to avoid and dispute the associated irrational beliefs in order to achieve HIGH FRUSTRATION TOLERANCE.

discomfort depression dejection and gloom induced by an individual's belief that she has lost some element of personal comfort in her life and now conditions are too harsh, uncomfortable or difficult to endure. By experiencing SADNESS in relation to such a loss, she is able to accept the empirical reality of present conditions, adapt constructively to them instead of withdrawing from them and thereby realistically appraise how detrimental they are.

discomfort disturbance see DISTURBANCE.

disputation see DISPUTING.

disputing debating with clients the illogical, unrealistic and usually self-defeating nature of their irrational beliefs and helping them to construct logical, realistic and usually self-enhancing rational beliefs. Disputing involves SCIENTIFIC THINKING as clients are encouraged to provide evidence to support or falsify their irrational ideas and through the same process to test the efficacy of their new rational ideas. Disputing helps clients to achieve, ideally, an ELEGANT SOLUTION to their problems, i.e. surrendering their rigid and absolute philosophies (MUSTS) for ones based on wishes and desires (PREFERENCES). For clients who find, for whatever reason, philosophical disputing beyond their ability can opt for an INELEGANT SOLUTION to their problems, e.g. challenging their INFERENCES while leaving intact the underlying musts. REBT hypothesises that philosophical disputing promotes greater emotional stability and enduring therapeutic change.

disputing of irrational beliefs technique used to teach clients the steps involved in challenging and changing their self-defeating ideas. Disputing clients' irrational beliefs (IBs) is usually the primary task of REBT therapists. Disputing can be divided into four sub-categories. (1) Detecting means identifying IBs, usually in the form of musts, shoulds, have to's, got to's, that lead to emotional disturbance. (2) Debating consists of the therapist asking the client to provide evidence in support of her IBs until she acknowledges the lack of such evidence; however, there is sufficient evidence to validate her rational beliefs (wishes, wants, preferences, hopes). (3) Discriminating involves teaching the client how to distinguish between her irrational and rational beliefs and how the former lead to unhealthy negative emotions about negative A's while the latter lead to healthy negative emotions about these same negative events. (4) Defining refers to the therapist assisting clients to make accurate definitions in their use of language, e.g. 'I am a failure' means she will always fail if the statement is true. A more accurate depiction of reality would be: 'I am a person who has failed on this particular occasion'. A formal method of challenging self-defeating ideas is known as DIBS (Disputing Irrational Beliefs), which uses forms to guide clients through the ABCDE model of emotional disturbance and its remediation. DIBS 'is one example of cognitive homework that is frequently given to clients to do between sessions after the client has been trained to use them [forms]' (Ellis & Dryden, 1987, p.47). Disputing involves a MULTIMODAL APPROACH and for those clients who find disputing difficult, rational COPING SELF-STATEMENTS are used.

disqualifying the positive rejecting beneficial experiences or comments in order to maintain one's negative outlook. An inferential distortion stemming from underlying MUSTS, e.g 'When people tell me "you can learn from your mistakes" they are only trying to cheer me up and conveniently overlooking the fact that I absolutely shouldn't have made any mistakes in the first place'. Burns (1980) states that disqualifying the positive 'is one of the most destructive forms of cognitive distortion. You're like a scientist intent on finding evidence to support some pet hypothesis [e.g. 'I'm a complete failure in life']' (p.34). The only result that such 'evidence' usually brings is emotional misery.

dissonance-inducing intervention technique which shows clients that their irrational beliefs are either in conflict or disharmony with their constructive behaviours or other ideas they hold, e.g. 'You say that you find it absolutely unbearable when you don't drink yet by your own account you haven't touched a drop in two months without any adverse effects'. Clients are liable to dismiss such evidence in order to maintain an existing equilibrium between their thoughts and actions or between their beliefs and ideas, but therapists can continue to present dissonance-inducing evidence to

weaken clients' irrational beliefs and gradually strengthen their rational alternatives (see INTELLECTUAL INSIGHT). Dryden and Yankura (1993) advise therapists to proceed cautiously with such interventions as they may lead to clients developing SECONDARY EMOTIONAL PROBLEMS, e.g. with regard to the above client, he may now feel ashamed because he believes he has been exposed as a liar (see COGNITIVE DISSONANCE THEORY).

distinctive features of REBT characteristic aspects of this therapeutic approach. Comparing REBT with other cognitive-behavioural approaches shows these features in strong relief. Such features include: focusing upon the rigid and flexible philosophies that individuals construct when appraising themselves, others and the world – other forms of cognitive-behavioural therapy (CBT) appear to lack this philosophical perspective; encouraging clients to strive for a profound philosophical change rather than mere symptom removal; emphasizing the need for disputing clients' disturbance-creating MUSTS rather than challenging only their INFERENCES which, REBT hypothesises, stem from underlying musts –antimusturbatory disputing uproots clients' rigid ideologies whereas anti-empirical or inferential disputing usually leaves them intact; keenly discriminating between unhealthy and healthy negative emotions which, respectively, block and facilitate goal-attainment – other forms of CBT do not have such a clear-cut taxonomy of emotions; highlighting more than other CBT approaches, the need to search for SECONDARY EMOTIONAL PROBLEMS and tackling these first if they block clients from focusing upon their primary emotional problems. Another distinctive feature of REBT is its sparing use or avoidance of techniques, which are deemed to be, among other things, inefficient or actually reinforce clients' irrational beliefs, e.g. respectively, inordinate accounts of ACTIVATING EVENTS and gradual desensitisation instead of FLOODING methods to overcome LOW FRUSTRATION TOLERANCE.

distraction diverting attention away from examining one's disturbance-creating ideas. Distraction is viewed as a short-term and superficial method of change (e.g RELAXATION, THOUGHT STOPPING) because distraction helps clients to avoid focusing on and changing their underlying musturbatory philosophies, which are the main cause of their psychological problems.

disturbance emotional and behavioural problems largely created by irrational beliefs. REBT posits two fundamental forms of human disturbance: ego and discomfort. Ego disturbance involves individuals making demands upon themselves, others and the world and when these demands are not met to indulge in self-damnation, e.g. 'As I can't have your love, which I must have, this means I'm no good'. The rational alternative to self-damnation is UNCONDITION-AL SELF-ACCEPTANCE as a fallible human being. Discomfort disturbance involves individuals making demands upon themselves, others and the world that comfortable life conditions must exist, and when they do not clients experience and exhibit low frustration tolerance ('I can't stand living under such conditions!'). The rational alternative to LFT is high frustration tolerance ('I can stand it but I don't like it'). Ego and discomfort disturbance are not discrete categories but can significantly overlap in emotional problems (see SECONDARY EMOTIONAL PROBLEMS).

disturbance about disturbance chain exacerbating primary emotional problems (e.g. anxiety about anxiety) or experiencing several emotional and/or behavioural problems linked in a single activating event, e.g. a client becomes angry over a colleague's insult, then becomes ashamed of his own angry response, and then experiences anxiety

because he wonders what his colleague will think of his behaviour. REBT therapists usually work on the part of the chain that clients wish to start with. However, therapists may offer a rationale to start elsewhere in the chain if it is clinically indicated or if the therapeutic focus is continually interrupted, e.g. a client wants to talk about her anxiety but keeps expressing her anger at having the problem in the first place (see CHAINING; SECONDARY EMOTIONAL PROBLEMS).

disturbance matrix derived from Dryden (1990c), a means of representing the conditions in which psychological distress is created. REBT hypothesises that the two fundamental forms of human DISTURBANCE are ego and discomfort, which are largely produced by individuals' DEMANDS upon themselves, others and LIFE CONDITIONS (see Figure 2). By constructing such a matrix, therapists are able to have an overview of emotional disturbance as well as place an individual client's problems within the appropriate category(ies), e.g. a man who says he is depressed because nothing seems to go right in his life may be experiencing ego disturbance because he is demanding that life conditions should be easy for him and, as they are

	Ego Disturbance	Discomfort Disturbance
I must	1	4
You must	2	5
Life conditions must	3	6

Figure 2 The disturbance matrix (see entry)

not, this means he is a complete failure (3); a woman who is angry with her colleagues' indifference to her heavy workload may be experiencing discomfort disturbance because she is demanding that her colleagues must make life conditions easier for her (5).

dogmatism a rigid insistence on the correctness of a particular viewpoint. Dogmatism usually takes the form of absolutist musts or shoulds which can lead to emotional disturbance. Clients' dogmas (e.g. 'I must always be in a relationship otherwise I am completely useless') are treated as hypotheses and therefore subjected to SCIENTIFIC THINKING with clients encouraged to develop the role of a PERSONAL SCIENTIST. If clients can discover that their dogmas are untenable then they can introduce flexibility into their thinking and construct psychologically healthier points of view.

doing v. trying a commitment to undertaking an activity in contrast to only attempting it. When clients agree to carry out HOMEWORK assignments, they frequently say 'I'll try to do them' rather than 'I'll do them'. The former attitude implies a good chance of failure or at least only half-hearted attempts; the latter attitude indicates a commitment to undertaking assignments and the probability of making faster progress and achieving deeper change. When a client uses the word 'try', the therapist can ask her to try and stand up but not actually stand up in order to get this therapeutic point across.

double systems therapy a two-stage therapeutic approach to problem-solving. First, REBT therapists help clients to remove their emotional disturbances about their practical problems (e.g. a man depressed about not having a girlfriend; a couple angry with each other over their unsatisfactory relationship).

Second, from their emotionally undisturbed viewpoints, clients can focus on what practical and constructive steps can be taken to increase their level of satisfaction in life and fulfil their desires (in the above examples, the man can learn assertiveness skills; the couple can undertake negotiation and communication training).

dreams a series of images, thoughts or emotions passing through the mind during sleep. Analysing clients' dreams is generally avoided in REBT because it is long-winded, time-consuming and indirect, and therefore inefficient. Emotional reactions about specific life events are much preferred as a basis for discussion. However, Dryden (1990b, p.55) advances two criteria when it can be used: '(1) it does not predominate in the therapeutic process and (2) the therapist has a definite purpose in mind in using it'. An example might be using dream material to tease out faulty inferences and irrational beliefs.

dysfunctional actions self-defeating behaviours which stem from an individual's irrational beliefs, e.g. a man who wishes to engage in love affairs is stymied by his belief 'I must not be rejected' and therefore is reluctant to approach suitable partners. By challenging and changing such a belief, clients can develop FUNCTIONAL ACTIONS.

dysfunctional beliefs attitudes which usually lead to unhealthy negative emotions, counterproductive behaviours and impede goal-attainment, e.g. a woman who loses her job and believes 'this absolutely should not have happened' becomes depressed, withdraws from the job market and thereby hampers her desire 'to find another job as quickly as possible'. By disputing such beliefs, clients are able to construct self-helping and goal-oriented FUNCTIONAL BELIEFS (see IRRATIONAL BELIEFS).

eclecticism see THEORETICALLY CONSISTENT ECLECTICISM.

educational approach teaching individuals how to acquire a rational philosophy of living. REBT is primarily a PSYCHOEDUCATIONAL approach to tackling emotional distress with REBT therapists in the role of authoritative (not but authoritarian) teachers. Explaining the ABCDE model to clients teaches them the causation, maintenance and eventual remediation of emotional disturbance. REBT not only helps individual clients but also seeks to attract and influence a wide audience with its educational message through such methods as self-help materials and public workshops. Indeed, ELLIS has frequently stated that 'REBT's future best involves widespread public education of its principles and practices' (Palmer, Dryden & Ellis, 1993, p.52). REBT has been introduced into the curricula of some American schools to provide schoolchildren with an emotional education in addition to the standard academic one. The most ambitious example of this policy was seen at the LIVING SCHOOL (see RATIONAL-EMOTIVE EDUCATION).

effects the new cognitive, emotional and behavioural results achieved by internalising a rational outlook. Effects are the 'E' in the ABCDE model of emotional disturbance and its amelioration, and are achieved by clients after successfully DISPUTING their irrational beliefs. This rational outlook based on PREFERENCES, reflects a non-devout and flexible attitude towards life, which is more likely to be self-enhancing, goal directed and lead to greater happiness than a rigid outlook based on MUSTS.

efficiency the maximal use of time and effort expended by therapists and clients to achieve effective client outcomes. ELLIS (1985a) lists the following as characteristic of efficient psychotherapy. BREVITY – achieving good client results in a relatively short period of time. DEPTH-CENTREDNESS – dealing with the deeply rooted 'causes' of emotional disturbance; in REBT this would be irrational beliefs. PERVASIVENESS – not only helping clients to deal with their present problems but also equipping them with a 'therapy for life'. EXTENSIVENESS – to decrease clients' emotional problems and increase their happiness as well as the potential for a more fulfilling life. MULTIMODAL APPROACH – the selective use of cognitive, emotive and behavioural methods to tackle clients' problems. MAINTAINING COUNSELLING GAINS –not only have clients' presenting problems been ameliorated, they also maintain their therapeutic gains after formal therapy has ended. PREVENTION – to provide clients with a therapeutic philosophy to minimise future emotional problems. ELLIS's zest for efficient psychotherapy may derive from his claim that 'I have a gene for efficiency' (Ellis, 1993a, p.12).

effort conscious exertion of physical and/or mental energy. REBT urges clients to work hard, often with maximum effort, if they wish to overcome their emotional and behavioural problems. This philosophy of effort can be summed up as: 'There's no gain without pain' and is particularly aimed at clients with LOW FRUSTRATION TOLERANCE beliefs.

egalitarianism doctrine advocating equality for all human beings. The REBT counselling relationship is based on the view that both therapist and client are equal in their humanity (neither is inferior nor superior), but unequal in their abilities and skills to tackle emotional problems. However, by the end of therapy, this skills inequality will usually have been greatly reduced or eliminated by the client becoming her own counsellor. Openness is also a feature of the egalitarian relationship and clients are free to ask about any aspect of REBT. Therapists are not averse to disclosing personal information for therapeutic purposes unless they believe that some clients might use this information in detrimental ways either to themselves or to the therapist (see THERAPIST SELF-DIS-CLOSURE).

ego anxiety worried state resulting from clients' demands that they must achieve success or gain approval and consequently will denigrate themselves if these goals are not realised, e.g. 'I must pass this exam otherwise I will be an utter failure'. The rational antidote to ego anxiety is for clients to experience CONCERN about the possibility of failure or rejection, unconditionally accept themselves if these events do occur and thereby engage in constructive coping behaviours.

ego depression state of melancholy induced by the belief that one's self-respect or self-worth has been lost, e.g. 'As my business collapsed, as it absolutely should not have done, this proves how worthless I now am'. The rational alternative to ego depression is for clients to feel SADNESS about such events thereby accepting themselves and the grim reality of what has occurred. From such a position of ACCEPTANCE, clients can adapt constructively to adverse events.

ego disturbance see DISTURBANCE.

elegant solution a therapeutic outcome where clients not only tackle their presenting problems but also strive to effect a profound philosophical change in their lives by surrendering their irrational ideologies and internalising a rational belief system to minimise future emotional problems. As 'musturbation [musts] is the essence of human disturbance' (Ellis, quoted in Bernard, 1986, p.47), the elegant solution is the method of change that REBT therapists prefer clients to choose. Clients are urged to accept themselves and others as fallible human beings and avoid appraising themselves, others and the world with a single global RATING thereby signalling their understanding of the complexity of human beings and the world in which they live. In addition to self-acceptance, an elegant solution involves the client staying largely with a preferential outlook, an anti-awfulising philosophy and exhibiting HIGH FRUSTRATION TOLERANCE. Acquiring and maintaining the elegant solution is a lifelong challenge. Obviously not all clients will wish to embark on such an ambitious undertaking and therefore may choose to pursue a less elegant or an INELEGANT SOLUTION. As indicated in the last sentence, the elegant solution can refer to different therapeutic outcomes and therefore might best be viewed as a continuum: a super elegant solution at one end which involves a permanent removal of emotional disturbance because clients have achieved an enduringly profound philosophical change (Weinrach & Ellis, 1980) – it is not anticipated that any human being, including Albert ELLIS, will achieve this solution for any sustained period; an elegant solution in the middle of the continuum where clients are able to minimise present and future emotional problems by internalising a largely preferential philosophy of living; and at the other end, a less elegant solution which involves more frequent eruptions of emotional disturbance because clients have only adopted a wavering preferential philosophy.

Ellis, Albert (1913-) the founder of REBT. The pioneering work of ELLIS in cognitive-behavioural approaches to therapy helped to launch other cognitive-behavioural schools and in recognition of this Dryden (1991b, p.7) has called him 'the father of rational-emotive [behaviour] therapy (RE[B]T) and the grandfather of cognitive-behaviour therapy (CBT)'. ELLIS had originally practised PSYCHO-ANALYSIS but became increasingly disillusioned with the inefficiency and ineffectiveness of this approach. He gave up psychoanalysis in 1953 and experimented with other methods of tackling emotional distress before founding REBT (originally called RATIONAL THERAPY) in 1955 – in its early form, a fusion of philosophical insight and behaviour therapy. Since that time, ELLIS has continually revised and refined the theory and practice of REBT in order to make it one of the most effective and efficient therapies currently available (see EFFICIENCY). Now in his 80th year, at the time of writing, ELLIS still works long days (usually from 9 am to 11 pm) seeing clients individually or in groups, presenting workshops, writing books, articles, engaging in correspondence, etc. Along with his vigour, his passionate but non-devout commitment to the role of musturbatory (MUSTS) thinking in largely creating emotional disturbance remains

undiminished (ELLIS, lecture, 1993).

embarrassment a state of self-conscious distress. An UNHEALTHY NEGATIVE EMOTION and a milder form of SHAME. Embarrassment stems from DEMANDS that a person should not have revealed a weakness or behaved stupidly in public (e.g. tripping over) and therefore condemns himself for such behaviour. Behavioural responses in embarrassment include withdrawal from the situation if possible or avoiding the gaze of others (see REGRET).

emotional consequences affective states resulting from one's beliefs, e.g. the guilt-inducing attitude 'I absolutely should not have done such a bad thing but because I did this makes me a bad person'. Emotional consequences are derived from both rational and irrational beliefs. Irrational beliefs about negative A's can produce unhealthy negative emotions such as anxiety, depression, guilt, hurt, and their associated self-defeating behaviours which tend to block goal-attainment. Rational beliefs about these same events can lead to more healthy negative emotions and act as alternatives to the above which are, respectively, concern, sadness, remorse, disappointment. These emotions usually have self-helping behaviours which aid goal-attainment (see NEGATIVE EMOTIONS).

emotional disturbance affective disorder stemming from irrational beliefs, e.g. the anxiety-provoking attitude 'I absolutely must not be rejected because it will be a terrible experience to endure'. The target for intervention in REBT and classified as UNHEALTHY NEGATIVE EMOTIONS (e.g. anger, morbid jealousy) because 'they lead to the experience of a great deal of psychic pain and discomfort; they motivate one to engage in self-defeating behaviour; and they prevent one from carrying out behaviour necessary to reach one's goals' (Dryden, 1990c, p.7). The irrational beliefs underpinning emotional disturbance are challenged and changed to create rational beliefs in order to produce EMOTIONAL HEALTH (see DEMAND).

emotional episode an eight step model proposed by Wessler and Wessler (1980) that breaks or separates a feeling state into its component parts. The emotional episode is an expanded model of the ABC's of REBT. The eight steps are: (1) a covert or overt stimulus that starts the episode; (2) input and selection as individuals become aware of the stimulus and also attend to other stimuli competing for attention; (3) thoughts or verbalised statements which describe the stimulus; (4) interpretations or INFERENCES made about the perceived stimulus and along with steps 1, 2, and 3 comprise the ACTIVATING EVENT (A); (5) appraisal 'is a crucial step in the emotional episode' (*ibid*. p.7) because the nature of the evaluative BELIEFS (B) will determine at steps 6 and 7, respectively, the EMOTIONAL and BEHAVIOURAL CONSEQUENCES (C); (8) reinforcing consequences of action occur as a result of the emotional episode and have important effects upon subsequent emotions and behaviours. IRRATIONAL BELIEFS at step 5 in the emotional episode are the focus for REBT therapists in their attempts to effect constructive change.

emotional health affective stability resulting from rational beliefs, e.g. the concern-producing attitude 'I would prefer not to be rejected but there is no reason why I must not be. If I am, it will be bad but not terrible'. Not all emotions are targeted for change in REBT. Certain emotional reactions to negative events (e.g. annoyance, non-morbid jealousy) can be seen as desirable and helpful and therefore are classified as HEALTHY NEGATIVE EMOTIONS because 'they alert one that one's goals are being blocked but do not immobilise one; they motivate one to engage in self-enhancing behaviour; and they encourage the successful execution of behaviour necessary to reach one's goals' (Dryden, 1990c, p.7). In order to attain emotional health, it is important for clients to distinguish between the cognitive underpinnings of disturbed and non-disturbed negative emotions (see PREFERENCE).

emotional insight refers to the stage in therapy where a client's rational beliefs are deeply and consistently held, e.g. 'I not only think it in my head but also feel it in my gut'. Though emotional insight does not originate in the intestines, this expression means that clients, through HARD WORK AND PRACTICE, are now comfortable with their new beliefs which help them to achieve their goal-directed behaviours (see INTELLECTUAL INSIGHT).

emotional reasoning advancing arguments or drawing conclusions based upon one's feelings, e.g. 'Because I feel like a failure, therefore I am a failure and this means I'll never achieve anything in life'. Clients assume that their feelings are true accounts of reality but therapists need to point out that feelings are not facts and draw clients' attention to the central role of irrational ideas in largely creating their emotional problems. Therefore the client's irrational belief 'I must not fail' leads to disturbed negative feelings which the client labels 'I feel like a failure' and uses to prove to himself that he is a failure.

emotional responsibility the concept that people are primarily responsible for their emotional reactions to life events. Clients come to therapy frequently blaming other people or circumstance, e.g. 'My wife makes me so angry!' The therapist in order to teach emotional responsibility might restructure his statement thus: 'How do you make yourself angry about your wife's behaviour?' The therapist can use various examples to show that other people or events do not directly cause our emotional responses, ~ 'Would twenty people who all los' jobs on the same day experi~

same emotion like depression, for example?' When clients accept responsibility for their emotional problems they empower themselves to overcome these problems (see PSYCHOLOGICAL HEALTH; THERAPEUTIC RESPONSIBILITY).

emotions feelings; affective states. Disturbed negative emotions such as DEPRESSION OR ANXIETY are the starting point for therapeutic intervention by providing cognitive data for examination, challenge and change in order to produce nondisturbed negative emotions such as SADNESS and CONCERN (respectively, rational alternatives to the above). Clients frequently complain of feeling, for example, 'trapped' or 'rejected' which, in REBT terms, are INFERENCES about reality rather than feelings about it – such 'feelings' do not appear in REBT's taxonomy of NEGATIVE EMOTIONS. In order to elicit how clients genuinely feel about adverse events in their lives, therapists can ask: 'How do you feel about this idea that you're trapped?' If clients reply 'angry' or 'depressed' then therapists can start work on uncovering the disturbance-creating beliefs. Some clients may say their emotional problems involve DISAPPOINTMENT or REGRET which, from the REBT viewpoint, are healthy negative emotions underpinned by PREFERENCES. If clients' accounts confirm the healthy nature of these emotions, then the search would continue for disturbed emotions. Other clients may state, for example, that ANNOYANCE is the problem but on closer examination therapists discover that ANGER (the irrational alternative to annoyance) is the more clinically accurate emotion or, alternatively, express anger about a negative event when only annoyance is really indicated. If a therapeuitc ALLIANCE is to be forged, it is important for the therapist and client to agree on a shared emotional vocabularly with the associated cognitive correlates, e.g. guilt is underpinned by DEMANDS; remorse, its rational alternative, is underpinned by PREFERENCES.

REBT is primarily concerned with solving emotional problems first before moving on to consider their practical aspects (see Bard, 1980).

emotive techniques methods which are designed to engage clients' emotions by disputing forcefully and energetically their irrational beliefs in order to move from intellectual to emotional insight. Such methods include IMAGERY, RATIONAL ROLE REVERSAL and SHAME-ATTACKING EXERCISES. REBT therapists employ emotive methods such as offering clients' unconditional acceptance as fallible human beings (though not accepting bad or obnoxious behaviours from clients); using HUMOUR to show clients they frequently take themselves and their problems too seriously; and disclosing to clients similar problems which they have had and how they overcame them by adopting a rational philosophy of living (see THERAPIST SELF-DISCLOSURE).

empathy the ability to understand and communicate a client's viewpoint accurately. REBT therapists offer clients two kinds of empathy: affective empathy where they demonstrate that they understand how clients feel, and philosophical empathy where they show that they understand clients' BELIEFS which underpin their feelings (see CORE CONDITIONS).

empirical approach an approach which relies upon the collection and evaluation of data in order to determine if clients' beliefs and attitudes are consistent with reality. Empirical disputing requires clients to provide evidence in support of their irrational beliefs while the therapist seeks to challenge such evidence, e.g. a client may say she 'can't stand living on my own' but the therapist points out that she actually 'can stand it' though obviously greatly dislikes living on her own. (The term 'empirical disputing' can be a source of confusion in REBT because it also refers to challenging only clients' INFERENCES). Clients' rational beliefs are reality-tested in order to show that their desires and wishes for, among other things, approval, love, success can be empirically validated but not their DEMANDS for these things. Clients are encouraged to see their beliefs as hypotheses rather than facts and develop SCIENTIFIC THINKING by subjecting their beliefs to logical and empirical scrutiny.

empirical disputing see EMPIRICAL APPROACH.

empty chair exercise a Gestalt therapy technique whereby a client imagines a significant person in her life, about whom she has unresolved feelings, sitting in a vacant chair in the consulting room and tries to engage in a 'dialogue' with that person. She may play both roles and switch chairs. Such a technique might be used in the REBT assessment process to uncover disturbed negative emotions and their associated dysfunctional cognitions when more traditional assessment methods have proved ineffective. The empty chair exercise is used as part of REBT's approach to THEORETICALLY CONSISTENT ECLECTICISM.

encounter marathons group interactions often of a vigorous and forceful kind which usually run for a 10-, 12-, or 14-hour period over the course of a single day, and are designed to give participants insights into their problems and methods to tackle them. The aim of the encounter marathons is twofold: 'first, to provide a maximum encountering experiences for all the group members; and second, to include a good measure of cognitive and action-oriented group psychotherapy that is designed not only to help the participants feel better but also to get better' (Ellis & Dryden, 1987, p.180). Under the direction of the group leader(s), various exercises are undertaken to 'loosen up' possibly inhibited group participants and thereby help to make them more amenable to discussing and examining their problems in greater

depth within the framework of the ABC model. The leader frequently intervenes to explain REBT concepts to the group as well as guide the investigation as individual participants attempt to unravel their problems with encouragement and comments from other group members. Participants frequently find that an individual's disturbance-producing ideas (e.g. a demand for APPROVAL) are also the source of their own problems. Tasks are assigned to individuals to carry out within the marathon to combat the irrational ideas that have been revealed. The closing procedures of the marathon include 'smoking out' members who have been relatively quiet during the day and encouraging them to present a major problem to the group; and asking group members to assign HOMEWORK tasks to each other. A follow-up session (of about 4 hours) is schedule 6–10 weeks ahead for group members to discuss whether or not the marathon has brought about in their lives some measure of constructive change. Latterly, very large group experiences which have a decided educational focus are preferred to encounter marathons. Known as intensives, these experiences are more highly structured than encounter marathons but share the latter's aim in providing a comprehensive cognitive — affective — behavioural experience for participants.

encouragement act of giving hope or confidence to. REBT endorses active encouragement of clients to tackle their emotional problems. As ELLIS (1985a, p.76) says: 'Coaching and pushing clients to change are a regular part of RE[B]T and are especially useful for working with difficult clients'. Therapists can encourage clients in their efforts by showing confidence that REBT not only works but can bring rapid results (but not all the time).

ending stage of individual therapy ʳ to the final sessions of therapy ⁱ

55

the client ideally shows proficiency at becoming her own REBT counsellor and is now ready to tackle problems on her own. The therapist remains alert to any lingering irrational beliefs of the client's: for example, that she still needs the therapist's help in facing her problems; not showing or suppressing her emotions (e.g. sadness) about the end of the relationship because she will condemn herself as weak. Dryden (1990b, p.45) urges REBT therapists to 'Be problem-focused to the very end!' 'Booster' or follow up sessions can be arranged if clients want them.

enlightened self-interest a position where individuals put themselves first most of the time in pursuit of their goals, without exploiting or manipulating others as part of their goal-directed endeavours. Individuals exist within a wider community and are encouraged to respect the wishes and desires of others. As enlightened self-interest is a flexible philosophy, it involves a person putting the interests of others before her own at times. In the REBT lexicon, enlightened self-interest is not a synonym for selfishness but a realistic approach to achieving happiness in life.

environmental problems practical difficulties that clients encounter in their daily lives. Clients often present in therapy with environmental problems they wish to tackle, e.g. noisy neighbours, poor housing. However, as REBT focuses on emotional problem-solving, its specific form will not be of much assistance unless clients are emotionally disturbed about these environmental problems (angry about noisy neighbours, depressed over poor housing). A major obstacle to client change is when clients cling to the idea that environmental problems directly cause their emotional reactions and thereby disregard or dismiss the crucial role of evaluative cognitions in mediating emotional responses to events (see ABC; A-C THINKING).

Epictetus (c.55–135 AD) stoic philosopher. A former slave, Epictetus taught, *inter alia*, a robust faith in willpower to overcome external misfortunes in life and obtaining inner freedom through submission to natural law and a rigorous detachment from everything not in our power. ELLIS credits Epictetus with being an important PHILOSOPHICAL INFLUENCE ON THE DEVELOPMENT OF REBT particularly with the quote that forms the heart of REBT: 'Men are disturbed not by things, but by the views which they take of them' – we are mainly disturbed by our attitudes towards events and not by the events themselves. Such a view of the causation of emotional disturbance is often very difficult for clients to grasp and/or accept as they usually exhibit A-C THINKING. Epictetus also made the uncompromising remark that 'A life not put to the test is a life not worth living' but with alteration can translate into REBT terms as: 'It is highly desirable (but not absolutely necessary) for individuals to test themselves in life in order to maximize their chances of a happier and more fulfilling existence'. While admitting that Epictetus has been a significant influence upon him, ELLIS has also stated that he 'clearly opposes many of Epictetus's semiascetic philosophies' (quoted in Bernard and DiGiuseppe, 1989, p.211) which are in direct conflict with REBT tenets, e.g. 'he [Epictetus] did not usually advocate changing obnoxious conditions that can be changed; he was utopian . . .' (*ibid*. p.215).

epicureanism philosophy of Epicurus (BC 341–270) which included advocating ethical hedonism. Epicureanism emphasised attaining enduring rather than transient pleasures and the avoidance of pain through prudence and discipline in order to reach the supreme goal of wisdom: peace of mind. Influenced by Epicurus, REBT hypothesises that as humans are essentially hedonistic in their wish to stay alive and pursue happy, fulfilling lives this is best achieved through responsible or LONG-RANGE HEDONISM, i.e. striking a balance between enjoying the pleasures of the moment and planning constructively for the future. Clients who sabotage future happiness for immediate gratification are indulging in the usually self-defeating philosophy of SHORT-RANGE HEDONISM. With regard to REBT's philosophical influences, ELLIS has stated that REBT 'is in many ways more Epicurean than Stoic' (quoted in Bernard and DiGiuseppe, 1989, p.211) because of its advocacy of long-range hedonism (see STOICISM).

epistemology the study or theory of the origins, nature, methods and limits of human knowledge. For some clients, therapy might be the first time that the basis for their beliefs has come under scrutiny in the search for evidence to confirm or disconfirm their beliefs. DiGiuseppe (1991a) gives three examples of client epistemologies. (1) Authoritarian – that knowledge comes from a higher source, e.g. God, parents. (2) Narcissistic – that something is true just because a client thought of it, e.g. 'I think life is a bleak journey – therefore it is'. (3) Constructivist – all viewpoints of reality are equally valid in spite of evidence to the contrary, e.g. 'I don't care how unrealistic it sounds, my opinion is just as good as anyone else's'. REBT encourages clients to adopt a scientific epistemology, i.e. knowledge can be acquired in more accurate and rigorous ways by subjecting beliefs to logical, empirical and pragmatic examination in order to test their truth and validity. Through this process, irrational beliefs can be uprooted and alternative views of the world (rational beliefs) can be constructed which clients can see are more self-helping, problem-solving and goal-oriented.

e-prime a semantic position in which the verb 'to be' is removed from the English language in order to avoid overgeneralisation. E-prime is used in particular in REBT to discourage clients from labelling self and others, e.g. instead of saying 'I am a failure', the e-prime version would be 'I sometimes act in ways that result in failure'. The use of e-prime in REBT attempted 'to provide an understanding of our tendency to overgeneralise (and to abuse the verb "to be") and to show the tremendous influence that those tendencies can have on our actions and emotional lives' (Ellis, 1977a, p.xii). Four books were written in e-prime during the 1970s but according to Wessler and Wessler (1980, p.249) 'it proved to be an awkward mode of writing and he [Ellis] later abandoned the practice' but not the concept of LABELLING (see GENERAL SEMANTICS).

escalation act of increasing, intensifying or enlarging by stages. REBT asserts that individuals make themselves prone to emotional disturbance when they escalate their PREFERENCES into DEMANDS, e.g. 'I very much want my colleagues' approval therefore I absolutely must have it'. However, there has been some confusion as to whether or not escalation really implies a transformation from one state to another which is ELLIS's meaning of the term. Echoing Gilmore (1986), ELLIS has suggested that to avoid confusion TRANSMUTATION is the more accurate term to use. Woods (personal communication) prefers the term 'changing' rational beliefs to irrational beliefs. He argues that 'escalation' implies that rational and irrational beliefs are on a single continuum. The term 'changing' suggests that they are, more accurately, located on separate continua as are the unhealthy and healthy negative emotions.

ethical humanism the position that human beings are neither subhuman nor superhuman and that human interests should take precednece in directing our lives rather than the interests of gods, nature or lower animals. With regard to the former, REBT stresses that all humans are equal in their humanity but not in their actions or traits; with regard to the latter, REBT advocates that we do not become insensitive or callous to these other interests or the religious beliefs of individuals.

ethics system or set of moral principles or values. REBT does not advance any absolute or prescriptive ethical principles for clients to follow (if it did it would undermine its own flexible and nondevout philosophical position). REBT adopts a relativistic stance with regard to ethics: questions of good or bad and right or wrong are dependent upon the specific situation and serve to determine if the client's moral values help or hinder the attainment of her goals, e.g. the client is angry about her loveless marriage and would like to have an affair but believes it is utterly wrong to be unfaithful. Therapists would help such a client tackle her ethical dilemma by subjecting it to logical, empirical and pragmatic scrutiny. REBT does not encourage or remain indifferent to clients who wish to act in socially irresponsible or harmful ways. By constructing an HEDONIC CALCULUS, for example, clients can usually see that such actions not only impede reaching their goals but also may rebound on them, e.g. a man who wants a wide circle of friends but believes he should exploit them when necessary eventually finds himself rejected and despised by them. REBT avers that if individuals act in ways that are both personally and socially responsible they are more likely to realise important life goals as well as help to produce a more equitable society in which to live (see ENLIGHTENED SELF-INTEREST).

etiology of irrational thinking causes or origins of self-defeating attitudes. ELLIS (1976) asserts that humans have a BIOLOGICALLY-BASED TENDENCY to think irrationally and thereby disturb themselves. ELLIS's evidence for his etiological view includes the prevalence of CROOKED THINKING both among the rationally raised and in all societies and cultures that have been studied. REBT does acknowledge the important familial and societal influences upon human irrationality but emphasises individual responsibility for such disturbance, e.g. a person who has had a lonely upbringing may well construct out of his experiences a rigid outlook involving the disturbance-producing belief 'I absolutely should not have been subjected to such loneliness and because of it, I'll never be happy'. Another person with a similar upbinging may emerge from it relatively happy and stable without such an irrational philosophy. Therefore irrational thinking is not directly caused by adverse life events but by our innate ability to disturb ourselves about these events. REBT's view of the biological basis of irrational thinking is not a fatalistic one (there is nothing we can do to resist human irrationality) because we also have a second innate tendency to rational thinking which can significantly reduce or limit our ability to disturb ourselves.

evaluative beliefs attitudes which are appraisals of self, others or the world and constitute the cognitive core of individuals self-helping or self-defeating ideas. These can be divided into two kinds: (1) rigid and absolute evaluations couched in the forms of musts and shoulds are known as irrational beliefs with their associated evaluative conclusions, e.g. 'I must always be successful otherwise I will be completely worthless'. These rigid evaluative beliefs are termed irrational because they will usually lead to emotional disturbance and inhibit goal-attainment. (2). Flexible and nonabsolute evaluations couched in the form of preferences and desires are known as rational beliefs with their associated evaluative conclusions, e.g. 'I would prefer to always be successful but I don't have to be. When I'm not successful it will be bad but hardly awful'. These flexible evaluative beliefs are termed rational because they are less likely to produce emotional upsets and facilitate goal-attainment.

exaggeration state of magnifying something beyond the limits of truth; overstate. Usually used as a form of HUMOUR in disputing irrational beliefs, e.g. a client might say 'I've done an awful thing and you will be shocked' at which point the therapist might hide under the table to prepare for the 'shock'. Humorous exaggeration is aimed at the client's irrational beliefs, not the client, and depends on the therapist's judgement whether or not its use is productive with clients.

existentialist stance the position which states that individuals have free will and largely create their own worlds as well as give meaning to them. They accept their own mortality and are responsible for the lives they make for themselves. As individuals are primarily in charge of their own emotional destiny, predeterministic features like fate or fortune are discounted in favour of self-sabotage in emotional unhappiness, e.g. a therapist may say 'REBT does not agree that it is your fate to be unhappy. Instead we can look at how you are preventing yourself from being happy'.

expectations act or state of looking forward with anticipation. These refer to both the client's and the therapist's. Clients' expectations include the relationship or BOND they wish to forge with the therapist, the degree of historical and biographical information they want to provide before a problem-solving focus is adopted, and the pace of therapeutic intervention in relation to their learning styles (how slowly or quickly they process information). REBT therapists demonstrate flexibility in meeting clients' expectations but are also alert to the fact that some expectations can reinforce existing problems (e.g. seeking a great deal of WARMTH from the therapist can strengthen a client's dire needs for approval). Therapist expectations from therapy may include succumbing to certain irrational beliefs such as 'I have to be greatly respected and loved by all of my clients' (Ellis, 1985a) which can prevent therapists from encouraging clients to work hard or making therapy uncomfortable for them. Regular monitoring of both client and counsellor expectations is an important feature of the REBT process (see Wessler and Wessler, 1980). Dryden (1993) suggests that expectations can have a threefold meaning which is not usually classified in the counselling research literature or in the practice of counselling. (1) Anticipation – e.g. a client expects that the therapist will blame everything on her childhood. (2) Preference – e.g. however, her desire is to focus on the problems that presently exist in her life. (3) Demand – e.g. her hopes of therapy were not realised as, implicitly suggested, they absolutely should have been. If the word 'expectation' is not clarified 'there is a reasonably good chance that they [counsellor and client or trainer and trainee] will misunderstand each other with unfortunate consequences for the subsequent process of counselling or training' (*ibid.* p.33).

exposure confronting situations that have been previously avoided in order to overcome one's fears about them. Exposure is used to challenge and change the irrational ideas underpinning behavioural avoidance, e.g. travelling on underground trains to prove 'I can stand it' or being rejected by the opposite sex to show that it is not an 'awful' or 'terrible' experience. REBT favours (but does not insist upon) full exposure or FLOODING techniques when negotiating with clients *in vivo* desensitisation tasks (see BEHAVIOURAL TECHNIQUES).

extensiveness the state of not only minimising clients' disturbed emotions (e.g. depression, anxiety) but also maximising their potential for a happier and more fulfilling life. Extensiveness is considered to be a hallmark of EFFICIENCY in psychotherapy. ELLIS (1985a) suggests that while intensive therapy deals with clients' current emotional distress '"extensive" therapy also deals with exploring and augmenting pleasure, sensuality, and laughter' (p.129). REBT includes intensive and extensive treatment approaches.

externalisation of voices a technique whereby clients learn to dispute powerfully and rationally irrational beliefs and messages either supplied by themselves or the therapist in order to enhance their disputing skills and respond rapidly to their own irrational ideas. An EMOTIVE TECHNIQUE derived from Burns (1980).

fable a short tale conveying a clear moral lesson. Fables, along with STORIES, PARABLES, ANALOGIES, MOTTOES, are used in disputing irrational beliefs and 'are dramatic ways of getting a point over' (Ellis, quoted in Dryden, 1991b, p.66). When the therapist has used a fable, it is important that she obtains feedback from the client that he has understood the point of it.

facilitating the working through process helping clients to internalise their newly acquired rational beliefs. This is achieved by clients using FORCE AND ENERGY to dispute their irrational beliefs in a number of problematic contexts in order to weaken such beliefs and thereby strengthen their rational ideas e.g. staying in highly uncomfortable situations in order to overcome 'I-CAN'T-STAND-IT-ITIS' and develop a philosophy of HIGH FRUSTRATION TOLERANCE. A variety of HOMEWORK assignments are negotiated to combat clients' irrational ideas and, as Dryden (1990c) observes, help 'to sustain his [the client's] interest in the change process' (p.66). Clients are taught the NON-LINEAR MODEL OF CHANGE to counter any ideas they may have that change will be a smooth process or that BACKSLIDING does not occur. As clients develop greater skill in disputing their irrational beliefs, it is important for therapists to 'ease off' so that clients can start devising their own homework tasks as part of REBT's aim to encourage them to become SELF-THERAPISTS for present and future problem-solving. REBT working through is the bridge from INTELLECTUAL INSIGHT to EMOTIONAL INSIGHT and 'constitutes the heart of RE[B]T [and] . . . is where most of the therapist's energy and time are directed and where longlasting change takes place' (Grieger & Boyd, 1980, p.122).

failures in REBT refers to clients who have been unable to engage with or profit from this form of psychotherapy. Dryden (1987b) examines some of his therapeutic failures by looking at the various domains within the therapeutic ALLIANCE. Goals – clients who insist that change in others is the goal of therapy and it is these others who 'make' the clients emotionally disturbed rather than the clients themselves. Bonds – clients who believe they need love or excessive warmth from the therapist (rather than the unconditional acceptance they are offered) and leave therapy when they do not receive it. Tasks – clients who do not accept the REBT view of emotional disturbance but blame other factors, e.g. external events, fate; clients who want to explore the historical roots of their present problems rather than focus on how these problems are being maintained in the present; clients who are not prepared to work

51

hard particularly with HOMEWORK tasks in order to overcome their emotional problems. Ellis's (1983b) conclusions regarding therapeutic failure include highly disturbed clients who were unable or unwilling to show any persistence in disputing their irrational beliefs; angry, rebellious or resistant to what was required of them (e.g. taking responsibility for their emotional problems) and generally avoiding the hard and uncomfortable work involved in the change process. As Dryden (1987b p.71) remarks 'clients who could most use therapy are precisely those individuals whose disturbance interferes with their benefiting from it'.

fallibility the inherent capability of human beings of getting things wrong and making mistakes. REBT urges clients to accept themselves and others unconditionally as complex and fallible human beings and not to harshly judge or condemn themselves and others when mistakes are made or wrong decisions taken, e.g. 'I am fallible human being who makes mistakes. I'm too complex as a person to give myself a single global rating like 'useless' or 'incompetent' on the basis of a few mistakes'. Clients who do not acknowledge their fallibility (e.g. 'I must always succeed at everything I do') are more likely to experience emotional disturbance when things go wrong. Life is also seen as complex and fallible where our desires and expectations will not always be met and therefore to avoid rating life, for example, as 'totally rotten' or 'completely crap' on the basis of our disappointments.

'false' emotions when clients present in therapy with emotions they do not actually experience but believe they are supposed to feel. These are 'false' emotions. For example, 'clients may believe that they must feel guilty in order not to commit some moral or social transgression or that they must feel frightened of failure in order to assure achievement' (DiGiuseppe, 1988, p.24). Other 'false' emotions may include clients feeling depressed in order to elicit pity from others or acting pre-emptively to denigrate themselves before others do it. 'False' emotions may be difficult for therapists to identify but 'they should be alert to their existence, particularly when 'something does not seem to ring true' about clients' accounts of their emotional experiences'' (Dryden & Yankura, 1993, p.55).

falsifiability the condition which allows statements to be tested by experiment and rejected if they fail the test. Popper (1959) considered that falsifiability is the hallmark of science and which distinguishes it from non-science. ELLIS, the founder of REBT, had largely followed the doctrine of LOGICAL POSITIVISM (which attempted to verify statements) but in the mid-1970s he switched to the Popperian camp of seeking to falsify them. For example, it is impossible to conclusively verify a client's universal statement that 'I must always be successful' because the client may have been successful up to now yet fail in the future, whereas it only takes a single instance of failure to falsify the belief thus allowing the therapist to start 'chipping away' at the client's irrational ideas. The principle of falsifiability is also applied to RATIONAL BELIEFS and they may need to be changed or modified in the light of observation or experience. REBT examines its own theories in order to falsify them (e.g. not every case of emotional disturbance invariably stems from musturbatory thinking) and thereby keep them flexible, sceptical and open to constant scrutiny (see VERIFIABILITY).

family therapy the therapeutic arena in which members of the family are counselled. While seeing the family as a unit or organization that can break down or become dysfunctional because of, for example, relationship problems, REBT primarily focuses on the emotional and behavioural problems of individual family members - as individuals in their own right rather than as members of a family system. Once individual family members identify, challenge and change the irrational ideas underlying their emotional problems (and help other members to do the same), then they can tackle the practical problems that still exist (e.g. squabbling over which television programmes to watch) and which prevent them from becoming a happier and more cohesive family unit (see Ellis and Dryden, 1987).

fear emotional agitation or distress caused by an individual's demands that an anticipated dangerous or frightening event must not occur. Hauck (1981a) states that the two most common fears are fear of rejection and fear of failure: 'The fear of rejection is probably more prevalent than the fear of failure but the two are very close. People are often afraid to fail for the very reason that they might be rejected if they do' (p.6). These two fears form the basis of many clients' anxieties. Clients are taught to overcome these fears by surrendering their DEMANDS that these fears must not occur, removing the 'horror' (emotional disturbance) if they do occur and striving to accept themselves unconditionally as fallible human beings in the face of failure or rejection.

feedback comments on or responses to an individual's progress, competence, performance, etc. to aid evaluation and correction, e.g. a therapist may say 'Client feedback can help me to improve my clinical skills and, if necessary, revise some of my methods.' As part of REBT's open and non-mystical approach to psychotherapy, therapists regularly ask for feedback from clients in order to determine the quality of the therapy offered and the effectiveness of their own performance – a kind of customer satisfaction questionnaire. Therapists also give feedback to their clients, for example, by informing them how they are progressing. Such feedback is deemed to be educative and corrective and not intended to be disparaging in any way.

feeling better usually superficial and temporary improvement in an individual's emotional state. REBT hypothesises that if clients seek or therapies provide only palliative methods to reduce emotional disturbance this may result in clients feeling better but not GETTING BETTER because their underlying disturbance-producing ideas remain unexamined, e.g. instead of challenging a woman's belief that 'I can't stand being stuck in traffic jams' the therapist encourages her to wear headphones and listen to soothing music.

feeling language an emotional vocabulary which distinguishes between healthy and unhealthy negative emotions and which therapists and clients agree to use. Misunderstandings can arise in REBT when therapists and clients do not use the same emotional vocabulary. A client may use the term 'sadness' when, in REBT terms, he really means 'depression' and vice versa. In order to minimise this misunderstanding, therapists teach clients the REBT taxonomy of emotions (unhealthy as opposed to healthy negative emotions) and their cognitive underpinnings of, respectively, demands and preferences. Even when unhealthy negative emotions have been identified, clients will not necessarily want to relinquish them or agree that they are self-defeating. Unless therapists present clear rationales for adopting healthy negative emotions, e.g. moving from anger to annoyance (non-damning anger) does not mean that people will 'walk all over' a client, therapeutic impasses can occur (see NEGATIVE EMOTIONS).

feminism doctrine advocating women's rights, interests, and equality with men especially in political, social and economic contexts. According to Wolfe

(1985, p.105), 'More than any other school of therapy, RE[B]T seems to come closest to meeting the criteria for effective feminist therapy.' Such criteria include tackling the LOVE-SLOBBISM (the dire need for love and the self-denigration that follows if it is not obtained) inherent in sex-role propaganda, stopping women from condemning themselves for their emotional and behavioural problems, and encouraging autonomy rather than dependence. REBT forms the springboard for attempts to achieve greater personal and economic power for women in their striving for self-actualisation (realising one's potential).

fixed role technique derived from Kelly (1955), this technique encourages clients to act (after a preliminary rehearsal period) as if they already have a new rational attitude, e.g. 'I would prefer my friend's approval but I don't need it', in order to learn alternative and more self-helping ways of thinking, feeling and behaving.

flamboyant therapist actions strikingly bold behaviours executed by a counsellor in order to make a therapeutic point. Dryden (1990b) provides a personal example of such flamboyance by flinging himself to the floor during therapy and barking like a dog in order for the client to answer the following question: 'Does behaving stupidly make you a stupid person?' Such actions can help clients to discriminate vividly between rating their behaviours and rating themselves on the basis of their behaviours (see VIVID REBT).

flexibility quality of being able to adapt or respond to changing conditions. Flexibility is viewed as a criterion of PSYCHO-LOGICAL HEALTH (mental attitudes which promote individual well-being). REBT views rational beliefs as flexible because they help clients to revise their goals or devise new ones when their existing goals are blocked or thwarted in some

way; irrational beliefs are characterised by their rigidity and usually prevent clients from adapting constructively to events when they fail to achieve their goals. REBT therapists demonstrate flexibility in their relationships with clients, e.g. those clients who only wish to make change in their INFERENCES about negative events in their lives rather than pursue PROFOUND PHILOSOPHICAL CHANGE; or adapting their style of intervention (e.g. formal v informal) to the requirements of clients. Therapist flexibility is tempered with caution as too much flexibility can sometimes reinforce clients' problems, e.g. a therapist agrees to go slowly in disputing a client's irrational beliefs because she 'can't bear too much pressure'.

flooding the concept of 'jumping in at the deep end straight away' rather than gradually working up to it. REBT encourages clients to face fully their fears in order to help them rapidly overcome their disturbance-producing ideas particularly LOW FRUSTRATION TOLERANCE ones, e.g. 'I can't stand too much discomfort in facing my fears'. ELLIS tries 'to get my clients to talk to ten or twenty new people a week, rather than merely one if they are afraid of rejection. Or if they are afraid of elevators, I encourage them to go into twenty elevators a day rather than one every twenty days. I find that those who are willing to act against their phobias implosively, overcome them much more quickly, and as far as I can see much more thoroughly' (quoted in Dryden, 1991b, p.36). Clients who are reluctant to use flooding (implosion) methods may prefer gradual desensitisation, 'dipping their toes in at the shallow end to start with' (see BEHAVIOURAL TECHNIQUES; CHALLENGING, BUT NOT OVERWHELMING).

focusing on the negative concentrating only on things that lack positive features; unrelieved pessimism. An inferential distortion stemming from underlying MUSTS, e.g. 'Because things in my life are not running smoothly, as they must do, everything is a complete mess'.

focus on changing emotional C's a major target for therapeutic intervention is disturbed emotional consequences. Therapists elicit from clients disturbed negative emotions rather than non-disturbed ones, e.g. respectively, anxiety v concern, depression v sadness, and assess clients' motivation to change these emotions as well as to help them see the benefits of such change. Therapists avoid vagueness in clients' descriptions of their emotions, e.g. 'I feel bad' by clarifying which emotion(s) this statement refers to – it might mean depression, guilt, shame or all three. Statements such as 'I feel abandoned' do not refer to emotions but INFERENCES. In order to find the emotion, therapists might ask: 'How do you feel about being abandoned?' If clients are unable to identify clear disturbed emotions, such techniques as the EMPTY CHAIR EXERCISE can be used to uncover them (see BEHAVIOURAL CONSEQUENCES).

follow-up counselling sessions which are arranged after formal therapy has ended to monitor clients' progress and assess how effective they have become as their own counsellors. Dryden (1990b, p.44) points out 'there is no absolute end to the rational-emotive counselling process' as clients may return to therapy at a later date with problems they have been unable to tackle successfully.

force and energy the use of vigour and exertion in attacking one's self-defeating attitudes. Some clients cling tenaciously to their disturbance-producing musturbatory (MUSTS) philosophies, even when they acknowledge the distress such thinking causes. REBT therapists use the principle of force and energy to dispute clients' irrational beliefs powerfully and vigorously if therapeutic movement is to occur. Therapists urge clients to use these same methods in their cognitive, behavioural and emotive assignments in order to move from INTELLECTUAL INSIGHT TO EMOTIONAL INSIGHT (see Ellis, 1985a).

fortune telling act of foretelling the future which clients usually claim only holds unhappiness or misery for them. An inferential distortion derived from underlying MUSTS, e.g. 'Because I have been rejected in love, as I absolutely should not have been, I can see myself being miserable for the rest of my life'. Clients are asked to provide solid evidence to support their negative predictions rather than indulging in what Burns (1980) calls 'mental magic'.

free speech argument challenging a client's contradiction between her claim that all humans have the right to express freely their opinions and her demand that a certain individual absolutely should not be saying the things that he does. Her restrictions on free speech in this particular instance are determined by her emotional disturbance (e.g. anger) about his comments, e.g. 'Of course I believe in free speech but that bastard should keep his mouth shut!' By pointing out the conflict between her democratic ideas and rigid beliefs, the therapist hopes to use such a DISSONANCE-INDUCING INTERVENTION to weaken her disturbance-producing beliefs and thereby construct rational beliefs which both express her strong dislike of his comments and support the principle of freedom of speech, e.g. 'I would greatly prefer that he did not make such comments but there is no reason why he must not make them. He is a fallible human being whose comments are highly unpleasant but he is not damnable because of them'.

free will philosophical concept that individuals are free to work out their own destiny. Despite our biological predisposition to irrationality (Ellis, 1976) and the effects of adverse environmental conditions in contributing to emotional and behavioural disturbance, REBT hypothesises that human beings can still exert considerable (but not complete) free will in choosing to work hard in order to overcome their self-defeating thoughts, feelings and behaviours. Clients who devoutly believe they are 'victims' of their genes (e.g. 'I'm a born addict') or environment (e.g. 'My upbringing made me depressed') may be very reluctant to accept the REBT view that we are largely responsible for our emotional problems. The free will argument can be used as part of the DISPUTING process: if such clients agree they have some degree of free will the therapist can ask, 'How does it follow then that you play no part in creating your emotional reactions to events?' (see A-C THINKING).

friday night workshops these are weekly public demonstrations of REBT given by Albert ELLIS on Friday evenings at the Institute for RET in New York. Volunteers are invited from the audience to discuss their problems with Ellis in order to show REBT in action; audience members may also absorb REBT principles to tackle their own problems. At the end of each interview members of the audience are encouraged to speak to the volunteer and therapist to gain further understanding of REBT theory and practice. According to Dryden and Backx (1987, p.155), 'REBT is well suited to this form of public workshop. It is a non-mystical type of therapy where the therapist is very open about his or her interventions'. Friday night workshops are not meant to supplant individual therapy but act as a means of PSYCHOEDUCATION within a public arena.

friend dispute challenging a client's double standards by pointing out that while he condemns himself as a 'complete failure' for losing his job he says he would be sympathetic and supportive if a friend of his also lost his job. Clients usually acknowledge the self-defeating nature of their double standards. The therapist can stress that if the client was as compassionate to himself as he would be to his friend, he might stand a better chance of overcoming his problems.

frustration state of having one's hopes, efforts, plans, etc. thwarted or nullified. When clients report that they 'feel frustrated', frustration in REBT is usually viewed as an ACTIVATING EVENT, e.g. a client is frustrated about his partner never heeding his wishes. In order to determine if the client's frustration is self-helping or self-blocking in tackling his problem, the therapist might ask: 'How do you feel about being frustrated at A?' to elicit either a disturbed or non-disturbed negative emotion, e.g. respectively, anger v. annoyance. If a disturbed emotion is identified, this is targeted for change.

frustration tolerance the amount of discomfort individuals believe they can tolerate in their lives particularly in the face of negative or unpleasant events. REBT identifies LOW FRUSTRATION TOLERANCE as a principal source of human disturbance and HIGH FRUSTRATION TOLERANCE as a major criterion of PSYCHOLOGICAL HEALTH.

'fun as psychotherapy' using humour in counselling to make therapeutic points. This refers to Ellis's contention (1977b) that 'emotional disturbance largely consists of taking life too seriously' and that one of the best methods to remedy this is to reduce irrational beliefs (not the person holding them) to humorous absurdity, e.g. getting a client to take responsibility for her inability to stick to a diet by asking her: 'Do those cream cakes really fly themselves out of the fridge and down your throat without you being able to prevent it?' (see HUMOUR).

functional actions self-enhancing behaviours which stem from an individual's rational beliefs and aid goal-attainment, e.g. a person with agoraphobia walks to the local shops on his own because he believes 'I can stand being uncomfortable even though I don't like it' (see DYSFUNCTIONAL ACTIONS).

functional beliefs attitudes which usually lead to healthy negative emotions, constructive behaviours and promote goal-achievement, e.g. a woman who loses her job and believes 'I would have preferred this not to happen but there is no reason why it must not happen' experiences SADNESS but is able to 'plunge' herself into the job market in order to achieve her desire 'to find another job as quickly as possible' (see DYSFUNCTIONAL BELIEFS).

functional disputing a form of debating where clients are asked to evaluate if holding on to their irrational beliefs will help them to achieve their goals or solve their problems. What useful or beneficial functions do these beliefs serve? The same kinds of questions can be asked with regard to the adoption of rational beliefs. Through such a functional analysis of clients' belief systems, clients usually agree that holding rational beliefs is more likely to help them realise their short- and long-term goals (see PRAGMATISM).

'garland of rational songs' ELLIS's (1977c) audio cassette collection of his rewritten lyrics of popular songs (e.g. 'I am Just a Love Slob' to the tune of 'Annie Laurie') in order to highlight clients' irrational beliefs and help them to internalise new rational beliefs – or 'sing your way to rationality' (see RATIONAL HUMOROUS SONGS).

'gateway' emotions emotions which act as entry points to other emotions that are usually more clinically significant for the REBT therapist, e.g. a client's anger towards her husband over his decision to go on holiday alone (as he absolutely should not want to do) reveals her underlying feelings of (1) hurt – that she has been treated in an uncaring, undeserved way and therefore must not receive such treatment; and (2) depression – she now believes she is worthless because she has lost her husband's love.

generalising gains from REBT insights which clients gain in therapy that can be used in all areas of their lives when they experience emotional and behavioural problems. For example, that demandingness is at the core of emotional disturbance and that force and energy coupled with SCIENTIFIC THINKING can remove these demands and replace them with a philosophy of preferences in order to reach important life goals. Clients are encouraged to remember that when they seriously upset themselves they will almost always 'sneak in' a must or absolute should to their thinking as this is a natural human tendency (see ELLIS, 1984a).

general REBT one of the two forms of REBT which helps clients to effect change at a non-philosophical level (see PREFERENTIAL REBT). ELLIS (1980b) has argued that general REBT 'is synonymous with broad-based cognitive-behaviour therapy (CBT)'. By this, ELLIS means that general REBT, *inter alia*, tackles clients' inferences about their problems rather than their disturbance-producing irrational philosophies; seeks symptom removal rather than profound philosophical change; teaches conditional self-esteem rather than unconditional self-acceptance; does not clearly discriminate between unhealthy and healthy negative emotions; and uses gradual desensitisation methods rather than implosive ones. There has not been unanimous agreement among REBT practitioners on the use of such terms as 'general' and 'preferential' because these terms 'are value-laden and may offend other cognitively-orientated practitioners, I prefer to avoid their use and thus distinguish between rational-emotive [behaviour] therapy and other forms of cognitive-behaviour therapy' (Dryden, 1987b, p.72).

general semantics one of the major philosophical sources of REBT which considers the important ways in which language influences thought and which, in turn, affects emotions. The imprecise use of language can lead to difficulties in rationally appraising and responding constructively to events, e.g. 'I am completely inadequate because I can't stop smoking' – such an overgeneralisation is hardly an encouragement to quit and may help to create emotional problems (e.g. depression). The statement 'I am completely inadequate' is an example of what general semantics calls the 'is of identity': the person is equated with the label. To avoid this labelling and linguistic inaccuracy, the verb 'to be' is discarded and the preferred mode of expression might be, 'I frequently act in ways that make it difficult for me to stop smoking but it is certainly not impossible to stop. My present inability to stop smoking does not make me as a person completely inadequate'. Omitting the verb 'to be' in writing is called E-PRIME and several REBT books were written in this style. As with general semantics, REBT promotes clear thinking and semantic precision in the use of language which will help clients to make more accurate assessments of reality and thereby reduce their propensity to emotional disturbance through exaggeration, distortion and overgeneralisation.

genuineness the quality of openness or congruence. When REBT therapists are being genuine they are 'not being phoney or trying to play roles' (Walen, DiGiuseppe & Dryden, 1992, p.60). REBT therapists are open to any questions about, or criticisms of, REBT and will disclose personal information if deemed to be clinically relevant; equally they will challenge or disagree with clients – honesty informs every aspect of the therapeutic relationship. In forging a BOND with clients, the idea of the therapist as an 'AUTHENTIC CHAMELEON' (Kwee & Lazarus, 1986) is used as long as it

does not lead to the development of a non-genuine therapist persona and thereby has the potential for undermining therapy, e.g. using a particular client's 'street slang' in order to build rapport but the client finds the therapist condescending and false and leaves therapy.

getting better usually deep and enduring improvement in one's emotional state. REBT hypothesises that if such a change is to occur, the clients need to remove through DISPUTING their disturbance-producing ideas, e.g. 'I must be loved'; 'I've got to be certain of success before undertaking important tasks', and replace them with rational alternatives based on PREFERENCES. Such a profound philosophical change usually leads to emotional stability and a significant increase in goal-directed behaviours: in the above example, ANXIETY is supplanted by CONCERN as the client tackles her dire need for love and acquires the rational belief 'I would like to be loved but being loved is not a necessity' (see FEELING BETTER).

global evaluations these are negative ratings that clients make of themselves, others and the world when their DEMANDS are not met, e.g. 'I am worthless', 'You are a bastard', 'The world is a cruel, rotten place'. Such evaluations or RATINGS attempt to define the totality of an individual or the world with a single label and thereby deny the complexity and FALLIBILITY of human beings and the world in which we live. Clients are encouraged to rate only aspects of themselves, others and the world, e.g. 'I failed at a few things but that doesn't make me a failure as a person' and give up all forms of global evaluations including positive ones, e.g. 'I am a good person' is equally simplistic and inaccurate for the reasons outlined above (see ACCEPTANCE).

Gloria the 1965 film of Albert ELLIS, the founder of REBT, Fritz Perls and Carl Rogers in which they demonstrate their therapeutic approaches with the eponymous client. For many counselling professionals and students this film is their first glimpse of REBT, and often provokes unfavourable criticism from those who object to ELLIS's 'aggressive' style in particular and the active-directive approach in general. ELLIS has stated that *Gloria* misrepresents his style and REBT: 'What I did in *Gloria* never was my therapeutic style . . . my style normally is much more relaxed as shown in other films that I have made . . . I deliberately stuck mainly to RE[B]T cognitive methods and I didn't use many of our emotive and behavioural techniques, which we usually employ in RE[B]T' (quoted in Bernard, 1986, pp. 258–259). ELLIS (Palmer & Ellis, 1993, p.173) has recently said that the film 'was the worst session of recorded psychotherapy I ever had'.

goals the aims or objectives that clients want from counselling. Goals are made explicit and not assumed, and specific rather than vague or unrealistic, e.g. 'I want to be able to ask women out' as opposed to 'I always want to be happy'. The treatment goals of REBT focus on the emotional aspects of the problem first (e.g. anxiety about approaching women) before moving on to the practical aspects of the problem (e.g. lack of social and assertion skills). Some clients may say they wish to feel 'less anxious' as a goal; however, from the REBT viewpoint, less anxiety still indicates the presence of lingering irrational beliefs and, therefore, clients are encouraged to choose a healthy negative emotion as their goal such as concern (the rational alternative to anxiety). Clients are also discouraged from choosing indifference towards negative events as a goal or feeling unrealistically happy about them. Bordin (1979) stresses the prime importance of a shared understanding between the therapist and the client of the latter's goals for change in building a successful therapeutic ALLIANCE.

got to verb expressing obligation or necessity. Dogmatic and absolute got to's are called IRRATIONAL BELIEFS, e.g. 'I've got to be sure that my friends like me'. Such got to's are targeted for DISPUTING (see DEMAND).

gradualism the practice in psychotherapy of helping clients to tackle their problems in gradual or incremental stages. ELLIS (1983a) has criticised gradualism in therapy for creating the impression that change can only be brought about in a slow and painless way and thereby actually reinforcing clients' LOW FRUSTRATION TOLERANCE beliefs (that they cannot stand much discomfort in facing their problems). Gradualism can, from this perspective, increase clients' problems rather than diminish them. REBT encourages clients (with their agreement) to use FLOODING methods to confront immediately and fully their problems in order to achieve rapid amelioration of them and significantly increase their tolerance level for discomfort. When clients refuse to undertake flooding assignments, a therapeutic compromise is reached which involves clients carrying out tasks which are CHALLENGING, BUT NOT OVERWHELMING.

group therapy the therapeutic arena in which clients who are not related to one another are counselled. This involves group members, through the vigorous active-directive leadership of the therapist, not only uncovering and disputing their irrational beliefs but also helping other group members to do the same. Some homework tasks can be carried out in the group, e.g. a silent group member speaking up. Small-scale groups act 'as a kind of laboratory where emotional, gestural and motor behaviour can be directly observed' and some clients, who are able to hide their feelings from individual therapists, 'can often be more easily unmasked in group, where they are asked to interact with several of their peers' (Ellis & Dryden, 1987, p.156). Group members give feedback to each other on their self-defeating thoughts, feelings and behaviours and through this 'collective wisdom' offer more possible solutions to problems than they might normally receive in individual therapy. REBT includes its FRIDAY NIGHT WORKSHOPS as a form of group therapy in providing PSYCHOEDUCATIONAL methods for emotional problem-solving.

guilt moral condemnation of an action or inaction as well as of oneself. An UNHEALTHY NEGATIVE EMOTION. Guilt stems from demands that individuals make upon themselves for breaking their moral codes, e.g. 'I absolutely should not have done such a bad thing as hurt someone's feelings and I am a bad person for doing so'. Guilt also stems from demands that individuals should have done good or helpful acts but damn themselves for not doing so. Behavioural responses in guilt include individuals attempting to make amends for their 'badness', punishing themselves through self-harm or withdrawing into substance use to ease or temporarily remove their guilt feelings (see REMORSE; Dryden 1994a).

gullibility the idea that human beings easily deceive or persuade themselves into believing the irrational messages of others, e.g. parents, teachers, political and religious teachers, fashion magazines. This tendency to gullibility is partly caused by humans' innate ability to disturb themselves (Ellis, 1976) and strong environmental and cultural reinforcement. For example, some parents may say to their children 'You won't be worth anything unless you get a good job'. Clients who come to REBT therapy seeing themselves as failures for not getting 'good' jobs are shown that they have chosen to accept and maintain the irrational messages of their parents. They also have the choice to challenge these irrational messages and replace them with rational and self-helping messages (see BRAINWASHING).

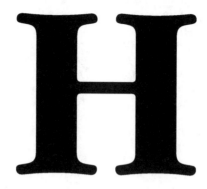

habituation to irrationality the process whereby clients have become accustomed to thinking and behaving in irrational ways, e.g. a client believes 'I must be liked otherwise I am no good' and always tries to please everyone even though he remains friendless. Even when clients acknowledge their irrational ideas and seek to change them, they still require considerable FORCE AND ENERGY to uproot these ideas and persistence in becoming habituated to rational ways of thinking, feeling and behaving.

happiness state of feeling or expressing contentment and pleasure. REBT 'is a system of psychotherapy designed to help people live longer, minimize their emotional disturbances and self-defeating behaviours, and actualize themselves so that they live a more fulfilling, happier existence' (Ellis & Bernard, 1985, p.5). From this perspective, rationality will significantly aid this process while irrationality will significantly impair or block this process. REBT hypothesises that happiness is maximised when humans achieve a relatively harmonious balance between short- and long-term goals without one jeopardising the other (see HEDONISM; PSYCHOLOGICAL HEALTH).

hard-learned lessons wisdom or insight derived from difficult or exacting therapeutic experiences. Hauck (1980b)

offers some hard-learned lessons for other therapists to consider: 'Study them carefully and apply them judiciously. I believe they will prove worthy of effort' (p.218). These lessons include: 'don't accept history as an excuse' – e.g. one's or others' obnoxious or objectionable behaviour requires action now to change it not an explanation justifying why it exists in the first place such as 'The reason for my violent behaviour is because my parents never loved me'; 'unconscious problems as red herrings' – e.g. a husband may blame marital problems on his wife's unconscious conflicts which, he claims, need to be uncovered and dealt with if marital harmony is to be restored; however, such reasoning usually indicates that he is avoiding the hard work required on his part to help effect change in the marriage; 'don't lose faith in your theory' – maintain a nondevout adherence to REBT theory in explaining the reasons for clients' problems despite their insistence that the theory is wrong or does not apply in this case, e.g. showing persistence in finding and revealing a client's anxiety-provoking thoughts when she is firmly convinced that her anxiety 'just appears out of the blue'.

hard work and practice maximum or strenuous effort and repeated action are required to internalise a rational philosophy of living. One of the THREE MAJOR

REBT INSIGHTS. If individuals wish to achieve enduring personality change by eradicating their irrational beliefs, then persistent and lifelong hard work and practice will be necessary to achieve this aim and avoid BACKSLIDING (see PERPETUATION OF DISTURBANCE).

hate an extreme form of ANGER, e.g. 'You absolutely should (must) not have behaved like that towards me and I'm going to kill you for it.' ELLIS has suggested 'there is an emotional variable of intensity which goes with the must' (quoted in Dryden, 1991b, p.20) and in hate it is probably at its most intense. Hate frequently goes hand-in-hand with revenge and their corrosive effects have led to some individuals experiencing 'an enormous amount of suffering which was far in excess of the suffering they received at the hands of others' (Hauck, 1980a, p.89). The rational alternative to hate is ANNOYANCE or non-damning anger (though probably strongly expressed if clients are to be encouraged to surrender their hate) and assertive behaviour, as well as increasing their tolerance of frustrating situations and the obnoxious behaviour of others.

have to verb expressing obligation or necessity. Dogmatic and absolute have to's are called IRRATIONAL BELIEFS, e.g. 'I have to succeed at everything I do'. Such have to's are targeted for DISPUTING (see DEMAND).

'head-gut' issue this refers to the stage in REBT where clients' newly acquired rational beliefs have intellectual credibility but lack emotional conviction, e.g. 'I believe it in my head but don't feel it in my gut'. In order to fuse the head-gut split, clients are urged to undertake HARD WORK AND PRACTICE so they can both think and feel the efficacy of their rational beliefs (see EMOTIONAL INSIGHT; INTELLECTUAL INSIGHT).

health see EMOTIONAL HEALTH; PSYCHOLOGICAL HEALTH.

healthy negative emotions these are emotions underpinned by rational beliefs (desires and preferences) about negative A's and are called healthy because they aid goal-attainment, increase one's ability to enjoy life and lead to self-helping behaviours. They are seen as negative rather than positive emotions because individuals will still experience some emotional discomfort. Such emotions include CONCERN, SADNESS and REGRET (see EMOTIONAL HEALTH; NEGATIVE EMOTIONS).

healthy resistance client resistance to change which is non-pathological (deriving from preferences). These clients resist change because they refuse to accept a therapist's insistence on a particular point of view, e.g. that they are consumed with self-hatred or their unhappiness stems from their parents' divorce. Instead of being led up these cul-de-sacs, they may healthily resist until some therapist flexibility emerges or leave treatment altogether (see RESISTANCE).

hedonic calculus a technique in which clients are invited to weigh up the short- and long-term advantages and disadvantages of a particular course of action in order to arrive at a healthy and rational balance between pursuing the pleasures of the present and not jeopardising those of the future, e.g. excessive party going and reluctance to study may result in future exam failure and diminished job prospects.

hedonism philosophy of achieving personally meaningful goals. While acknowledging that the pleasure principle is a driving force in life, REBT views hedonism not as a life of carnal pleasure but as those pursuits which are important or significant for individuals. REBT advocates a philosophy of responsible hedonism: that individuals seek to achieve both their short- and long-term goals rather than indulge in instant gratification at the expense of future happiness, e.g. an individual wants to lead a drug-free lifestyle but is reluctant to stop using drugs because it will mean a lot of discomfort which he is not prepared to tolerate. Responsible hedonism also involves not exploiting or harming others – making the world a harsher place to live may well militate against individuals' long-term interests.

helplessness state of being unable to help oneself. Some clients believe they are powerless and helpless to effect any amelioration of their problems and therefore are reluctant to examine the irrational ideas underpinning them, e.g. 'It won't make any difference, as it absolutely must do. Therefore nothing will ever change.' In order to test clients' hypotheses of helplessness, Grieger and Boyd (1980) suggest clients carry out tasks which are virtually guaranteed to succeed and have some positive impact on their lives which will help to stimulate further constructive activity.

here and now immediate present time. REBT focuses on how clients' problems are being maintained in the present through REINDOCTRINATION rather than how they were acquired in the past. Even if clients acquire insight into how their problems developed (e.g. 'I unquestioningly accepted my parents' view of me as a failure') this is usually insufficient to bring about enduring change in their lives. In order to achieve this, insight is coupled with HARD WORK AND PRACTICE to remove such a self-defeating belief (see AHISTORICAL APPROACH).

heuristic disputing debating which encourages clients to investigate whether or not their beliefs help or hinder the attainment of their goals, e.g. 'Does your belief "I must always be in control" actually help you to be self-confident and assured?' By examining the self-defeating nature of their irrational beliefs and the self-helping nature of their rational beliefs, clients frequently find that heuristic disputes rather than logical or empirical ones are the most persuasive in encouraging them to bring about constructive change in their lives (see PRAGMATISM).

hidden A's (activating events) the most clinically relevant inferences in clients' presenting problems which are difficult for them to identify or pinpoint. For example, a male client may say he is anxious every time he enters a public lavatory but is not sure why – 'I might be mugged. That could be it.' However, by INFERENCE CHAINING, for example, the therapist is able to reveal that what the client is most anxious about is being propositioned in the lavatory and agreeing to engage in homosexual acts that he will later condemn himself for. The disturbance-producing ideas implicit in the hidden A are targeted for DISPUTING. Hidden A's can also refer to UNHEALTHY NEGATIVE EMOTIONS (e.g. anger, guilt) which can be concealed by AVOIDANCE BEHAVIOUR (e.g. procrastination).

hidden agendas the covert but real reasons why some clients enter therapy rather than the ostensible ones they disclose to the therapist, e.g. an illicit drug user claims he wants help to give up drugs but actually seeks a favourable report from the therapist for a pending court case: 'I don't want to stop drugs but I have to tell lies to the therapist to get what I need.' By giving all clients unconditional acceptance as fallible human beings, ELLIS (1985a) suggests that REBT provides a therapeutic milieu which makes it more likely that clients will reveal their hidden agendas and undertake disputing of their associated irrational beliefs. However, for some clients who reveal their real reasons for entering therapy, this will not necessarily secure a satisfactory outcome for them (in the above example, a favourable court report) and therefore they may terminate therapy.

high frustration tolerance (HFT) the ability to tolerate or withstand a great deal of difficulty or discomfort in one's life without making oneself emotionally disturbed about it. A criterion of PSYCHOLOGICAL HEALTH and one of the three major derivatives from primary preferences, e.g. 'I would prefer not to be in this very uncomfortable situation but I can stand it even if I don't like it.' From this perspective, individuals are prepared to tolerate frustration because it is worth doing so to achieve their goals. Individuals with HFT accept grim reality; seek to distinguish between adverse events they can change and accept those they cannot; refrain from damning others for obnoxious behaviour without being prepared to put up with such behaviour; and giving themselves and others the right to be wrong (see LOW FRUSTRATION TOLERANCE).

high-level disputing challenging clients' irrational beliefs. High-level disputing seeks to effect a profound philosophical change in clients' lives by encouraging them to surrender their musturbatory ideologies (e.g. 'I must have easy conditions in my life') and replace them with preferential ones (e.g. 'I very much desire easy conditions in my life but there is no reason why I must have what I desire'). For clients who find this level of disputing unproductive, the therapist can switch to inferential or LOW-LEVEL DISPUTING.

historical development of REBT significant past events that have contributed to the evolution of this therapeutic approach. REBT was founded in 1955 by Albert ELLIS (b. 1913), an American clinical psychologist. The personal origins of this approach can be traced back to when Ellis, at the age of 19, forcefully acted against his fears of public speaking and meeting women. From 1947 to 1953, he practised as a psychoanalyst but became increasingly disenchanted with what he considered to be an ineffective

and inefficient form of psychotherapy – long-winded, time-consuming and wrong about its view that emotional disturbance is caused by early childhood experiences. When he finally abandoned psychoanalysis, he experimented with active and directive approaches to psychotherapy informed by his love of philosophy. It was a Stoic philosopher, EPICTETUS, who provided the cornerstone of REBT: 'People are not disturbed by things but by the views which they take of them' (1st Century AD); in other words, it is our beliefs and attitudes about events rather than the events themselves that largely create our emotional difficulties. A combination of philosophy and behaviour therapy launched REBT in 1955, and though it was initially called 'RATIONAL THERAPY', ELLIS emphasised from the outset that thoughts, emotions and behaviours were interdependent processes. Since 1955, the theory and practice of REBT has been, and is, continually revised (including name changes: 1961–1993 Rational-Emotive Therapy; 1993- REBT) to ensure that it remains a vibrant and dynamic approach rather than a static one.

Hitler argument the Nazi dictator (1889–1945) as an example, albeit an extreme one, of human fallibility. REBT takes the view that there are only bad deeds but not bad people (see GLOBAL EVALUATIONS; LABELLING). The logical outcome of this argument is that Hitler (and other tyrants such as Stalin and Pol Pot) committed many evil acts but was not himself an evil or bad person; in short, he was a fallible human being. Whenever the Hitler argument surfaces, either brought up by the REBT therapist/trainer or clients/trainees, it frequently leads to heated discussion. Hauck (1980a, p.79) suggests that people behave badly for three reasons: stupidity, ignorance, and disturbance. Therefore, 'we have the perfect and proper right to forgive anyone any kind of miserable and improper action. It is possible to forgive Hitler for killing millions of people, because he must have been pretty insane to feed people into gas chambers.' Some REBT therapists/trainers have considerable difficulty with accepting and defending the Hitler argument and openly express this to their clients and trainees.

homework this refers to the activity assignments clients carry out between therapy sessions. These assignments usually accelerate the process of constructive change through clients putting into practice their newly acquired rational beliefs, and thereby gaining confidence and competence in tackling their problems and reducing the potential for dependency upon the therapist. Homework is a key aspect of REBT: in fact, what happens outside of therapy sessions is usually considered more important than what happens inside of them – homework is the bridge between INTELLECTUAL INSIGHT and EMOTIONAL INSIGHT. Homework tasks are negotiated between the therapist and client and are based on the work done during a particular session. REBT therapists often say that homework tasks offer a 'no lose' formula in that if clients do their homework that is obviously useful, and if they do not do it that is useful too in that their irrational beliefs which block them from doing the assignments are revealed, challenged and targeted for change. REBT frequently uses OPERANT CONDITIONING methods (rewards and penalties) in order to encourage clients to undertake their agreed multimodal (cognitive, emotive, behavioural, imaginal) assignments.

homosexuality sexual preference for or sexual activity with members of one's own sex. ELLIS's (1965) earlier view of homosexuality emphasised its ubiquitous potential for emotional disturbance when individuals developed 'obsessive-compulsive necessities' for homosexual sex rather than allowing the possibility to exist of bisexual relations because they

were scared of developing relationships with women. This view was later revised so that 'I [Ellis] now hold that people may rationally *prefer* either an exclusively heterosexual or a homosexual life but they may be irrational when they *absolutely insist* that they cannot under any condition enjoy *any* kind of homosexual or heterosexual participation [original author's italics]' (Ellis, 1987b, p.197). Ellis adds that individuals can experiment with bisexual relations but there is no necessity to do so and they can remain exclusively, but not rigidly, hetero- or homosexual without developing emotional problems.

hostility see ANGER and HATE.

'hot cognitions' these are evaluative irrational beliefs in the form of commands and demands and frequently produce emotional and behavioural disturbances, e.g. 'You absolutely must not treat me like this. You are an utter bastard for doing so!' – such intensity may well lead to anger and retaliation. Clients are taught how to identify and modify their hot cognitions and thereby 'lower the temperature' to create 'WARM COGNITIONS' (preferences and desires) which are less likely to create emotional upsets. One problem with the distinction between hot and warm cognitions is that it implies that warm cognitions are less strong than hot cognitions, whereas rational beliefs can be held very strongly, but not rigidly (see 'COLD COGNITIONS').

humanism the view, endorsed by REBT, that human interests or values rather than superhuman ones should guide our behaviour and progress. It is also known as ETHICAL HUMANISM. Humans have intrinsic value or importance simply because they are alive and the best way to achieve happiness and fulfilment is through a life governed by reason – attained in REBT through SCIENTIFIC THINKING. Humanism usually rejects religious beliefs and though Albert ELLIS, the founder of REBT, is a well-known atheist, he has recently reformulated his objections to religion: 'I no longer believe that religion creates emotional disturbance but now believe that what I call religiosity – which I define as the devout, dogmatic believe [sic] in any theological or atheistic creed – tends to lead to neurosis' (Ellis, 1992, p.38).

humour the ability to express or appreciate the comic or amusing. ELLIS (1977b, 1980a) has frequently stated that emotional disturbance largely consists of taking life too seriously and exaggerating the significance or importance of events: 'that is what I have called, with humor aforethought, catastrophizing, awfulizing, or horribilizing' (Ellis & Abrahms, 1978, p.145). REBT therapists use humorous attacks on clients' irrational beliefs but not on the clients themselves. These therapists use such humorous techniques as taking things to extreme, reducing them to absurdity, paradoxical intention (e.g. agreeing with clients that they are the only people in the world who make mistakes), puns, witticisms, irony, slang, and the jocular use of profanity (see Yankura & Dryden, 1990).

hurt emotional anguish stemming from a perceived injustice to oneself. An UNHEALTHY NEGATIVE EMOTION. Hurt largely stems from DEMANDS that a person absolutely should not have been treated in an unfair way and it is awful to be treated in a way that is totally undeserved. Dryden (1987a) notes three hurtful reactions: self-pitying – e.g. 'Poor me'; depressed – e.g. 'I'm worthless for being treated in this manner'; angry – e.g. 'You're a bastard for treating me this way'. Behavioural responses in hurt usually involve retreating into silence or sulking (see *The Incredible Sulk*, Dryden, 1992) in the hope of getting back at or punishing the other person in some way (see DISAPPOINTMENT).

hypnosis artificially produced sleep-like state which increases an individual's susceptibility to therapeutic suggestion. REBT usually sees hypnosis as an INELEGANT vehicle for change because the therapist suggests rational beliefs to the client while she is relaxed rather than her arriving at these beliefs through conscious and vigorous disputing of her irrational beliefs. Also some clients with LOW FRUSTRATION TOLERANCE beliefs (e.g. 'Change is much too hard, as it absolutely shouldn't be. I can't stand the discomfort involved') may seek hypnosis as a method of bypassing the hard work usually required to overcome their problems (e.g. giving up smoking) and thereby actually strengthen their disturbance-producing ideas. However, hypnosis is sometimes used with clients who find traditional REBT methods unhelpful. Hypnotherapy sessions are usually recorded so clients can review the material between sessions with particular emphasis on how irrational beliefs can be challenged by listening to how the therapist undertakes it (see Ellis & Dryden, 1987).

hypothesis testing any statement, proposition, or belief which is viewed as a provisional explanation of events, circumstances, etc., and is submitted to observation and experiment in order to confirm or reject it. REBT views scientific thinking as the best way to achieve PSYCHOLOGICAL HEALTH and therefore treats clients' beliefs as hypotheses about reality rather than as facts. Irrational beliefs (e.g. 'I must never be without love') are subjected to logical, empirical (reality-testing) and functional (usefulness) scrutiny in order to demonstrate that such beliefs are insupportable. Rational beliefs (e.g. 'I would prefer never to be without love but there is no reason why I must have what I prefer') are equally subjected to logical, empirical and functional scrutiny to demonstrate that such beliefs are supportable. Clients learn to test their hypotheses as part of their developing roles as PERSONAL SCIENTISTS. *Hypothetico-deductive assessment* is the therapist's assumptions about a client's beliefs and/or emotions during the assessment stage and asks for client feedback regarding the accuracy of his assumptions, e.g. 'By what you've told me so far, it seems that you are feeling very angry over what happened. Would you go along with that?' If the client says 'no', the therapist collects further evidence to suggest another hypothesis or returns to his previous one because the evidence still points to anger.

iatrogenic techniques methods which inadvertently induce problems for clients or exacerbate their existing ones. This usually means any procedures which reinforce clients' irrational beliefs and therefore are generally avoided, e.g. therapists who give undue warmth to their clients can strengthen clients' needs for approval and lead to dependency upon the therapist; gradual desensitisation rather than implosion (FLOODING) can reinforce clients' demands for comfort in carrying out difficult or unpleasant tasks. REBT therapists are alert to the iatrogenic potential in the techniques they may use.

I-can't-stand-it-itis the jocular term for LOW FRUSTRATION TOLERANCE and refers to clients' demands for ease and comfort in life and their abhorrence of discomfort. Taken literally, I-can't-stand-it-itis can mean imminent client demise, but usually suggests that clients cannot envisage happiness in their lives while this discomfort exists. One method of disputing I-can't-stand-it-itis is to point out to clients how long they have actually been withstanding or putting up with their discomfort and are still able to achieve some measure of happiness.

ideology a system or body of ideas that forms a particular point of view or way of looking at the world (e.g. communism,

capitalism). REBT primarily focuses upon a client's 'musturbatory' (MUSTS) ideology which, it hypothesises, is at the core of her emotional disturbance and engages her in DISPUTATION of this ideology and helps her to adopt and act on an ideology based on PREFERENCES.

illogicality mental approach which is devoid of logic; unreasoning. A major criterion of irrationality. Illogical thinking occurs when clients' desires or preferences are transmuted (the form is changed) into demands, e.g. 'I want a new car therefore I must have one'. Clients are asked to demonstrate how the demand for a new car logically follows from a preference for one – such demands cannot be logically validated. Similarly some clients' premises (propositions) may be true, e.g. 'I have had some failures in my life', but they illogically conclude 'therefore I am a failure as a person'. Such a conclusion can lead to emotional problems (e.g. depression, shame). Clients are taught how to develop the skills of logical thought and reasoning in order to tackle such disturbance-producing illogic (see NON SEQUITUR; SYLLOGISM).

image of the person conception of how humans function. REBT asserts that humans are basically hedonistic: their major goals are to stay alive and pursue happiness though the nature of this happiness is individually defined. From this viewpoint, REBT defines rationality as that which aids goal-attainment and irrationality as that which blocks goal-attainment. Humans are viewed as essentially fallible: they make mistakes, have character faults and engage in self-defeating behaviours. Human perfectibility is probably an impossible goal. Humans have a biologically-based tendency towards irrationality (Ellis, 1976) and therefore an innate ability to disturb themselves; however, they also have a biologically-based tendency towards rationality and can minimise such disturbance-creating ideas and behaviours. REBT sees emotions, behaviours and thoughts as interdependent processes but does give primacy to thoughts, particularly evaluative beliefs (rational and irrational), as largely responsible for a person's emotional reactions to life events. Humans have the ability to realise their potential by actively (rather than passively) pursuing their life goals and vigorously counteracting their self-limiting beliefs, emotions and behaviours.

imagery techniques methods which use mental images or pictures to challenge clients' irrational beliefs. These are used as part of REBT's EMOTIVE TECHNIQUES. The main techniques involve using RATIONAL-EMOTIVE IMAGERY (Ellis and Maultsby versions). Using imagery can demonstrate to clients that they have considerable control over their emotions through cognitive modification and such techniques are readily given as HOMEWORK assignments (see HYPNOSIS; TIME PROJECTION).

implosion see FLOODING.

inappropriate negative emotions see UNHEALTHY NEGATIVE EMOTIONS.

incomplete sentences a technique to encourage clients to 'fill in the blanks'

left by the therapist's unfinished sentence in order to make explicit their dysfunctional thinking. For example, a client says his wife does not love him any more and the therapist may ask: 'And that would mean . . . ?' The client might reply that he now considers himself to be 'worthless'. Another use of this technique is 'to help patients become aware of the reinforcers operating to perpetuate a problem' (Walen, DiGiuseppe & Dryden, 1992, p.172), e.g. 'What I enjoy about cocaine is . . .' This can be asked until the client has exhausted all possibilities.

indifference lack of interest or concern. Clients frequently assume that if they surrender their demands (MUSTS) then the only alternative is to feel indifferent, calm or passive in the face of negative life events. REBT teaches clients a philosophy of preferences and desires (mild, moderate, strong) as a middle way between these approaches. Preferences encourage clients to express their dislike of negative events as well as to take constructive action to ameliorate the situation (if possible); whereas indifference implies that clients are trying to suppress their rational desires for unpleasant events not to occur and lack of action may make a bad situation worse.

individual therapy the therapeutic arena in which a person is counselled. REBT includes an early emotional problem-solving focus (practical problems are usually considered later in therapy) as part of clients' SOCIALIZATION into this therapeutic approach. Clients may generate a problem list which is then prioritised. Each problem is placed within the ABC model of emotional disturbance in order to elicit the clients' disturbance-creating ideas, e.g. the depression-inducing belief 'As my girlfriend left me for someone else, as she absolutely shouldn't have done, this means I'm a complete failure.' Therapists employ, and hope that clients will emulate, FORCE

AND ENERGY in challenging irrational beliefs and constructing rational alternatives, e.g. 'I would have strongly preferred that my girlfriend had not left me for someone else, but there is no reason why she must not leave me. My relationship failed but that certainly does not make me a failure as a person.' Multimodal HOMEWORK techniques are negotiated, e.g. behavioural tasks such as 'STAY-IN-THERE' EXERCISES in order for clients to develop competence and confidence in tackling their problems and which enable them to move from INTELLECTUAL to EMOTIONAL INSIGHT. When clients have become adept at SELF-THERAPY, termination of counselling is agreed and any lingering irrational beliefs are 'smoked out', e.g. 'As I am having difficulty coping on my own as I must not, I'll never be able to manage on my own' for disputing. Booster or follow-up sessions can be arranged. Therapy is tailored to the requirements of the individual client to achieve concord within the various domains of the therapeutic ALLIANCE, e.g. the therapist elicits from the client the kind of BOND he wishes to forge with her.

indoctrination process of uncritically accepting the frequently expressed ideas of others, e.g. 'People have always told me that I'm a "total loser" and I've always believed them.' Clients frequently state that other people make them believe what they do and therefore they are responsible for the clients' emotional problems, e.g. 'Who wouldn't be depressed if you're continually told how useless, no-good and worthless you are?' While agreeing that it might be difficult to withstand such a vituperative onslaught from others, therapists point out that clients are ultimately responsible for not only accepting such ideas but also for maintaining them. Therefore if clients wish to achieve emotional stability and relative happiness in their lives they are encouraged to undertake DEINDOCTRINATION, i.e. uprooting their self-defeating ideas through logical, empirical and pragmatic examination and replacing them through the same process with self-helping ideas, e.g. 'No doubt the same people will continue to insult me, but I now realise that I have the power to choose how I respond to such insults' (see A-C THINKING; BRAINWASHING).

induction introducing and preparing clients for REBT. This can take different forms. For example, Woods (1991) uses mini-lectures on the ABC's of REBT to provide a common conceptual framework and language on the causation and remediation of emotional disturbance. Grieger (1991) provides his clients with a booklet showing the sequential steps of REBT and 'literally guides clients through their psychotherapy' (p.37). Macaskill (1989) employs individually tailored induction procedures that teach clients what REBT 'has in store for them' including the release of powerful emotions in order to reduce 'misconception, confusion, or emotional overload' (p.88). All the above authors agree that effective preparation of clients for REBT frequently leads to improved client outcomes.

inductive reasoning argument which moves from particular instances to a general law or statement without proving its conclusions. 'Rational-emotive [behaviour] theory rejects logical positivism and its emphasis on induction' (DiGiuseppe, 1991b, p.153) because ELLIS eventually came to share Popper's (1959) view that no scientific (or client) statement could ever be proved with decisive finality (i.e. was not demonstrative) but it could be FALSIFIED.. Thus they both are opposed to inductive verification and suggest that science or knowledge advances by hypothetico-deductive methods, i.e. with regard to REBT, therapists use its theory to formulate and present to clients hypotheses about their disturbance-creating ideas which can then be confirmed, rejected or modified in the light of incoming information and clients' comments. If these hypotheses are confirmed, they have only temporary validity as they may be falsified at a later stage in therapy; whereas inductive methods of client assessment would tend to seek confirmation rather than disconfirmation of their hypotheses. Also inductive assessment is time-consuming because of its lengthy data gathering procedures and therefore, from the REBT viewpoint, is inefficient because it does not quickly test hypotheses by zeroing in on the clients' underlying irrational beliefs (see DEDUCTION).

inefficient procedures methods which prevent or distract clients from rapidly focusing upon and disputing the cognitive core (IRRATIONAL BELIEFS) of their emotional problems. Such procedures include: extensive dream analysis and free association (expressing whatever comes to mind) which are considered to be long-winded, time-consuming and indirect; lengthy rumination upon clients' past history distracts them from examining how their present problems are being maintained (rather than how they were acquired) by irrational thinking; endless discussions of clients' feelings instead of discovering the cognitive determinants of these feelings; encouraging positive thinking rather than challenging irrational beliefs to achieve REALISTIC THINKING (clients' problems will not always be satisfactorily resolved).

inelegant solution different therapeutic outcomes which involve challenging and changing distorted inferences about ACTIVATING EVENTS (A's), effecting behaviourally-based change, or changing adverse A's rather than confronting them – each outcome is achieved without concomitant philosophical change (see Dryden, 1987b; ELEGANT SOLUTION). For example, a client says she has no friends and is therefore miserable. The therapist seeks evidence to prove that her claims

of friendlessness are probably a distortion of reality rather than an accurate depiction of it (inferentially-based change). REBT views this process as inelegant because the client has not been encouraged to ASSUME THE WORST, i.e. that she has no friends and learns how to cope with this situation without regarding it as AWFUL. As this example shows, REBT therapists often have to make compromises on their preferred goals for client change. REBT hypothesises that the inelegant solution has limited generalisability to the client's other problems because she has not learnt any coping strategies if her inferences turn out to be true (see COMPROMISES IN REBT; GENERAL REBT; PREFERENTIAL REBT).

inference a perception of reality which goes beyond the information immediately available to an individual and is personally significant, e.g. 'None of my friends have contacted me in the last week. They probably all hate me'. The first sentence is a description of events; the second is what the individual infers or draws conclusions from these events. Inferences can be accurate or inaccurate. Inferences are generally seen in REBT as non-evaluative because they do not appraise how the individual views the event. REBT hypothesises that distorted negative inferences usually stem from underlying MUSTS, e.g. 'As I failed my exam, as I absolutely should not have done, therefore I will be sacked from my job' which will, in turn, primarily determine the individual's emotional reaction (e.g. depression). Inferences are seen as peripheral rather than central to emotional problems (see INFERENCE CHAINING; INFERENCE-EVALUATIVE BELIEF CHAIN).

inference chaining a technique of linking a client's INFERENCES in order to discover which one triggers her irrational beliefs. For example, Therapist: Let's assume that your work colleagues are sniping at you behind your back. Then what? Client:

Well, it might mean they don't like me; Therapist: Okay, let's assume that. Then what? Client: Well, they might stop talking to me, ignore me; Therapist: And if they did do that, then what? Client: That would mean I am a totally unlikeable, despised person. Oh God! The therapist keeps on asking 'Let's assume ... THEN WHAT?' questions until the irrational belief is identified, e.g. 'I must not be ignored and if I am, this means that I am a totally unlikeable, despised person. I couldn't stand that' which will account for the client's emotional disturbance (e.g. anxiety).

inference-evaluative belief chain the supposition that each INFERENCE in a chain contains an implicit rigid appraisal based on a MUST or SHOULD which in INFERENCE CHAINING is deliberately overlooked by the therapist in the wider search for the client's most clinically relevant inference. However, the interlocking nature of inferences and irrational beliefs requires in certain disorders (e.g. panic) to have each belief challenged and changed in order to show the client how her panic is created as well as diffusing the impending sense of catastrophe, e.g. inference –'I can't breathe'; irrational belief – 'I must be able to breathe freely'; inference – 'I'm going to pass out'; irrational belief – 'I must not pass out in front of these people' (see Dryden, 1989) (see INFERENCE CHAINING).

inferential distortion illogical and anti-empirical (unrealistic) INFERENCE stemming from underlying MUSTS, e.g. 'If I fail to give a wonderful speech, as I must not, I will be completely incompetent'. Inferential distortions include ALL-OR-NOTHING THINKING and JUMPING TO CONCLUSIONS.

inferentially-based change challenging and changing only clients' distorted INFERENCES to reduce emotional disturbance rather than attempting to remove it by examining the underlying irrational ideas from where these inferences derive. For example, a therapist may say 'Based on the available evidence, it does seem that your husband still loves you' instead of focusing upon the implicit irrational belief 'My husband must love me'. REBT hypothesises that inferentially-based change has limited generalisability to the client's other life problems: by leaving intact her core irrational philosophies she has not learnt any coping strategies if her inferences prove accurate (see COMPROMISES IN REBT; INELEGANT SOLUTION).

information-giving imparting to clients accurate information when they demonstrate ignorance about a particular issue or problem, e.g. the way a person brings an implicit MUST to his physiological arousal which marks the onset of a panic attack and results in him making increasingly distorted negative inferences such as 'I'm going to suffocate and die'. The therapist provides the client with information concerning how his implicit must can create distorted inferences, and if he disputes his must about the initial physiological arousal he is more likely to make increasingly accurate inferences regarding his arousal than if his must remains unchallenged.

insight discovery by clients of the central role of IRRATIONAL BELIEFS in largely creating their emotional disturbance. REBT is an insight and action-oriented therapy because it provides clients with a clear understanding of the true nature of their disturbance-producing ideas and what remedial steps can be taken. In particular, REBT presents clients with three major insights as to how they perpetuate their psychological problems: (1) human disturbance is largely determined by irrational beliefs. We mainly feel the way we think; (2) we remain disturbed in the present because we continually reindoctrinate ourselves with these beliefs; (3) the only enduring way to overcome our problems is through persistent hard work and practice – to think, feel and act against our irrational beliefs (Ellis, 1962). These three insights provide clients with a capsule account of REBT and act as a lifelong guide for emotional problem-solving.

Institute for RET centre for promoting this therapeutic approach. This was founded in New York in 1959 by Albert ELLIS (and originally called the Institute for Rational Living) and describes itself as a not-for-profit organization. The institute has other REBT centres in the USA as well as worldwide – it estimates there are over 12 000 practitioners of REBT and other cognitive-behavioural therapies. The institute offers training programmes for mental health professionals, and workshops and courses for the general public which cover a wide range of emotional and behavioural problems. The institute provides an extensive range of self-help books, pamphlets, audiotapes, videos, as part of its PSYCHOEDUCATIONAL approach. The institute sponsors an international quarterly journal entitled *The Journal of Rational-Emotive and Cognitive-Behavior Therapy* (published by Human Sciences Press). At the time of writing, the Institute has not changed its name to the 'Institute for Rational Emotive Behaviour Therapy'.

insults offensive remarks or acts. Clients often state that their emotional upsets directly stem from another's insults, e.g. 'Of course I'm bloody well angry. He called me a "lying bastard"'; 'She made me depressed when she called me a "poor excuse for a man".' Therapists point out that clients largely disturb themselves because either they DEMAND that others must not insult them or they actually agree with these insults. Therefore it is not insults *per se* that cause such offence or disturbance but an individual's rigid appraisal of them.

intake interview this refers to the therapist's initial assessment of a client's presenting problems and the mutual decision to undertake counselling.

Hauck (1980b) calls the intake interview 'the most important session you will have with a client. Sometimes you have only one opportunity to do your thing and if you spoil it, you don't get another chance' (p.45). Hauck favours 30-minute interviews (though this is not an REBT requirement) because this time is generally sufficient to gain an understanding of the client's problem, the cognitive dynamics underpinning it, some basic teaching of REBT, a summary of the interview and negotiating a homework assignment. Longer sessions than half an hour can often duplicate the material discussed in the first 30 minutes. Such a compact and seemingly comprehensive intake interview can quickly gain the client's confidence and trust and encourage the view that her problems are remediable rather than insuperable.

intellectual fascism 'is the arbitrary belief that individuals possessing certain traits (such as those who are intelligent, cultured, artistic, creative, or achieving) are intrinsically superior to individuals possessing certain other traits (such as those who are stupid, uncultured, unartistic, uncreative, or unachieving)' (Ellis, 1984b, p.1). The belief of the intellectual fascist is arbitrary because there is no objective evidence to confirm it – only the individual's value judgments or prejudices. REBT argues that all humans have intrinsic and equal importance simply because they are alive and not because of any extrinsic achievements or personal traits. However, some individuals have particular traits or abilities which make them superior in specific situations, e.g. the intellectual skill to become a chess grand master. Emotional stability and psychological health are derived from individuals choosing to accept themselves and others unconditionally as fallible human beings and avoiding all RATINGS of their selves but not of their particular traits or actions. The intellectual fascist, on the other hand, not only condemns certain others for their intrinsic 'inferiority' because they lack certain qualities (e.g. a literary sensibility) but also runs the risk of being hoist with his own petard when he fails to meet his own criteria of 'superiority' (e.g. his peers inform him that his literary sensibility is practically nonexistent) and thereby becomes, for example, depressed and/or ashamed.

intellectual insight refers to a client's RATIONAL BELIEFS that are only lightly and intermittently held – 'I believe it in my head but not in my gut'. Intellectual insight is usually insufficient to bring about enduring change (Ellis, 1963). This can be achieved by clients using FORCE AND ENERGY to put into practice, through a variety of multimodal methods, their rational beliefs and thereby reach EMOTIONAL INSIGHT.

intellectualisation a defence mechanism whereby clients provide seemingly plausible but overly intellectual explanations of their problems and bypass or avoid talking about their emotional reactions to these problems, e.g. a husband who discovers his wife's infidelity may describe it as the natural consequence of a deteriorating relationship and deny he feels emotionally upset. With such intellectual clients, Dryden and Yankura (1993, p.239) suggest counsellors introduce gradually into the session 'a productive level of affect . . . and employ emotive techniques, self-disclosure and a good deal of humour'.

interactionism the theory that various phenomena have a continuous reciprocal influence, e.g. the ongoing interaction between an individual and his environment. COGNITIVE INTERACTIONISM suggests that various cognitions such as inferences, problem-solving thinking, beliefs, act reciprocally but, REBT hypothesises, evaluative beliefs (irrational and rational) are central in influencing other cognitions, e.g. the source of a client's distress who infers that no one likes him really stems from his underlying irrational belief: 'I must be liked in order to be worthwhile'. PSYCHOLOGICAL INTERACTIONISM refers to thoughts, feelings and behaviours as being interactive and interdependent processes: thoughts will contain emotional and behavioural components; feelings and behaviours will each have elements of the other two. Even though all three processes are powerfully implicated in determining the level of human functioning, thoughts (specifically, evaluative beliefs) in REBT are considered to be first among equals – you feel as you think – and therefore are given prominence in tackling and ameliorating emotional distress.

interactive style the type of relationship or approach adopted by the REBT therapist based upon the client's relationship preferences in order for the client to achieve her outcome goals for change. For example, one client may favour a formal relationship highlighting the therapist's expertise and credibility; another client prefers an informal relationship emphasising trust and friendliness. However, REBT therapists would be wary about implementing a particular style that may reinforce a client's problems, e.g. being overly friendly to a client who expressed approval needs. The therapist's interactive style can be varied throughout therapy depending on the client's mood and behaviour at any given time (see BOND).

internal dialogue see SELF-TALK.

'interpersonal nightmare' technique devised by Dryden (1980) to encourage clients to imagine vividly and enact an unclear but anticipated 'dreaded' event in order to discover the client's irrational beliefs and associated disturbed negative emotions, e.g. a client is asked to write a vignette about an impending meeting with her estranged sister and to let her 'fear run riot'. She is asked to write down words and phrases articulated by her sister about which she would particularly disturb herself. An actress then records on tape the sister's words and phrases and this is then used as a stimulus which enables the woman to practise her new rational beliefs (see VIVID REBT).

interpretation drawing out meaning from a client's behaviours, dreams, utterances, life events, etc. in order to present to the client explanations for his present problems. REBT takes 'a very forthright stand on interpreting patients' verbalisations and are able to use them to make fundamental changes in some important aspects of their functioning and malfunctioning' (Ellis & Abrahms, 1978, p.23). For example, REBT does not view past events or influences as the 'cause' of a client's present emotional problems; rather, REBT interprets (i.e. explains) the client's interpretations (i.e. views) of these events as the real cause, e.g. 'You demanded that your parents must always love you and you made yourself depressed when they withdrew their love. You still demand today that your wife must always love you with similar results when she doesn't. If you want to overcome your depression, then give up your demands.' Interpretation is also used by REBT therapists as a synonym for INFERENCE but Dryden (1994b) suggests an important difference between the two: both are hunches about reality that go beyond the immediately available information but only inferences indicate personal significance, e.g. 'I think our company is going to merge sooner or later' as opposed to 'I think our company is going to merge sooner or later and all the subsequent upheaval may well have an adverse impact on my job.' In this sense then, teasing out clients' inferences about, rather than their interpretations of, events are more likely to reveal IRRATIONAL BELIEFS.

in vivo counselling these are counselling sessions conducted in the situations or settings where clients experience their emotional problems in order for the therapist to collect assessment data (such information has not been obtained by sitting in the therapist's office), e.g. a client with agoraphobia is able to pinpoint her fear-producing cognitions of being looked at while walking down the street with the therapist. *In vivo* counselling sessions are also used sometimes to conduct therapy.

in vivo desensitisation encourages clients to expose themselves to a feared object or situation in order to decrease their anxiety and eventually extinguish it. REBT favours implosive (FLOODING) rather than gradual desensitisation as it helps to rapidly remove clients' disturbance-creating ideas and raise their tolerance level for discomfort, e.g. a man who fears travelling on the underground in case he has a panic attack, extensively travels on the underground system in one day to prove to himself that 'I can stand it even if I still greatly dislike it' (see LOW FRUSTRATION TOLERANCE).

involuntary clients these are clients who reluctantly come to therapy at the insistence of others, e.g. parents, partners, courts, employers, and claim they have no emotional or behavioural problems. REBT therapists can, for instance, construct an HEDONIC CALCULUS with such clients to show them how their present behaviour may have short-term advantages but definite long-term disadvantages and therefore is self-defeating, e.g. a youngster who says truancy from school and shoplifting is 'a good laugh' can be shown how his problems are piling up and threaten to overwhelm him. Ellis (1985a) suggests agreeing with involuntary clients that the world or others are against them in order to gain their cooperation and help them to change.

irony saying the opposite of what is actually meant. REBT therapists often use irony as a HUMOROUS technique to challenge clients' irrational ideas, e.g. a client claims that anger is the driving force behind all of his major achievements in life and therefore is reluctant to give it up. The therapist ironically lists the client's 'achievements' including ending up in therapy as an indirect way of prompting the client to reappraise the usefulness of anger in his life.

irrational see IRRATIONAL BELIEFS.

irrational beliefs evaluative cognitions couched in the form of rigid, dogmatic and absolute musts, shoulds, have to's, got to's, oughts, and are found at the core of emotional disturbance. Irrational beliefs can be grouped into three major musts (demands): 'I must . . .'; 'You must . . .'; 'The world must. . .'. When these demands are not met, irrational conclusions usually follow from the irrational musts or premises – primarily AWFULISING, LOW FRUSTRATION TOLERANCE and DAMNATION, e.g. 'I must always get what I want in life otherwise I will be a total and pathetic failure' (damnation). Such an irrational belief may well create (1) anxiety about the possibility of failure and (2) depression when failure is experienced. IRRATIONALITY in REBT is usually defined as that which prevents people from reaching important life goals because their belief systems underpinning their goals are seen as illogical, unrealistic and lack utility (usefulness) and therefore are not adaptable when existing goals are blocked or thwarted, e.g. a client who failed to get into medical school makes herself depressed because she believes 'I must be a doctor at all costs otherwise my life will be finished'. Irrationality is not defined in any absolute sense in REBT, but as relative to each client's goal-blocking beliefs.

jargon the language, especially vocabulary, peculiar to a particular group, class or profession. The term 'jargon' is often used disparagingly to mean incomprehensible, pretentious or obscure language. As REBT advocates an EDUCATIONAL APPROACH to understanding emotional disturbance and its amelioration, this is usually best achieved by avoiding REBT jargon and rendering its ideas into clear language that will be understood by clients, e.g. realistic instead of empirical; unhelpful ideas rather than irrational beliefs; useful instead of pragmatic, functional or heuristic. Clarifying subcultural jargon is also necessary in order for the REBT therapist and client to agree on a shared meaning of the client's vocabulary, e.g. one of the present authors (MN) works with illicit drug users and some popular phrases for anger or rage include 'I just lost it and went into one' and for depression 'It's doing my head in'.

jealousy resentment or unease about the possibility of rivalry or unfaithfulness; apprehensive about the loss of another's exclusive devotion; possessiveness. REBT divides jealousy into morbid and non-morbid types. Morbid jealousy is an UNHEALTHY NEGATIVE EMOTION and stems from demands that a person must have the exclusive romantic interest of his partner otherwise he may condemn himself as worthless if he does not have it (depressed jealousy) or damn his partner and/or the third party for taking it away from him (angry jealousy). Behavioural responses include seeking reassurance that he still is the sole romantic interest in his partner's life, checking on and/or restricting her movements, retaliating against her presumed or actual infidelity by having an affair himself. Non-morbid jealousy is a HEALTHY NEGATIVE EMOTION and stems from preferences that a person has the exclusive romantic interest of his partner but does not insist upon it. If he fails to secure or keep his partner's exclusive interest he views this as bad but not awful and refrains from damning himself, his partner and/or the third party. Behavioural responses include acting assertively to express his desires for his partner's fidelity and being able to constructively carry on with his life if his partner leaves. A person who experiences non-morbid jealousy is more likely to look for evidence of his partner's infidelity rather than naturally assume it as in morbid jealousy. Hauck (1982, p.138) says that 'few emotional disturbances are as painful, constant or self-defeating as jealousy [i.e. the morbid type]. If you suffer from the green-eyed monster, you know it'.

jehovian derived from Jehovah, a name of God in the Old Testament. The term is frequently used by Albert ELLIS, the founder of REBT, to convey the absolute (God-like) and implacable nature of people's commands, demands and necessities they construct from their preferences and wishes, and thereby refuse to accept the sometimes grim reality of life with the risk of creating emotional problems for themselves. Some Christians may object to this meaning of jehovian because it implies an unloving and unforgiving God. Ellis, however, is not attacking religious beliefs as such: he uses the term to embrace all beliefs which are held dogmatically and rigidly – which Ellis (1983c) calls 'religiosity'. The concept of religiosity includes secular religions (e.g. fascism, communism) and personal belief systems. In order to remove religiosity from a belief system, individuals are encouraged to develop SCEPTICISM.

jokes things said or done to provoke laughter. Jokes are used as part of REBT's HUMOROUS techniques to challenge irrational thinking (jokes are not aimed at the clients themselves), e.g. the therapist might nickname a client 'Michael the Musturbator' in order to remind him of the demands he makes upon himself when he gets upset.

journal periodical dealing with specialist subjects. A journal specialising in REBT was established in 1966 and originally called *Rational Living* until 1983 when it changed its name to the *Journal of Rational-Emotive Therapy*; in 1988 its name changed again to the *Journal of Rational-Emotive and Cognitive-Behavior Therapy*. The journal 'seeks to pro-vide a forum to stimulate research and discussion into the development and promulgation of Rational-Emotive Therapy (RET) and other forms of cognitive-behavioral therapy' (from the journal's statement of intent). The journal used to include an 'Ask Dr Ellis [the founder of REBT]' column but this ceased in 1988. The journal, sponsored by the Institute for RET, is published quarterly in the calendar year by Human Sciences Press.

jumping to conclusions quickly assuming an outcome that is not justified by the facts of a particular situation. An inferential distortion stemming from underlying MUSTS, e.g. 'As I have been rejected by my partner, as I must not be, I'll never find happiness again' (see NON SEQUITUR).

'just reasonably content' level term used by Hauck (1983) to indicate emotional equilibrium in a romantic relationship. However, disequilibrium occurs at 'that point below [the JRC level] which we are starving for emotional and psychological satisfactions' (Hauck, 1991, p.201). If individuals do not respond to their 'hunger pangs', Hauck (1991) suggests three consequences will follow: (1) they will become unhappy and probably emotionally disturbed; (2) they will begin to fall out of love; (3) they will want to end the relationship. In order to return to the JRC level, individuals are encouraged to pursue a course of ENLIGHTENED SELF-INTEREST by constructively tackling the frustrations and dissatisfactions within the relationship or removing the psychological blocks that prevent them from leaving it to find new relationships.

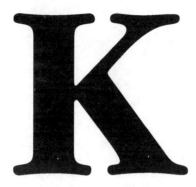

keywords words that have significance or importance. Such words include 'must', 'should', and 'ought' because they frequently express irrational thinking, e.g. 'I must never fail at important tasks in my life'. REBT therapists bring clients' attention to these words to demonstrate how they are implicated in the client's emotional problems, e.g. 'Next time you are really upset, look for a 'must' or 'should' in your thinking. There's the culprit.'

'knee-jerk' disputing a quick and ill-considered challenge by the therapist to clients' statements. Novice REBT therapists are particularly prone to 'pounce' on certain words or statements (e.g. 'must', 'should', 'it's awful', 'I can't stand it') because, they believe, these words are irrational and therefore indicate the presence of emotional disturbance. Clients are challenged to present evidence to support their 'musts' or 'awfuls', e.g. 'Where's the evidence that it is awful to be stuck in a traffic jam?' As Walen, DiGiuseppe and Dryden (1992, p.212) caution: 'This reaction frequently misses the point. Remember that these words are harmful because of the concepts that they stand for, not their face value.' In the above example, the 'awful' may only mean irritating or annoying rather than the REBT definition of awful:

worse than it could conceivably be. Even if the client did mean awful in the REBT sense, it may not be clinically relevant to the client's presenting problems or a problem the client wishes to discuss. REBT therapists remain alert to the disturbance-producing potential of these (and other) words and statements but gather evidence first to determine if they are legitimate targets for DISPUTING.

knowledge the body of information, truth, and principles acquired by an individual, group or culture. The knowledge base underpinning clients' irrational beliefs is subjected to logical and empirical examination in order to test the validity of these beliefs. REBT teaches clients that there are more rigorous and accurate ways of acquiring knowledge than the often haphazard and self-limiting ways they use, e.g. 'You say you could never go to a party on your own and enjoy yourself. Let's devise an experiment to test this out and see how true it is.' By adopting SCIENTIFIC THINKING, clients can reality-test their beliefs as hypotheses not facts and these can be confirmed, changed or modified in the light of observable results. Knowledge obtained through scientific thinking helps clients to form rational (and therefore self-helping) beliefs (see EPISTEMOLOGY).

labelling to describe or categorize (as if) with a label. Labelling is an inferential distortion stemming from underlying musts, e.g. 'Because I have failed, as I absolutely should not have done, this makes me stupid.' As can be seen in the above example, labelling is an extreme form of overgeneralization whereby an individual affixes to himself a negative label ('stupid') on the basis of certain actions or events (failure) – thus he equates himself with the label and is therefore more likely to experience emotional problems (e.g. depression) than someone who only labels the event or action but not himself, e.g. 'I have failed, which is bad, but I am not stupid'. REBT teaches clients to see themselves and others as fallible human beings who are too complex to be given or summed up with a single label.

language body of words used and understood by a particular people, nation, etc. An important feature of REBT is for the therapist and client to use the same vocabulary, i.e. both agree on the use of certain words and their meanings in order to avoid confusion, misconception and to facilitate the therapeutic alliance, e.g. irrational in REBT means 'that which blocks the client's goals in life' and does not mean, as many clients assume, 'mad' or 'psychotic'. Similarly, feeling words in REBT, such as 'depressed' and 'sad', are not seen as synonymous but have separate meanings of, respectively, DEMANDS and PREFERENCES. In order to arrive at what Dryden (1986) calls 'a shared meaning framework', REBT therapists seek regular FEEDBACK from their clients that they have both understood and agreed with the meanings of various words and concepts used in therapy. REBT also encourages clients to be more precise in their use of language and thereby avoid overgeneralisation with its potential for emotional disturbance, e.g. 'I failed to get the job but that doesn't make me a failure' instead of 'Because I failed to get the job I'm a total, pathetic failure'. As Ellis remarks (quoted in Dryden, 1991b, p.64): 'Irrational thinking and sloppy language continually interact.'

leads these are direct and concise statements or questions which guide clients to provide specific information required by the therapist. Such information will assist the therapist in understanding the ABC's of the client's presenting problems, e.g. 'Can you give me a recent example of your unease at work?' (A); 'What thoughts were going through your mind at the time?' (B); and 'Which emotion best captures your feelings of unease?' (C). Such leads help to reduce clients' vagueness, prolixity or irrelevant information and keep the therapy session structured and problem focused (see Grieger & Boyd, 1980).

learning the acquiring of knowledge or skill. As REBT has a PSYCHOEDUCATIONAL approach to emotional-problem solving, it is vitally important that therapists discover the learning styles of individual clients in order to tailor therapy to their particular needs, e.g. how fast or slow to proceed, what language to use or avoid. REBT therapists who disregard clients' learning styles may well pay the price in client apathy, disaffection or early termination of therapy (see BOND).

lecture formal presentation of a subject, especially for instruction, usually delivered to an audience or class. Lectures are given to clients by REBT therapists which cover the general principles and practices of REBT: the acquisition, perpetuation and eventual remediation of emotional problems. Lectures can provide information to clients much more quickly than the drawn out procedures of SOCRATIC questioning, e.g. informing clients that enduring change is achieved through hard work and determination rather than them arriving at a similar conclusion through questions and answers. However, too many therapist lectures can overwhelm clients, turn them into passive recipients of therapy rather than active collaborators in it. Whenever a lecture is delivered, it is important for REBT therapists to obtain feedback from their clients that they have understood the content of the lecture and can put it into their own words (see DIDACTIC APPROACH; INFORMATION-GIVING).

life conditions the state or circumstances of an individual's life or life in general at any given time. REBT hypothesises that disturbed clients make three basic demands (musts): on themselves, others and life conditions - in the last category, clients refuse to accept the empirical reality of their lives because it is not the way it must be and AWFULISE about the wretchedness of their existence. Such an attitude can lead to feelings of self-pity and hurt and behavioural problems such as substance abuse and procrastination. By surrendering their demands about life conditions and substituting preferences about them, clients can learn to distinguish between life conditions which can be changed and those which cannot as part of their new philosophy of ACCEPTANCE.

'life history inventory' devised by Lazarus and Lazarus (1991) as a series of questions to obtain a comprehensive picture of a client's background. Parts of the questionnaire ask clients to specify how therapists should ideally interact with their clients and what personal qualities they should possess. Such information can be used by REBT therapists to forge productive BONDS with their clients (e.g. a formal v. informal therapeutic relationship) in order to help them achieve their goals for change.

limitations of REBT the limits, weaknesses and shortcomings of this particular therapeutic approach. Limitations noted by Dryden (1984b) include clients who refuse to take responsibility for their emotional disturbances (an REBT requirement for change) and blame others for causing their problems; clients who expect undue warmth or love from the therapist (and viewed in REBT as reinforcing their dire needs for APPROVAL) rather than the unconditional acceptance they are offered. ELLIS (1980a) lists certain conditions that REBT is usually ineffective with: 'extreme mental deficiency, childhood autism, acute schizophrenia, dyslexia, epilepsy, and acute mania' (p.29). REBT's ambitious aim of seeking profound philosophical change in clients (replacing irrational beliefs with rational ones) is often thwarted because of, among other factors, client fallibility and their innate tendency to disturb themselves: in this case, over the kind of change preferably required of them. REBT therapists endeavour not to disturb themselves over the inherent limitations of their own therapeutic approach (see FAILURES IN REBT).

listening skills therapist proficiency in considering which aspects of clients' accounts of their problems are clinically significant. This means listening for the ABC's of clients' problems; in particular, listening for irrational ideas is 'the most crucial issue in psychodiagnosis' (Grieger & Boyd, 1980, p.62) as they largely create clients' emotional disturbances. For example, the therapist might infer that a client's main irrational idea producing her depression about her boyfriend's lack of interest in her is: 'He must love me, and as he doesn't any more, this means I'm worthless'. This is presented to the client as a hypothesis not as a fact to account for her depression and can be revised, rejected or defended in the light of further information.

living school a private school founded in 1969 at the Institute for RET in New York to teach ordinary schoolchildren the basic principles and practices of REBT. This emotional educational programme, integrated into the school's standard academic curriculum, was designed with the hope that, after several years of training in REBT, the school children would 'have a significantly lesser chance of developing mild or severe personality maladjustment than they might otherwise commonly develop' (Ellis, 1973a). The school's teachers were trained and supervised by REBT therapists. The school wanted children from the first grade (6-years-old) to the eighth grade to see how they progressed; there were only two classes with about ten pupils in each. Research projects were initiated to determine if the children's attitudes had constructively changed as a result of the REBT training. However, there was a high turnover rate as parents sent their children to bigger and better equipped schools (most of the children left after two or three years). Such a turnover rate interfered with the long-term follow-up studies -there was also no control group to compare the children with – and the school was closed in 1974. For ELLIS (Ellis & Dames, 1991, p.248), the Living School 'was an interesting experiment and it seemed to work'. REBT educational materials have been, and are continuing to be, introduced into more traditional American schools (see EDUCATIONAL APPROACH).

locus of control perceived source of control over one's behaviour. Many or most clients seen in REBT stress an external locus of control, i.e. someone or something directly causes their emotional difficulties, e.g. 'The weather makes me depressed', 'My daughter makes me feel guilty'. Such a view often indicates that clients experience little sense of control over their lives. Conversely, REBT emphasises an internal locus of control, i.e. that individual's largely create their own emotional problems: 'How do you make yourself depressed about the weather?' 'What do you tell yourself in order to feel guilty towards your daughter?' Teaching clients to switch from an external to an internal locus of control is the first step in REBT towards accepting EMOTIONAL RESPONSIBILITY and achieving greater control over their lives (see A-C THINKING; ATTRIBUTIONS).

logical disputing see LOGICAL THINKING.

logical positivism the philosophical doctrine whose most distinctive feature was its verifiability principle: any statement which could not be proven true or correct through observation or experience was therefore meaningless. Although ELLIS, the founder of REBT, originally followed (to some extent) a logical positivist approach, he eventually came to the conclusion 'that scientific statements are not empirically confirmable [can be shown to be true through reality-testing]' (quoted in Jacobs, 1989, p.184). Having abandoned logical positivism, REBT's scientific approach since 1976 is modelled on 'Popper's . . . critical realism . . . which focuses on critically assessing theories and trying to learn by falsifying them rather than on striving for their "truth" or "validity"' (Ellis, 1993a, p.10) (see FALSIFIABILITY).

logical thinking the ability to use reason in an orderly and demonstrable way. Illogicality is a major criterion of irrationality, e.g. 'Because I want a lot of friends therefore I must have them.' Clients are introduced to the principles of logical thinking by REBT therapists asking, for example: 'How does it logically follow that just because you want a lot of friends therefore you must have them?' Clients' preferences or wants can be logically validated and reality-tested but their demands (musts) are illogical and unrealistic and have the potential to produce emotional problems. By developing sound thought and reason, clients can tackle their disturbance-producing illogic (see DIALECTICS).

logico-empirical method using the principles of logic and reality-testing, REBT adopts a scientific approach to testing the validity of clients' irrational beliefs. This involves asking two questions. (1) Are they logically consistent?, e.g. 'Just because you want to be promoted at work, how does it logically follow that therefore you must be?' (2) Are their beliefs consistent with reality? 'You demanded that your wife shouldn't leave you. If your demands reflected reality, then she would have stayed rather than left'. The logico-empirical method is also used in constructing and testing the validity of clients' rational beliefs (seen as self-helping and goal-oriented). REBT hypothesises that if clients employ SCIENTIFIC THINKING they will be much less prone to making themselves emotionally disturbed than if they do not.

long-range hedonism the ability to plan constructively for the future as well as enjoy the pleasures of the moment, e.g. studying for one's college exams during the week and going to parties at the weekend. Clients who seek immediate gratification or SHORT-TERM HEDONISM frequently sabotage their long-term interests and goals thereby storing up trouble for themselves. To avoid this outcome, REBT encourages clients to achieve a balance between their short- and long-term goals (see HEDONISM).

long-term therapy psychological treatment applied over a considerable period of time. REBT advocates BREVITY (short duration) in its treatment approach: that effective results for clients can be achieved in a relatively short period of time by quickly focusing upon and changing their disturbance-producing irrational beliefs. As ELLIS remarks (1985a, p.126) 'the longer they [clients] take to overcome their disturbances, the more they and their associates are likely to suffer'. However, Ellis concedes that some clients 'have such rotten underlying philosophies and who hold on to them so rigidly that they often resist regular treatment and often require long-term treatment' (quoted in Dryden, 1991b, p.119).

loss detriment or disadvantage from a failure to keep, get or have. Loss is the major theme in DEPRESSION and stems from an individual's demands that a loss (e.g. death of a partner) must not have occurred and it is AWFUL that it did. REBT encourages individuals to make a constructive adjustment to their loss by examining and changing the irrational ideas underpinning their depression in order to experience SADNESS.

love profound tenderness, deep affection, warm attachment, sexual passion or desire towards others. ELLIS (1985b) has described the feelings of love as 'normally healthy and gratifying . . . it not only vitalizes human life and happiness but also helps to perpetuate and preserve the human race' (pp. 31–32). Problems with love arise when individuals create dire needs (absolute musts) from their desires for love and affection. Ellis lists various categories of pathological love (producing emotional disturbance) including: super-romantic love – idealised rather than realistic love, e.g. 'True romantic love lasts forever'; obsessive-compulsive love that involves more emotional pain than pleasure, e.g. 'If my beloved does not care for me or if he or she dies, life has no value and I might as well be dead'; jealousy and possessiveness – an individual's demand for the exclusive love of his partner, e.g. 'I must have a guarantee that you strongly love only me, and will continue to do so indefinitely'. REBT therapists show clients how to examine and change the irrational ideas underpinning their pathological love in order to achieve healthy love (based on preferences). REBT also deals with the self-created blocks (e.g. fear of rejection, fear of 'being hurt') that prevent clients from falling in love with suitable partners. REBT is concerned with showing individuals how to keep love alive by enhancing and perpetuating their feelings of love, e.g. deliberately acting in loving ways towards one's partner; realistically accepting that love can sometimes appear humdrum rather than always ecstatic or highly passionate.

'love slobbism' refers to ELLIS's (1977a) term for individuals who believe they must have love in order to be happy and validate their self-worth. Such is their dire need for love that they often believe their survival depends upon it, e.g. 'I must be loved in order to give my life purpose and meaning. Without love, my life is nothing and I'm utterly worthless.' REBT therapists show 'love slobs' how to maintain their strong desires for love while removing their dire necessities for it; that they still can be happy and survive without love and pursue other interests in life; the emotional problems arising out of their love slobbism actually makes it harder for them to find suitable partners.

low frustration tolerance (LFT) the perceived inability to put up with discomfort or frustration in one's life and to envisage any happiness while such conditions exist. LFT is one of the three major derivatives stemming from primary MUSTS, e.g. 'Things must be easy and comfortable in my life otherwise I can't stand it.' REBT views LFT as possibly the most important reason why individuals perpetuate their psychological problems – they avoid the hard work (and its associated discomfort) necessary to overcome their problems because they pursue a philosophy of SHORT-TERM HEDONISM (immediate gratification and comfort at the expense of longer-term goals). LFT beliefs are challenged and changed in order for clients to experience and maintain HIGH FRUSTRATION TOLERANCE.

'lft splash' is a visual model used by Dryden (1990b) to encourage clients to generate LOW FRUSTRATION TOLERANCE (LFT) attacking ideas (in this case, what would a young man have to say to himself to stand being soaked with water in order to achieve a particular goal?). Dryden suggests the model is useful 'in introducing to clients the idea of tolerating acute time-limited discomfort which, if tolerated, would help them achieve their goals' (p.61).

low-level disputing only challenging clients' inferences, e.g. 'Is it really true that your wife does not love you any more?' Such disputing leads to the INELEGANT SOLUTION in REBT because it avoids confronting the client's underlying musturbatory philosophy, e.g. 'My wife must always love me' which, REBT hypothesises, is the real cause of his emotional problems. If clients wish to achieve the ELEGANT SOLUTION in REBT, they are engaged in philosophical or HIGH-LEVEL DISPUTING.

magical thinking the idea that desirable effects or results can be achieved simply by wishing them to exist. Clients' magical thinking is challenged in order to produce REALISTIC THINKING, i.e. constructing their self-helping ideas on the basis of how reality actually is and not on how they demand it should be, e.g. a therapist may say 'Things are more likely to improve at work if you start facing your problems rather than demanding they shouldn't exist at all.' Magical thinking can make existing problems worse because some clients are reluctant or refuse to undertake the hard work usually required to overcome them.

magnification causing to seem greater or more important; attributing too much importance to. Magnification is an inferential distortion stemming from underlying MUSTS, e.g. 'I made a mistake in my exam, as I must not do, and it will mean I've failed my whole course.'

maintaining counselling gains preserving the therapeutic benefits from REBT not only during therapy but also after it has ended. This is achieved by, among other methods, clients using the three REBT INSIGHTS: (1) their emotional problems largely stem from irrational beliefs; (2) their problems are maintained by reindoctrinating themselves in the present with these beliefs; and (3) the only

enduring way to overcome their problems is through hard work and practice. Clients are urged to remember that when they upset themselves to look for a 'must' or absolute 'should' in their thinking and that BACKSLIDING is part of the normal pattern of progress as well as demonstrating their FALLIBILITY. The REBT methods they have used to tackle one set of problems can be similarly used for tackling other problems in their lives. Such methods are based on scientific thinking which REBT hypothesises is the most efficient route to PSYCHOLOGICAL HEALTH (see Ellis, 1984a).

marathon encounters see ENCOUNTER MARATHONS.

marriage counselling the therapeutic arena in which married couples are counselled. REBT distinguishes between couple dissatisfaction (e.g. lack of a social life; infrequent sexual activity) and couple disturbance (e.g. angry or depressed about these dissatisfactions). Such disturbance will usually prevent constructive problem-solving and is more likely to perpetuate an unhappy marriage. For this reason, couple disturbance is generally tackled before couple dissatisfaction. Frequently, REBT therapists will see married couples individually in order to help each one undisturb themselves about the other's behaviour before bringing both back into conjoint sessions. When both partners have made some progress reducing their emotional problems 'they are in a position to constructively look at ways of enhancing their degree of relationship satisfaction or to be helped to amicably separate' (Ellis & Dryden, 1987, p.118). REBT has no absolute prescriptions for a happy marriage but 'simply defines a good relationship as one that provides long-range satisfaction – that is, pleasurable experience – for the individuals in it' (DiGiuseppe & Zeeve, 1985, p.57). In order to achieve this aim, Hauck (1981b) has provided many helpful suggestions in his book *Making Marriage Work*.

mastery model in therapist self-disclosure see THERAPIST SELF-DISCLOSURE.

matching bringing together a corresponding or suitably associated pair to create a therapeutic alliance. Poor matching in REBT (e.g. the client prefers a younger therapist or one who is not so 'laidback') can lead to obstacles in the client's progress as she becomes more preoccupied with what she dislikes about the counsellor rather than focusing on her problems. If therapeutic impasse occurs, referral to another client-preferred counsellor can be arranged. Paradoxically, if client-therapist matching produces an enjoyable relationship this can lead to a tacit agreement to avoid the hard work of emotional problem-solving. Dryden (1987a) suggests that this 'problem can be largely overcome if counsellors first help themselves and then their clients to overcome the philosophy of low frustration tolerance implicit in this collusive short-range hedonism' (p.177).

meaning see JARGON; LANGUAGE.

means-ends thinking deciding on what steps will be necessary to reach one's goals, e.g. 'If I want to be drug free in three months' time, what do I need to start doing now in order to achieve this?'

Means-ends thinking is part of a group or set of problem-solving cognitions (others include CONSEQUENTIAL THINKING). Clients with this particular COGNITIVE DEFICIT may require skills training.

measures of irrationality these are methods used to determine the extent of clients' irrational thinking. The most commonly used include the 'Rational Belief Inventory' (Shorkey & Whiteman, 1977) and the 'Irrational Beliefs Test' (Jones, 1968). Criticisms of these measures (see Dryden, 1987b) include that they lack discriminant validity, i.e. the test scores correlate as highly with general measures of psychological disturbance as they do with other measures of irrational beliefs. How reliable are these and other measures as assessment or research tools? Warren and Zgourides (1989) suggest that, based on their research findings, the Malouff and Schutte (1986) Belief Scale, a single construct measure of irrational belief, 'provide[s] further evidence of construct and discriminant validities for the Belief Scale, and to support the basic tenets of the ABC theory of RE[B]T' (p.171). The work of Thorpe, Parker and Barnes (1992) on the central issue of discriminant validity in the Common Beliefs Survey III (Bessai, 1977), a 54 item inventory divided into six subscales, showed discriminant validity 'in that its subscales on self-criticism and perfectionism clearly differentiate clinical from nonclinical subjects' and 'in correlating more strongly with the other beliefs inventory [the Situational Self-Statement and Affective State Inventory (Harrell, Chambless & Calhoun, 1981)] than with most of the questionnaires [e.g. Beck Depression Inventory (Beck, Rush, Shaw & Emery, 1979)] on feeling states' (p.95). Both studies recommend further research into and refinement of these measures for clinical use (see Robb & Warren, 1990).

mediating goals these are objectives which act as stepping stones or intermediate stages to clients' ultimate goals for change, e.g. stabilising a client's erratic tranquilliser use and investigating the factors associated with it before undertaking a graduated reduction programme to achieve abstinence. The use of mediating goals offers some clients a more realistic way of achieving their often ambitious goals for change rather than the immediate success they demand.

medication medicines used to treat illness or disease. REBT does not expect all clients to be drug free during their course of therapy. Psychotropic drugs (e.g. antidepressants, tranquillisers) may be the only way to make severely depressed or anxious clients accessible to therapy. Medication may be a precondition for therapy in some cases (e.g. a depressed and suicidal client). ELLIS (quoted in Dryden, 1991b) suggests that it is only with medication that he is more likely to help psychotic clients 'eliminate their delusions, hallucinations, paranoid thinking, and other largely biologically based psychotic manifestations' (p.72). The combined use of REBT (or other cognitive-behavioural approaches) and psychotropic medication frequently produces better client outcomes than when each is used alone (Ellis, 1987a).

mementoes things that serve as reminders of past events, people, etc. Dryden (1990b) has used clients' mementoes (e.g. perfume, records) to uncover their disturbed feelings and irrational cognitions when traditional assessment methods have proved unsuccessful (see VIVID REBT).

mental filter picking out and dwelling upon the negative aspects of a situation thereby seeing the whole situation in the same light. An inferential distortion stemming from underlying MUSTS, e.g. 'Because I didn't get the job, as I should (must) have done, this proves that there was nothing good about my application.'

Burns (1980) likens a mental filter to one's vision of reality darkening 'like the drop of ink that discolors the entire beaker of water' (p.40).

metaphors figurative representations of reality, e.g. 'My problems keep me shackled to depression'. Metaphors are used to illustrate therapeutic points. A commonly used metaphor is the MONEY EXAMPLE (the loss, regaining and potential loss again of money) in order to teach clients the causation of emotional disturbance. FEEDBACK is obtained from clients to ascertain if they have understood the point of the metaphor (see Goncalves & Craine, 1990).

metatherapy issues 'issues concerning matters relating to therapy itself' (Golden & Dryden, 1986, p.372), e.g. discussions between the therapist and client as to whether the latter's goals for change are realistic; or how many sessions may be needed for the client to achieve a reasonable degree of progress. Golden and Dryden recommend 'the establishment and maintenance of a channel of communication between client and therapist which deals with metatherapy issues...' *(ibid.)*. Such a channel of communication is more likely to aid the development of a therapeutic alliance. The main responsibility for keeping this channel open lies with the therapist.

middle phase of individual therapy the concerns and problems encountered midway through REBT as well as the distinctive features of this particular phase. During this phase, the therapist and client work together to strengthen the latter's rational beliefs (wishes and preferences) and weaken her irrational beliefs (demands and commands). Obstacles to change are tackled, e.g. client discouragement due to her belief that she should be making faster progress. As the client, with the therapist's help, internalises and applies the ABCDE model of emotional disturbance and its remediation, COPING CRITERION is established with one problem before moving on to the next one. The therapist may be less directive as the client becomes more of her own counsellor and is able to set her homework tasks. The therapist helps the client to generalise REBT methods to her other problems and pinpoint the CORE IRRATIONAL BELIEFS linking them. It is important during this phase for the therapist to discover if the client is achieving philosophical change (removing her irrational beliefs) or empirical change (correcting her distorted inferences). Philosophical change is seen in REBT as the more enduring because the client has eradicated her disturbance-producing ideas; therefore the client would be encouraged to pursue this goal if her change is only empirically-based. As well as the hard work required to effect change, change itself can be an uncomfortable experience for some clients: putting their new rational beliefs into practice may seem unnatural and they conclude, for example, 'This isn't really me' (see COGNITIVE-EMOTIVE DISSONANCE). Difficulties in sustaining the change process are likely to result from clients' LOW FRUSTRATION TOLERANCE beliefs (see BEGINNING PHASE; ENDING STAGE).

mind reading the professed ability to discern another person's thoughts without the normal means of communication. Clients frequently claim to know what other people are thinking about them without any evidence to support their claims. Mind reading is an inferential distortion stemming from underlying MUSTS, e.g. 'I acted stupidly in front of other people, as I absolutely should not have done, and they all think I'm an idiot.'

minimization to undervalue the importance or contribution of someone or something; play down. An inferential distortion stemming from underlying MUSTS, e.g. 'Everyone sparkled in the

debate except me. I should (must) have done better. I only said one or two things which were mildly interesting.'

misconceptions about REBT mistaken ideas about the principles and practices of REBT. One of these ideas is that REBT turns clients into rational robots who do not experience emotions but live 'a life of the mind'. This is not true since REBT teaches (1) clients to discriminate keenly between unhealthy and healthy negative emotions (e.g. depression and sadness, respectively) and how the latter emotions aid goal-attainment; and (2) REBT urges clients to be actively involved in life and not passively detached from it. Another objection is that REBT teaches clients to be selfish. REBT views such an aim as self-defeating for both individuals and the wider community: individuals are likely to pursue SHORT-RANGE HEDONISM at the expense of their longer-term goals and such self-absorption may well have the effect of making the world a harsher and more uncaring place to live. Instead of selfishness, REBT advocates ENLIGHTENED SELF-INTEREST. Correcting these and other misconceptions is part of the portfolio of an REBT therapist/trainer (see Dryden & Gordon, 1990).

modelling behaviour serving as an example for others to follow. The therapist models a rational philosophy of living particularly with regard to UNCONDITIONAL ACCEPTANCE, i.e. the therapist accepts the client no matter how badly she behaves without always accepting her behaviour. By such therapist actions, it is hoped that clients will learn to accept themselves (and others) as FALLIBLE human beings. Another form of modelling is THERAPIST SELF-DISCLOSURE: the therapist tells clients how, for example, he overcame past problems and is tackling present ones in order to encourage them to confront their own problems in similar ways. Modelling can be counterproductive if, for example, a therapist models a particular trait (e.g. high frustration tolerance) without showing the client how to achieve it; the client may then denigrate herself because she believes she is inadequate when she compares herself with the therapist.

money example a three stage model used to teach clients how disturbed emotions are largely created. Attitudes (preferences as opposed to demands) to losing, regaining and potentially losing again a certain amount of money are contrasted in order to teach clients that an attitude based on PREFERENCES usually leads to healthy negative emotions (e.g. concern) while an attitude based on DEMANDS is more likely to produce unhealthy negative emotions (e.g. anxiety). This example is best used with clients who can understand abstract concepts rather than with clients who display concrete thinking (requiring actual instances rather than abstractions).

moral code ethical principles that guide conduct. Breaking one's moral code is the major theme in GUILT: doing something an individual considers to be bad (e.g. smacking a child) or not doing something an individual considers to be good (e.g. helping out a friend who is in trouble). REBT therapists do not seek to impose their moral values on clients; instead they help clients to remove the rigidity from their codes (e.g. 'I must never smack my child . . .') and to introduce flexibility (e.g. 'I would strongly prefer never to smack my child, but I'm not immune from doing so . . .') so that they experience only REMORSE when perceived bad events occur.

morbid jealousy see JEALOUSY.

motivation to change driving force that arouses and directs goal-seeking behaviour. REBT therapists assess clients' motivation to change their unhealthy negative emotions (e.g. anxiety and hurt) to healthy negative ones (respec-

tively, concern and disappointment). Clients often do not understand why their disturbed emotions are self-defeating and therefore are reluctant to change them (e.g. 'Feeling guilty will help to make me a better person'; 'If I'm not angry, other people will get the better of me'). Helping clients to understand the self-defeating nature of these emotions can be achieved by: asking clients what will be the likely consequences of continuing to experience them; constructing healthy negative emotions (not passivity, indifference, or defeatism as clients might assume) as alternatives; and undertaking a comparative analysis of the probable outcomes of experiencing both unhealthy and healthy negative emotions in the same situation. Such methods will help clients to increase their motivation to change their disturbed emotions.

mottoes pithy expressions which act as guiding principles, e.g. 'Never trust anyone who won't look you in the eye'. Mottoes serve to underscore important REBT principles, e.g. 'Enjoy the present and plan constructively for the future' (LONG-RANGE HEDONISM) and 'No gain without pain' (overcoming LOW FRUSTRATION TOLERANCE).

multimodal approach the use of various psychological modalities to effect change. REBT therapists encourage their clients to employ cognitive, emotive, behavioural and imaginal methods to challenge and change their irrational beliefs. Despite its emphasis on cognitive restructuring methods, REBT 'is practically always multimodal and consequently we would rarely only try to talk people out of their irrational ideas' (Ellis, quoted in Dryden, 1991b, p.41). ELLIS (*ibid.*) hypothesises that clients who employ the three main modalities of REBT (cognitive, emotive and behavioural) rather than a single modality 'would be the ones to get better quicker and more thoroughly and who would maintain their progress' (p.43). To reflect the mainly trimodal approach of REBT since its inception in 1955, Ellis, in 1993, changed its name from Rational-Emotive Therapy to Rational Emotive Behaviour Therapy.

multiple problem areas several or many problems that require intervention. REBT therapists would strongly prefer to achieve COPING CRITERION on one problem before tackling another. However, this is not always possible because some clients may switch prematurely to another problem and if the therapist does not agree to this change it can have an adverse effect on the therapeutic alliance. Other problems (e.g. suicidal behaviour) may supervene which require immediate therapist attention. The therapist may decide to switch before coping criterion is established because one problem (e.g. depression) is distracting the client from focusing upon and tackling her chosen one (e.g. anxiety). Clients who frequently jump from problem to problem may be exhibiting AVOIDANCE BEHAVIOUR and this itself becomes another problem to focus on (see Dryden & Yankura, 1993).

musts verb expressing necessity, compulsion or imperative requirement, e.g. 'I must keep my word'. REBT hypothesises that individuals are prone to experience emotional disturbance when they TRANSMUTE their desires, wants, and preferences into dogmatic, rigid, and absolutistic musts, e.g. 'Because I want your love therefore I must have it.' By adhering to a philosophy of musts, clients are likely to derive irrational conclusions from their primary musts, e.g. 'I must have your love; without it I'm utterly worthless.' REBT identifies three major musts (DEMANDS) at the heart of emotional disturbance: 'I must . . .'; 'You must . . .'; 'The world must . . .' Absolute musts and their DERIVATIVES are known as IRRATIONAL BELIEFS because they are illogical, unrealistic, lack utility (usefulness) and therefore block goal-attainment. Not all musts are targeted for disputation – only unconditional musts, e.g. 'I must always be successful'. Conditional musts may be rational, realistic and nondogmatic, e.g. 'I must get a move on if I want to get to the cinema on time'. REBT therapists should consider the meaning of a client's 'must' before deciding whether or not to dispute it. *'Musturbation'* is a comic term coined by Albert ELLIS, the founder of REBT, for a serious purpose: to emphasise to individuals the emotional and behavioural harm they inflict on themselves by musturbatory thinking and is encapsulated in his slogan – 'Masturbation is good and delicious, but musturbation is bad and pernicious' (quoted in Yankura & Dryden, 1990, p.85).

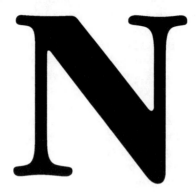

needs expressing necessity, urgency, the lack of something which must be filled. Individuals frequently disturb themselves when they convert their WANTS into dire needs, e.g. 'Because I want your approval therefore I must have it. Without it, I'm completely inadequate'. REBT teaches clients to distinguish between their healthy and rational wants (e.g. for love and success in life) and their unhealthy and irrational demands for these things. Certain needs for continued existence (e.g. food, water, shelter) are self-evident and obviously would not be disputed.

negative emotions feelings that can produce discomfort and interfere with individual functioning. ELLIS (1980a) divides negative emotions into INAPPROPRIATE and APPROPRIATE states with their cognitive correlates of, respectively, DEMANDS and PREFERENCES. (Some REBT therapists are unhappy with or object to the terms 'inappropriate' and 'appropriate' and instead prefer to use 'unconstructive' and 'constructive' and/or 'unhealthy' and 'healthy'.) The following table encourages clients to use the same emotional vocabulary as their therapists in order to reduce or avoid misunderstanding and confusion (if clients wish to use their own terms it is important that they reflect the REBT bifurcation of negative emotions).

TABLE OF NEGATIVE EMOTIONS

Inappropriate Emotions	*Appropriate Emotions*
Anxiety	Concern
Depression	Sadness
Anger	Annoyance
Guilt	Remorse
Hurt	Disappointment
Shame	Regret
Morbid jealousy	Non-morbid jealousy

Inappropriate negative emotions, not appropriate ones, are targeted for change. Vague expressions like 'I feel bad' are not considered helpful and clients are encouraged to 'select' from the above table in order to be precise about their affective state; this helps the REBT therapist to make a more accurate assessment of their underlying IRRATIONAL BELIEFS. The advantages of experiencing appropriate negative emotions and, therefore, more effective problem solving are delineated for the client in order to promote emotional change (see CONSTRUCTIVE AND UNCONSTRUCTIVE NEGATIVE EMOTIONS; HEALTHY and UNHEALTHY NEGATIVE EMOTIONS).

negative events occurrences which have unpleasant or adverse consequences. Individuals can make absolute evaluations about negative events in their lives (e.g. 'It absolutely shouldn't have happened. I can't stand it!') and then state in therapy that their goals are to feel indifferent (e.g. 'It happened. Who cares?'), or positive (e.g. 'I'm glad it happened. It's character building') about these events. REBT therapists teach clients to avoid suppressing their rational desires for negative events not to occur and to experience a HEALTHY NEGATIVE EMOTION (e.g. sadness) to help them adjust constructively to these events.

negative musturbatory evaluations thoughts which are absolute and dogmatic and appraise unfavourably a situation or event, e.g. 'I must not be the centre of attention in a group'. Derived from this evaluation are absolute negative INFERENCES, e.g. 'They are staring at me because they realise how inadequate I am'. The person may conclude with a negative absolute evaluation, e.g. 'I can't stand being stared at!' Negative musturbatory evaluations are seen as irrational because they are rigid and devout and therefore block goal-attainment (see COGNITIVE DISTORTIONS; DERIVATIVES).

negative preferential evaluations thoughts which are nonabsolute and nondogmatic and appraise unfavourably a situation or event, e.g. 'I'd rather not be the centre of attention in a group but there's no reason why I must not occupy such a position'. Derived from this evaluation are nonabsolute negative INFERENCES, e.g. 'I think that some people in the group may be looking at me.' The person may conclude with a negative nonabsolute evaluation, e.g. 'It's bad being stared at in the group but hardly awful.' Negative preferential evaluations are seen as rational because they are not rigid and devout and therefore aid goal-attainment.

negative thinking thoughts lacking positive attributes. REBT distinguishes between negative thinking based on PREFERENCES, e.g. 'I much prefer not to do that dreary task' and negative thinking based on DEMANDS, e.g. 'I must not do that dreary task under any circumstances.' The former type of thinking usually leads to a HEALTHY NEGATIVE EMOTION (e.g. annoyance) and constructive behaviour (reluctantly undertaking the task); the latter type of thinking can produce an UNHEALTHY NEGATIVE EMOTION (e.g. anger) and self-defeating behaviour (avoiding the task increases his work load). Negative thinking in REBT does not automatically mean the presence of EMOTIONAL DISTURBANCE.

neurosis psychological disturbance not due to any known neurological or organic impairment, e.g. guilt. ELLIS (quoted in Dryden, 1991b, p.28) asserts that the 'two main sources of just about all neurosis are, first, ego anxiety or self-damning, and second, discomfort anxiety, discomfort depression, or refusal to accept uncomfortable things in one's life. This is also known as low frustration tolerance (LFT).' As neurotic clients still maintain contact with reality, Ellis says he 'can help most of the neurotics change with relative ease . . . after about five or six sessions you can start convincing them that they really do upset themselves and are capable of not doing so . . .' (*ibid.* pp. 71–72). Greater difficulties are encountered by REBT therapists when dealing with clients suffering from a PSYCHOSIS (see SLOGANS).

'neurotic agreement in psychotherapy' term used by Hauck (1966) to describe a counsellor's failure or reluctance to challenge her client's irrational beliefs because she holds the same beliefs, e.g. 'I must have a romantic relationship in my life in order to be worthwhile.' Such a 'neurotic agreement' will leave important client problems unexamined unless the therapist is able to dispute her own irrational beliefs first (e.g. in supervision).

New Age therapy see TRANSPERSONAL THERAPY.

non-absolutism not following absolute or rigid principles. REBT hypothesises that flexible, logical, empirical, and pragmatic thinking is more likely to result in PSYCHOLOGICAL HEALTH. A philosophy of non-absolutism usually leads to healthy negative emotions (e.g. concern) and constructive behaviour when an individual's goals are blocked or thwarted. A non-absolutist outlook can be achieved by an individual disputing her ABSOLUTIST THINKING.

non-damning anger anger that is aimed at a person's actions rather than at the person, e.g. 'I deplore your bad behaviour but do not damn you as a bad or rotten person.' When a person experiences non-damning anger, she accepts that individuals do not have to always act in a proper or responsible manner and that their bad deeds do not adequately reflect the totality and complexity of their individual selves. Non-damning anger may help individuals not to hate themselves or others and to reduce their bad behaviour (see ANGER).

nonevaluative inferences hunches about reality that go beyond the immediately available information and are personally significant, but do not sum up or appraise a particular situation, e.g. 'That dog is running towards me and will jump up at me' – but the individual does not conclude whether this will be a good or bad thing. Inferences are usually nonevaluative when they are not relevant to our goals. However, in the above example, if the individual's goal is to avoid dogs he would negatively evaluate being jumped upon by the dog if it occurred.

nonevaluative observations descriptions of reality that do not go beyond the immediately available information or sum up or appraise a particular situation, e.g. 'It gets darker earlier in the winter months.' Observations are usually nonevaluative when they are not relevant to our goals. However, in the above example, if a woman was anxious about walking in the dark she would negatively evaluate the earlier nights.

non-linear model of change representation of movement from one state to another that does not follow in a straight line. REBT therapists teach clients that they will usually experience varying degrees of success in disputing their irrational beliefs in different situations and that BACKSLIDING is common. Change involves the amelioration, not eradication, of clients' emotional disturbances and therefore can be evaluated along three dimensions: (1) frequency – is the client less frequently disturbed than before?; (2) intensity – is the disturbance less intense than before?; and (3) duration – does the disturbance last as long this time? Clients are encouraged to use FORCE AND ENERGY in disputing their irrational beliefs in order to sustain the change process (see Ellis, 1984a).

non-morbid jealousy see JEALOUSY.

non sequitur Latin for 'it does not follow', this expression is usually applied only to the drawing of conclusions without even an appearance of valid argument. *Non sequiturs* are inferential distortions stemming from underlying MUSTS, e.g. 'Since I have been rejected, as I must not have been, I will never be happy again and am totally unloveable.' ELLIS (quoted in Dryden, 1991b, p.14) asserts that 'Humans have a great difficulty in keeping *non sequiturs* out of their thinking' but SCIENTIFIC THINKING can help to reduce their presence (see LOGICAL THINKING).

nonutopianism the view that any place or state of perfection is not achievable. Nonutopianism is seen as a criterion of PSYCHOLOGICAL HEALTH. Individuals realistically accept that not all of their desires and wishes will be realised, do not expect unalloyed unhappiness or seek to avoid discomfort and pain in their lives.

non-verbal communication information exchanged between individuals without the use of overt, spoken language. Ellis and Abrahms (1978) point out that REBT therapists are mainly concerned with the irrational ideas underpinning clients' non-verbal behaviours rather than just acknowledging that these behaviours exist, e.g. a client who continually looks at the floor may feel ashamed because she believes 'I shouldn't have this problem in the first place and am a weak and inadequate person for having to seek help'. This information would be presented to the client as an hypothesis for examination and possible challenge rather than as a fact. REBT therapists may also non-verbally communicate irrational ideas to the client, e.g. a therapist who is unsmiling, impatient, forever looking at his watch may signal 'I can't stand this client!' Such a self-defeating belief would usually be disputed in SUPERVISION.

'no cop-out therapy' term used by Ellis (1973b) to emphasise the REBT view that individuals are largely responsible for creating their emotional problems and this is the major focus in therapy. Clients who blame other factors (e.g. parents, partner, society) for 'causing' their emotional upsets are shown, by using the ABC model, that their disturbance-producing IRRATIONAL BELIEFS are the real culprits. If clients agree with this viewpoint, REBT considers that they have taken the first step towards EMOTIONAL RESPONSIBILITY and the likelihood of overcoming their problems.

normal resistance opposition in therapy to personality change that is seen as natural because it is 'statistically highly prevalent and . . . usually to be expected, at least to some degree, to occur' (Ellis, 1985a, p.6). Both rational and irrational beliefs are involved in normal resistance, e.g. the ultimately self-helping 'I wish it was easier to change and I really don't like the hard work involved but I understand it is in my best interests' accompanied by the self-defeating 'I shouldn't have to work this hard to change. I'm not going to put myself through this horrible experience.' REBT therapists pinpoint only the irrational beliefs behind such resistance and dispute them in order to help clients give them up and thereby effect constructive change (see HEALTHY RESISTANCE).

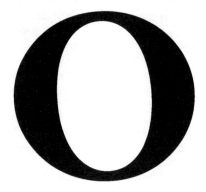

obstacles to client progress anything that interferes with or retards a client's ability to tackle her problems constructively. Dryden (1990c) identifies three main areas where obstacles to client progress can occur. (1) Within the counselling relationship, e.g. poor client-therapist MATCHING can produce a non-therapeutic relationship; clients who are reluctant or refuse to accept EMOTIONAL RESPONSIBILITY for their problems. (2) Within the client, e.g. some clients may exhibit LOW FRUSTRATION TOLERANCE with regard to the hard work they are expected to undertake in order to effect change. (3) Within the counsellor, e.g. 'Since I am doing my best and working so hard as a therapist, my clients absolutely should be equally hard working and responsible, should listen to me carefully, and should always push themselves to change' – a major therapist irrational belief identified by ELLIS (1985a) which can impede client progress. In order to overcome these obstacles, in the first case, a referral to another therapist or therapeutic approach may be considered; in the second case, the therapist needs to pinpoint, challenge and help change the client's progress-blocking beliefs; and, in the third case, the therapist needs to identify and dispute her own irrational beliefs or have them examined in SUPERVISION (see Dryden & Yankura, 1993).

Ockham's razor derived from William of Ockham (*c.* 1285–1349), the principle of applying economy in choosing between competing theories or explanations. The ABC model is a relatively straightforward explanation of emotional disturbance; however, its apparent simplicity has been criticised as taking Ockham's razor too far in accounting for the complexities of human behaviour (Ziegler, 1989). ELLIS (1985c) has agreed that the model can appear 'oversimplified' and has written extensively on the complexity and sophistication built into the model (see, for example, Ellis, 1991). 'Deceptively simple' might, therefore, be a more accurate description of the model. Ellis has applied Ockham's razor with dramatic economy in analysing some clients' problems, e.g. Client: How could my husband treat me so badly? Ellis: Easily. The reply 'easily' becomes the starting point for Ellis to teach the client that there is no law of the universe which forbids her husband from treating her badly and that he seemingly has no trouble in treating her in that way.

ontology the study of the nature of reality. REBT does not follow a RATIONALIST approach in its view of reality and therefore 'posits no absolutistic or invariant criteria of rationality' (Ellis, 1990, p.176). Instead REBT assumes a relativistic position: rationality is seen as that which aids individual goal-attainment; irrationality as that which blocks or interferes with individual goal-attainment. A person's view of reality is an experience which is mediated by his INFERENCES and EVALUATIVE BELIEFS. These beliefs are treated as hypotheses by the therapist (but regarded by the client as facts), e.g. a man is depressed because he truly believes 'I absolutely should not have lost my job and this makes me a total failure' and subjected to testing by both therapist and client to see if they are consistent with empirical reality – does the world conform to his demands? If it did, then he would still have his job. How does losing his job make him a total failure? If it did, then he would always fail at everything he attempted in his life. In this sense, empirical reality acts as an objective standard against which an individual's beliefs are examined to determine if they are self-helping or self-defeating (see CONSTRUCTIVISM).

open-ended questions questions which encourage individuals to explore a problem or situation in a spontaneous and unguided manner in order for them to achieve greater awareness. REBT therapists use open-ended questions to encourage clients to think for themselves (and not just repeat therapists' statements parrot-fashion) and to 'think about their thinking' in more logical, empirical, and pragmatic ways, e.g. 'What are the likely consequences of holding on to that particular belief?' However, open-ended questions will not automatically reveal to clients the role of irrational beliefs (MUSTS) in their emotional problems, e.g. 'What were you telling yourself about his behaviour to make yourself so angry?' to which the client might reply with an INFERENCE, e.g. 'Because it shows that he despises me.' In order for the therapist to tease out the implicit must (demand) in the client's most clinically relevant inference she may ask a THEORY-DRIVEN QUESTION or present a DIDACTIC explanation.

openness exposed to the general view; willingness to receive and consider (e.g. ideas, criticisms). REBT therapists discuss any aspect of REBT theory and practice with their clients and present clear rationales for their clinical behaviour. Equally they are often forthright in commenting upon their clients' behaviour but not in any disparaging sense: the intent is educative and corrective. Therapists may disclose, if clinically relevant, how they overcame similar problems in their own lives (see THERAPIST SELF-DISCLOSURE). REBT therapists 'try to get people . . . to be open about what their problems are, open with themselves and preferably also open with others . . . because if you try to hide a problem you will have to pretend to what you aren't and only get falsely accepted' (Ellis, quoted in Dryden, 1991b, p.51). Lack of openness, secrecy, usually increases anxiety and therefore interferes with effective problem-solving (see GENUINENESS).

operant conditioning a method of shaping new self-helping behaviours and reducing or extinguishing old self-defeating behaviours through a system of rewards and penalties. Clients can reward themselves for carrying out HOMEWORK tasks and penalise (but not punish) themselves if they do not. Operant conditioning methods can teach clients the pitfalls of short-term HEDONISM or instant gratification and that avoiding hard work or discomfort takes them further away from their goals rather than closer to them. Grieger and Boyd (1980, p.145) suggest that operant conditioning 'often provides the extra incentive that makes the difference between avoiding or completing it [homework]'.

operationalising problems having a clear understanding of a problem in order to implement an appropriate intervention. This means understanding clients' problems within the ABC framework, e.g. 'I'm fed up at work' is too vague for an REBT therapist and she might ask, 'What is it that you are fed up with at work and how do you feel about it?' The practical problem (A) is whatever he is fed up with; the emotional problem (C) is the unhealthy negative feeling (e.g. depression) he experiences about the work situation. The stage is now set for discovering the client's disturbance-producing beliefs at B.

other-acceptance the philosophy of displaying unconditional acceptance of other people (but not always of their behaviours) once an individual has learnt UNCONDITIONAL SELF-ACCEPTANCE. Acceptance of self and others is a criterion of PSYCHOLOGICAL HEALTH.

'other pity' see DEPRESSION.

ought verb expressing duty, moral obligation or condemnation. Dogmatic and absolute oughts are called IRRATIONAL BELIEFS, e.g. 'I ought to do the right thing on every occasion otherwise I will be despicable.' Clients who do not monitor or reduce their use of absolute oughts are liable to incur a greater risk or higher incidence of emotional disturbance because of developing 'hardening of the oughteries'. Such oughts are targeted for DISPUTING (see DEMAND).

outcome studies analyses of the results of a particular activity. Ellis (quoted in Dryden, 1991b, p.128) estimates there 'are now about five hundred studies that tend to show that RE[B]T and other forms of cognitive-behaviour therapy (CBT) get better results than a control group.' He concedes there is no conclusive evidence that REBT and CBT are more effective than other approaches. Studies of REBT have often been significantly flawed because, among other reasons, they have lacked an authoritative REBT treatment manual to follow, only focused upon the cognitive restructuring aspects rather than its MULTIMODAL APPROACH, failed to comment on the quality of the REBT practised and did not specify if PREFERENTIAL or GENERAL REBT was the mode of treatment. Haaga, Dryden and Dancey (1991) have offered various recommendations for improving REBT outcome research. Silverman, McCarthy and McGovern (1992) in a review of 89 outcome studies of REBT carried out between 1982–1989 concluded that 'this review coincides with . . . previous findings . . . that RE[B]T is a valuable, effective therapy that warrants increased research to broaden its application. Over the past 20 years, the research that has been concluded with RE[B]T has constantly verified its role as an efficacious therapy applicable in a variety of problem situations' (p.169).

overgeneralisation constructing invariant general rules from specific instances. This is an inferential distortion stemming from underlying MUSTS, e.g. 'If I don't pass this test today, as I must do, I will never pass it'. REBT therapists teach clients SEMANTIC PRECISION in order to tackle their overgeneralisations, e.g. 'If I don't pass this test today, as I hope to do, it does not mean that I will never pass it. It may mean that I have to work harder next time.'

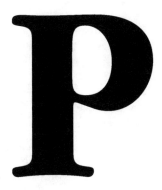

pace of interventions speed at which therapists help clients to tackle their problems. As REBT is primarily an EDUCATIONAL APPROACH, therapists adjust the pace of their interventions to how slowly or quickly clients process information and to their LEARNING styles. It is the therapist's responsibility to keep in step with the client's pace and to be alert to the verbal and non-verbal cues that may suggest the client is 'falling behind'. Failure to carry out this task may result in a rupture of the therapeutic ALLIANCE.

palliative methods procedures which lessen the adverse effects of a problem without removing its cause, e.g. relaxation and distraction methods in panic attacks. REBT views palliative methods as helping client to FEEL BETTER in the short-term but not to GET BETTER in the long-term because the use of these methods avoids identifying, challenging and changing the irrational ideas underpinning their problems.

parable short story which conveys indirectly a moral or lesson. Parables are used to underscore important REBT principles and teach clients the self-defeating nature of their irrational beliefs. When parables are used, it is important for the therapist to ascertain if the client has really understood the moral or lesson and its application to their own problems.

paradoxical techniques verbal or behavioural responses by therapists which are the opposite of what is actually meant, e.g. a client who severely berates herself for making mistakes is assured by the therapist that she is the only person in the world who ever makes mistakes and therefore everyone should keep away from her in case they contract the same 'disease'. Such HUMOROUS paradoxical statements are used to encourage the client to accept herself unconditionally as a fallible human being and DISPUTE the irrational beliefs underpinning her self-downing philosophy. It is important that the therapist obtains FEEDBACK from the client as to whether she has understood his paradoxical intention.

passionate self-statements vigorous declarations of intent used by clients in facing their problems, e.g. 'It's better to do than do well, so get the hell on with it!' (overcoming procrastination). Such statements are frequently used with clients who lack the intellectual skills involved in DISPUTING.

passivity meekly accepting; lacking in energy, will or initiative. REBT therapists are not passive listeners but employ an ACTIVE-DIRECTIVE STYLE in tackling clients' emotional problems. Such a style is frequently modified with passive clients in order to avoid reinforcing their passivity through increased therapist activity; instead, they are encouraged or PERSUADED to become collaborators in seeking ways to overcome their problems. Clients who choose passivity in the face of negative events as a therapeutic goal are shown that this will not help them adjust constructively to these events and are suppressing their rational desires for these events not to occur.

past history of clients significant events, details, biographical information, etc. covering earlier periods of clients' lives. REBT presents an AHISTORICAL APPROACH to understanding clients' problems: it is more concerned with how they are being maintained in the present rather than how they were acquired in the past (REBT therapists are not rigidly against an historical exploration of a client's present problems particularly if not doing so will harm the therapeutic ALLIANCE). Grieger and Boyd (1980) suggest that the REBT therapist who spends too long on a client's past history is inadvertently teaching the client that the problem and its solution lies in the past; and wastes therapeutic time in not focusing on the here-and-now to find ways of uprooting the client's currently held disturbance-producing beliefs.

payoffs from problems benefits or rewards derived from existing problems. REBT views this as one means of PERPETUATING PSYCHOLOGICAL DISTURBANCE, e.g. increased sympathy or attention from others when an individual feels depressed serves to maintain the problem; a woman is reluctant to overcome her shyness about meeting men because her greatest fear is being rejected. REBT therapists show clients that these payoffs are ultimately self-defeating rather than self-enhancing and help them to seek more constructive ways of addressing their problems.

penalties and rewards see OPERANT CONDITIONING.

perfectionism attitude that demands unrealistically high or flawless standards in one's self and work and rejects anything less as unacceptable. ELLIS (1988) distinguishes between task-and self-perfectionism: individuals can strive to be perfect at particular tasks but this does not mean that they are good or perfect if they achieve these tasks (or failures if they do not achieve them), e.g. 'I very much want to be a perfect lover but I don't have to be one in order to accept myself.' Individuals can accept themselves irrespective of whether or not they attain their goals. REBT therapists do not usually seek to lower clients' standards (except when they are superhuman) but help them to introduce some flexibility into their thinking about their standards.

perpetuation of psychological disturbance factors involved in maintaining an individual's emotional and/or behavioural problems. REBT's primary focus is on how psychological problems are perpetuated rather than on how they were acquired. Such perpetuation occurs because, *inter alia*, individuals lack the three major REBT INSIGHTS, have a philosophy of LOW FRUSTRATION TOLERANCE which prevents them from undertaking the hard work usually necessary to overcome their problems, and/or have problems about their original problems – these SECONDARY DISTURBANCES interfere with individuals tackling their primary ones. Unless clients confront the factors and ideas maintaining their emotional problems, little therapeutic progress is likely to be made (see Dryden, 1990c).

persistence continuing steadily or firmly on a course of action especially in the face of opposition, difficulties, etc. REBT therapists show persistence in DISPUTING clients' IRRATIONAL BELIEFS no matter how tenaciously they cling to them and thereby modelling for their clients HIGH FRUS-TRATION TOLERANCE. REBT therapists 'encourage clients to persist at change, to keep pushing them to work and work, not just at the beginning (as they might work at a diet), but to continue to do so, often for the rest of their lives . . . so the therapist keeps encouraging the client to persist and persist in a forceful manner . . .' (Ellis, quoted in Dryden, 1991b, p.43). Therapist persistence should be viewed by the client as supportive, not prosecutorial or threatening.

personality data form a means of collecting information on the irrational beliefs held by clients at the beginning of therapy by asking them how frequently they experience upsetting feelings in response to various questions relating to such issues as control, worth, certainty, and catastrophising. Such forms enable clients to provide background information rather than REBT therapists collecting it – they prefer to take an early problem focus in order to understand the ABC's of clients' presenting problems and thereby get therapy started.

personalisation assuming personal responsibility for the course of certain events. When these events are negative ones individuals are liable to make themselves emotionally upset (e.g. guilt, anxiety). REBT views personalisation as an inferential distortion stemming from underlying MUSTS, e.g. 'Because my clients don't work hard in therapy, as they must do, this proves I am a completely inadequate therapist who doesn't deserve any success with his clients.' Burns (1980) suggests that individuals have confused influence with control over others and therefore require help to 'overcome your tendency to personalize and trim your sense of responsibility down to manageable, realistic proportions . . .' (p.39).

personal qualities of effective REBT therapists the assumption in REBT that those of its practitioners who have certain characteristics will produce better client outcomes than those REBT therapists who lack these characteristics. Such characteristics include the ability to work comfortably within structured sessions in order to maximise therapy time; to have an intellectual or philosophical bent in order to dispute clients' irrational ideas and help them to construct rational ones; to be able to employ an often vigorous ACTIVE-DIRECTIVE STYLE in helping clients to overcome their problems. These characteristics are used flexibly, not rigidly, and are tailored to individual client requirements. The personal qualities which contribute to the effective practice of REBT are regarded as hypotheses and therefore viewed 'as both tentative and awaiting empirical study' (Ellis & Dryden, 1987, p.31).

personal scientist encouraging clients to adopt the methods of science by open-mindedly and flexibly examining the logical and empirical evidence for and against their beliefs. Clients are taught to view their beliefs as hypotheses about reality, not as facts, and thereby subject them to testing in order to try and FALSIFY them, e.g. a client who believes 'I couldn't stand staying in on my own for a whole week' finds she can stand the experience after undertaking it as a HOMEWORK assignment. Through such testing, REBT aims 'to make better scientists of our clients so that they can acquire correct information, use evidence logically, and construct sound, self-helping beliefs' (Walen, DiGiuseppe & Dryden, 1992, p.4). However, Ellis states 'that people are, often, rotten scientists!' (quoted in Dryden, 1991b, p.26) and will dogmatically select evidence to confirm rather than reject their self-defeating ideas, e.g. 'Because I failed to get the job I wanted so badly, this conclusively proves how useless I am.' Clients who are unable, for whatever reason, to develop SCIENTIFIC THINKING to tackle their problems can switch to constructing COPING SELF-STATEMENTS to reduce emotional distress.

person-rating the practice of applying (usually negative) global evaluations to oneself or others, e.g. 'Because I failed to get the job, as I absolutely should not have done, this means I am completely worthless.' Such ratings frequently lead to emotional disturbance, e.g. depression, shame. REBT therapists teach clients to avoid rating themselves or others on the basis of particular traits or actions because these can never adequately describe or appraise the complexity and totality of human beings. Clients can, however, legitimately rate their (and others') specific traits, actions or performances in order to determine if these will help or hinder the attainment of their goals, e.g. 'I am lazy in not carrying out my homework tasks and therefore will make little progress in therapy.'

perspective taking looking at a problem or situation from a standpoint that is different from the usual one. Clients who lack this cognitive skill are taught to look at their problems from a different perspective rather than the rigid and self-defeating one they are used to, e.g. 'Would your best friend relentlessly damn himself because his marriage, like yours, fell apart?' Such perspective taking helps clients to develop a realistic approach to tackling their problems.

persuasion being swayed by argument, reasoning or pleading to change one's opinions, course of action, etc. REBT therapists attempt to dissuade clients from holding on to their self-defeating irrational beliefs and persuade them to construct new self-helping rational beliefs. REBT makes no bones about using persuasion as a means of effecting attitude change: 'RE[B]T is largely a teaching or persuasive form of therapy. We are trying to persuade people to change their attitude, to change their feelings, to change their behaviour,

because even if they knew what to do before they came to therapy they weren't doing it. So we push them and persuade them . . .' (Ellis, quoted in Dryden, 1991b, p.66; see Wessler & Wessler, 1980).

pervasiveness influence, activities, presence, etc., spread throughout. Pervasiveness is considered by ELLIS (1985a) to be a major characteristic of EFFICIENCY in psychotherapy because its use by therapists not only deals with clients' presenting problems but also many other problem areas in their lives; in this sense, REBT will equip them with a lifelong therapeutic approach.

philosophical change to alter one's attitudes and beliefs to life. REBT therapists encourage clients to achieve an ELEGANT or profound philosophical change in their lives by uprooting their goal-blocking musturbatory philosophies (rigid musts and shoulds) and replacing them with goal-attaining preferential philosophies (flexible wishes and wants). Philosophical change in REBT can be specific to certain events or general towards all life events. Philosophical change occurs when clients accept EMOTIONAL RESPONSIBILITY, understand the central role of disturbance-producing irrational beliefs in their lives, dispute these beliefs through SCIENTIFIC THINKING and use a MULTIMODAL APPROACH to internalise their new rational beliefs for present and future emotional problem-solving (see COMPROMISES IN REBT).

philosophical influences on the development of REBT views or works of past and present philosophers which have had important effects on the evolution of this therapeutic approach. The STOIC philosopher EPICTETUS provided the cornerstone of REBT: 'Men are disturbed not by things, but by the views which they take of them' – it is our attitude towards events rather than the events themselves which largely creates our emotional problems about these events. Other philosophical influences include the EXISTENTIALISM of Heidegger (1949) which views the individual as the architect of his own emotional destiny – an important principle for clients to grasp if they are to make progress in overcoming their problems; and Popper's (1959, 1963) FALSIFIABILITY principle as the basic feature of scientific theory and falsifying hypotheses as the principal task of the scientist – in REBT, this means seeking to falsify clients' irrational beliefs that, for example, they must have love or approval in order to be happy (see Ellis & Dryden, 1987).

philosophy of effort the view that clients are much more likely to reach their goals in life through hard work and persistence. Even when their goals have been achieved, clients are still required to monitor their behaviour in order to avoid or minimize BACKSLIDING. The slogan 'There's no gain without pain' encapsulates the REBT philosophy of effort and REBT therapists encourage their clients to use it as a lifelong principle particularly for those clients who have LOW FRUSTRATION TOLERANCE beliefs.

phoneyism pretending to be something one is not. Clients often believe that their phoniness has been revealed when they, for example, let other people down or fail to reach their high standards. Phoneyism is seen as an inferential distortion stemming from underlying MUSTS, e.g. 'As I failed to deliver on my promise of help, as I should (must) have done, I am a real phoney, and will be seen as one.' REBT therapists show clients that their phoneyism is created by their rigid demands upon themselves and their refusal to accept their FALLIBILITY. Such ideas are challenged and changed through DISPUTING.

pleasurable pursuits activities which provide enjoyment or satisfaction. Clients who suffer from anhedonia (lack of pleasure or the capacity to experience it) are sometimes helped in REBT by therapists suggesting various pleasures they could pursue and how to engage in them. Ellis (1985a) states that he was able to help many anhedonic and/or depressed clients 'who resisted therapy for a long period of time, who mainly seemed to change because I finally helped them to commit themselves to a vital absorbing interest . . . such as a social or political course, writing a book, or becoming an auxiliary therapist' (pp. 78–79) (see PSYCHOLOGICAL HEALTH).

poems compositions in verse. Poems are sometimes used as an EMOTIVE TECHNIQUE in assisting therapists to dispute clients' irrational beliefs. Poems selected by REBT therapists offer clients a very different and often enjoyable way of examining their irrational ideas.

pollyannish thinking derived from the novel *Pollyanna* by Eleanor Porter, an attitude which is irrepressibly optimistic. Pollyannish thinking is generally avoided in REBT as it encourages clients to FEEL BETTER (e.g. 'If this person does not like me there will be others who do') rather than GET BETTER (challenging and changing the irrational idea that 'I must be liked in order to be happy'). Pollyannish thinking can convince (or deceive) clients that things in their lives are or will be better than they actually are and thereby avoid accepting the sometimes grim reality of adverse events. REBT therapists encourage clients to develop REALISTIC THINKING as it is more likely to prove self-helping in their goal-directed behaviours.

positive musturbatory evaluations thoughts which are absolute and dogmatic and appraise favourably a situation or event, e.g. 'I must be liked by everyone.' Derived from this evaluation are positive absolute INFERENCES, e.g. 'As everyone is talking to me, this means I am greatly liked.' The person may conclude with a positive absolute evaluation, e.g. 'I will always be liked and never have an enemy.' Positive musturbatory evaluations are seen as irrational because they are rigid and devout and therefore block goal-attainment (see COGNITIVE DISTORTIONS; DERIVATIVES).

positive preferential evaluations thoughts which are nonabsolute and nondogmatic and appraise favourably a situation or event, e.g. 'I would prefer to be liked by everyone but I don't have to be.' Derived from this evaluation are nonabsolute positive INFERENCES, e.g. 'As everyone is talking to me, this might mean I am liked by them'. The person may conclude with a nonabsolute positive evaluation, e.g. 'I like to be liked but it's hardly awful if I'm not'. Positive preferential evaluations are seen as rational because they are not rigid and devout and therefore aid goal-attainment.

positive thinking attitude that emphasises what is good, beneficial or optimistic about life events. Positive thinking is generally avoided in REBT because, among other reasons, it encourages self-rating, e.g. 'I will succeed sooner or later so therefore I'm still a good person' rather than UNCONDITIONAL SELF-ACCEPTANCE; it fails to show clients how to adjust constructively to unpleasant or adverse events in their lives and instead suggests that things will always get better; its philosophy indicates that failure equals worthlessness and therefore individuals have to keep on striving to prove themselves successful. Positive thinking can often translate into self-downing when things go wrong in an individual's life. REBT therapists teach clients a philosophical self-helping outlook based on REALISTIC THINKING (see Ellis & Abrahms, 1978).

'possible reasons for not completing self-help assignments' a questionnaire used to elicit clients explanations for not carrying through their homework tasks.

Clients are expected to fill out the questionnaire 'at the time that you feel a reluctance to do your assignment or a desire to put off doing it' (Dryden, 1990c, Appendix 1, p.94). Clients answer 'true' or 'false' to such questions as 'It seemed too hard', 'I did not have enough time. I was too busy', 'It's too much like going back to school again'. REBT therapists inform their clients that their rate of progress is usually dependent upon the number of homework assignments they are prepared to execute. Burns (1989) suggests that on the basis of studies that he and others have carried out 'compliance with self-help assignments may be the most important predictor of therapeutic success' (p.545).

postmodernism a late twentieth-century tendency in the arts characterised by cultural uncertainty and a loss of faith in authority, progress and societal absolutes, which are replaced by pluralism and a relativistic approach to values. REBT takes a postmodernist stance in its view of rationality: it offers no absolute certainty or authority in its use of the term but views it as a relative construct determined by and aiding a client's self-chosen goals for change. Irrationality is also viewed as relative to a client's goals but this time as blocking or thwarting them.

practical problems difficulties involving ordinary, everyday activities. REBT is a DOUBLE SYSTEMS THERAPY: it tackles first the emotional aspects of a problem before moving on to the practical aspects, e.g. depressed about being in debt. Once an individual has removed her emotional disturbance about being in debt, she is more likely to find constructive ways of dealing with her financial problems (see EMOTIONS).

pragmatic disputing see PRAGMATISM.

pragmatism a practical approach to problems and affairs. One of the three major criteria in challenging IRRATIONAL BELIEFS, e.g. 'Where is it going to get you holding on to the idea that you must always succeed?' The point of the pragmatic dispute is to show clients that all they are likely to 'hold on to' are self-defeating emotions and behaviours (e.g. performance impaired by anxiety) which will sabotage their goals. For many clients, the concreteness involved in delineating the pragmatic consequences of retaining their irrational beliefs is a more effective way of initiating change than LOGICAL or EMPIRICAL DISPUTING.

preconscious memories, thoughts, images, etc. which are currently outside of conscious awareness but are capable of being readily recalled when needed. ELLIS opposes the psychoanalytic view that our disturbance-producing beliefs and emotions are deeply embedded in the UNCONSCIOUS and suggests 'the more credible view [is] that many of our thoughts and bodily processes are automatic or preconscious but that few of them are deeply unconscious or repressed. RE[B]T assumes that many, perhaps most, of our disturbing thoughts – our rigid shoulds, oughts, musts, demands and commands – are by no means at our full conscious awareness, but instead are just below the level of consciousness and can fairly easily be inferred, looked for, and clearly brought to consciousness' (quoted in Dryden, 1991b, pp.105–106). INFERENCE CHAINING is one method used to bring clients' preconscious irrational beliefs into conscious awareness in order to start challenging and changing them. Such a process often takes only a few sessions to achieve.

prediction forecast; foretell the future. An inferential distortion stemming from underlying MUSTS, e.g. 'If this relationship fails, as it must not, then I will have an unhappy life' (see SELF-FULFILLING PROPHECIES).

preference evaluative belief couched in the form of a flexible wish, want, hope, desire, etc. Preferences form the basis of RATIONAL BELIEFS because they are seen as adaptable, aid goal-attainment and lead to healthy negative emotions such as concern, e.g. 'I would strongly prefer to have a lot of friends but I don't have to have them. If I only have few friends, it will be bad but hardly awful.' Rational preferences usually lead to rational DERIVATIVES (in the above example, evaluations of BADNESS rather than AWFULISING). Ellis has pointed out 'that if humans would stick to preferences they would not get into so much emotional trouble' (quoted in Dryden, 1991b, p.15). The potential for emotional disturbance arises when individuals TRANSMUTE their preferences into DEMANDS.

preferential REBT one of two approaches within REBT which seeks to effect a profound philosophical change in an individual's attitude by uprooting her irrational beliefs and replacing them with rational beliefs. Features of preferential REBT include: understanding the role of flexible and rigid evaluations in largely creating, respectively, emotional health and disturbance; striving to accept oneself and others unconditionally as FALLIBLE human beings; seeking PERVASIVE and long-lasting change rather than symptom removal; disputing the philosophical core (absolute musts and shoulds) of emotional disturbance rather than INFERENCES derived from these musts; keenly discriminating between inappropriate and appropriate negative emotions (depression and sadness, respectively). Clients who are unable, for whatever reason, to benefit from the preferential approach are switched to GENERAL REBT (see Ellis & Dryden, 1987).

premise proposition forming the basis of an argument or inference. Premises are usually seen as primary in the creation of emotional distress (e.g. 'I must always be liked') or emotional health (e.g. 'I would prefer to be liked but I don't have to be'). Rational and irrational conclusions or DERIVATIVES from these premises can be viewed as of secondary importance in creating emotional distress or health (e.g. 'If I'm not liked, as I must be, this means I'm completely worthless'). Dryden (1990b) urges REBT therapists to be cautious in challenging clients' premise language: not all musts or shoulds, for example, used by clients are irrational – only absolute, dogmatic, unconditional ones, e.g. 'I must never fail at anything' (unconditional) as opposed to 'I must train hard if I want to complete the London marathon' (conditional). With the unconditional 'must', this is DISPUTED if it is linked to the self-defeating emotions that the client wishes to change; if the conditional 'must' is disputed, the client might wonder what has happened to the therapist's common sense.

present behaviour current conduct. Clients often mistakenly believe that past events directly cause their present self-defeating behaviours, e.g. 'The reason I see myself as a failure today is because my parents always told me I would be one.' REBT therapists show clients that their present problems are being maintained by the irrational ideas they continue to believe about past events, e.g. 'Even though your parents said you would be a failure, you still chose to believe them and have carried this idea of being a failure in your head ever since.' When clients start to dispute their irrational ideas, constructive changes will usually be made in their present behaviours.

prevention keep from happening or existing; hinder. Prevention is a hallmark of EFFICIENCY in psychotherapy. By the time REBT treatment has ended, clients should have internalised a rational and anti-musturbatory philosophy of living which will teach them 'to see so clearly how they usually create their own emotional problems, and to understand so solidly what they can do to restore their own emotional equilibrium that they are able to approach the future with a basically unupsetting philosophy' (Ellis, 1985a, p.132).

problem categories difficulties which can be divided into classes or groups. Grieger and Boyd (1980) group clients problems into three categories to determine if they call for REBT intervention. (1) Career concerns – these include what vocation to pursue, whether to stay in a job or leave to find a better one. (2) Environmental concerns or problems in living – these include poor housing, unemployment, lack of a social life. (3) Emotional and behavioural concerns – these include emotional distress such as depression and guilt and behavioural problems such as procrastination and drug addiction. Category three is clearly the province of REBT therapists but career and environmental concerns may also be targeted if clients have emotional problems about these concerns, e.g. anxious about leaving present employment; depressed about poor housing. When the emotional aspects of these problems have been dealt with, REBT therapists can either help clients with the practical aspects of these problems or refer them to other agencies, e.g. a local council housing department. Clients are likely to tackle their practical problems more effectively if they are not emotionally disturbed about them.

problem list difficulties which are itemised. Clients can list which problems they want help with and in what order of priority. The therapist is usually guided by the client's choice of which problem to tackle first, and assists the client in translating his problem into a realistic goal, e.g. a significant reduction in panic attacks rather than their eradication. Such agreement helps to promote a productive working ALLIANCE. Sometimes a secondary emotional problem might interfere with working on the client's chosen one, e.g. ashamed about being anxious. If the client is not persuaded by the therapist's rationale to tackle shame first, the therapist would return to the anxiety in order not to disrupt the alliance.

problem matrix see DISTURBANCE MATRIX.

problems about problems additional difficulties created by clients in relation to their original difficulties. Clients frequently have SECONDARY EMOTIONAL PROBLEMS associated with their primary ones, e.g. ashamed about feeling anxious; angry about feeling hurt. These secondary problems 'usually exacerbate primary symptoms [problems], and they largely interfere with people clearly perceiving how they tend to create these primary symptoms and what they can do to uncreate them' (Grieger & Boyd, 1980, p.51). Such interference may mean that secondary problems have to be tackled first (with the client's agreement) if progress is to be made on overcoming their primary problems. Tertiary or third rank emotional problems may also occur, e.g. angry about being ashamed about feeling anxious; guilty about being angry about feeling hurt. It may be necessary for the therapist to work backwards: to identify, challenge and change the irrational ideas underpinning clients' tertiary and secondary emotional problems before developing a clear focus on the primary emotional problem – by this time some clients will have a better grasp of the principles of REBT and their problem-solving efficacy.

'problems of everyday living' title of weekly workshop held at the Institute for RET in New York to demonstrate the REBT approach to tackling emotional and behavioural difficulties routinely encountered by people. This workshop, before an audience of up to and sometimes exceeding a 100 people, is a form of GROUP THERAPY in which REBT therapists teach a PSYCHOEDUCATIONAL approach to the causation, maintenance and remediation of emotional problems (see FRIDAY NIGHT WORKSHOP).

problem-solving, REBT see SIMULATION.

problem-solving cognitions thoughts and attitudes that will usually help individuals to resolve their difficulties. Such problem-solving cognitions include considering the consequences of one's actions (CONSEQUENTIAL THINKING) and planning the sequence of steps necessary to achieve one's goals (MEANS-ENDS THINKING). Clients who lack these cognitive skills are taught them by REBT therapists. Whether or not clients have them, the emotional aspects of their problems are dealt with first in order to improve clients' chances of successfully using these skills, e.g. a man who overcomes his depression about living on his own is now more likely to undertake a plan of action to meet suitable partners.

procrastination act of deferring or delaying action. Procrastination is a form of AVOIDANCE BEHAVIOUR. REBT therapists encourage clients to imagine or carry out their avoided activities or tasks in order to 'release' the disturbed negative emotion(s) hidden by the procrastination, e.g. a client imagines confronting a colleague at work in order to discover why she is so anxious about it. Once the irrational ideas maintaining the anxiety have been identified, (e.g. 'I must have her approval') challenged and changed to self-helping rational ideas, the client will be more likely to face rather than avoid her difficulties at work. Wessler and Wessler (1980) suggest that LOW FRUSTRATION TOLERANCE is nearly always involved in procrastination, usually coupled with other emotional problems, as clients believe that the discomfort they will experience by engaging in the avoided tasks will be too much to bear (see Ellis & Knaus, 1977).

profanity quality of using swear-words. Albert ELLIS, the founder of REBT, is noted for his use of swear-words but this is not a requirement to practise as an REBT therapist. Ellis's use of profanity is not gratuitous but serves to, *inter alia*, build rapport with certain clients and thereby strengthen the therapeutic ALLIANCE as well as to highlight important points, e.g. 'Why the fuck do you always have to succeed?' Profanity, if used, is directed at clients' irrational beliefs and not at the clients (see SLOGANS).

progress review evaluation of the constructive change that a client has so far achieved and what further work is required to realise her therapeutic goals. Progress reviews enable therapists to determine how much INSIGHT clients have acquired into their problems, e.g. do they still believe that other people 'cause' their problems?; do they understand the central role of IRRATIONAL BELIEFS in largely creating their emotional disturbance? Therapists also seek FEEDBACK from clients on what they have found helpful and unhelpful about counselling. Progress reviews help to clarify what OBSTACLES TO CLIENT PROGRESS remain and how these blocks can be removed. Regular progress reviews can aid clients to prepare for TERMINATION.

proselytising, rational clients who teach others how to lead a more rational existence by following REBT's philosophy of living. Proselytising is one method whereby clients can become more rational themselves and thereby achieve EMOTIONAL INSIGHT. Grieger and Boyd (1980) list three cautions in using rational proselytising: (1) clients are to have this form of HOMEWORK only when they have understood the process of rational thinking otherwise they might teach nonsense or false ideas to others; (2) clients should be selective about who they proselytise to in case they hurt others or lose friends; (3) therapists should 'intermittently continue to roleplay with these clients in order to refresh their rational thinking and to reinforce their continued cognitive-emotive-behavioural reeducation efforts' (p.180).

'pseudo-rationality' a false or pretended acceptance of REBT's rational outlook. Clients who develop pseudo-rationality may well have an impressive intellectual grasp of REBT but fail to put it into practice outside of therapy thereby not achieving EMOTIONAL INSIGHT (enduring change is brought about by deeply held rational beliefs). Dryden and Yankura (1993) suggest that this lack of effort may be due to LOW FRUSTRATION TOLERANCE or the misapprehension that INTELLECTUAL INSIGHT (rational ideas lightly and intermittently held) alone is sufficient to effect fundamental change. Both ideas would be DISPUTED in order to help clients achieve genuine rationality, i.e. REBT's view of it.

psychoanalysis method of analysing unconscious processes and treating psychological problems that aims to bring these processes to individuals' consciousness by allowing them to talk freely about themselves especially early childhood experiences. ELLIS, the founder of REBT, practised as a psychoanalyst in the late 1940s and early 1950s but became increasingly disenchanted with the theory and practice of psychoanalysis in helping people to overcome their emotional problems. Ellis claims that 'psychoanalysis is probably the most wasteful form of therapy every invented, because it encourages clients to continue in treatment for years and years and to focus on long-winded and side-tracking free-associations, dream analysis and exploration of the past . . . The reason I gave it up was largely because it was inefficient and wasteful' (quoted in Dryden, 1991b, p.104). In developing the ACTIVE-DIRECTIVE approach of REBT, Ellis emphasised that emotional problems were maintained by current irrational thinking (absolute musts and shoulds) and such thinking was often located outside of conscious awareness in the PRE-CONSCIOUS. By bringing it to conscious attention, Ellis was able to realise his goal of psychotherapy 'not only to help people but to help them as quickly, effectively, intelligently, and elegantly as possible' (quoted in Bernard, 1986, p.15). Because psychoanalysis takes so long in many cases, Ellis (1993a) asserts that this leads to clients needlessly and painfully suffering.

psychoeducation the process of acquiring a rational and self-helping philosophy of living. Clients can frequently hasten and deepen their understanding of REBT by using psychoeducational materials such as self-help books, audiocassettes, videos. Such material is also available to the general public. Other psychoeducational activities include FRIDAY NIGHT WORKSHOPS. REBT is primarily an educative rather than a therapeutic approach to tackling emotional distress and because of 'the ubiquity of emotional disturbance' (Ellis, 1980a p.10) REBT ambitiously seeks 'a public education policy of disseminating some of the main elements of RE[B]T to the general populace [which] would effect a great deal of prophylaxis and treatment of emotional ills' (*ibid.* p.11). Indeed, ELLIS has often suggested 'the psychoeducational aspects of RE[B]T are more likely to be important in the future than the psychotherapeutic aspects. It [REBT] had better encourage public education and public acceptance of its principles and practices' (quoted in Bernard, 1986, p.271).

psychological disturbance mental attitude which largely produces emotional disorder or distress. REBT hypothesises that psychological disturbance is primarily created by individuals' rigid, dogmatic, and absolute 'musts', 'shoulds', 'oughts', 'have to's', 'got to's' – demands they make on themselves, others and the world, e.g. 'I absolutely must get this job

otherwise my life might as well be finished.' Because these BELIEFS are usually inflexible and unadaptable to changing circumstances, they are likely to block or impede individual goal-attainment and therefore are seen in REBT as IRRATIONAL. From these 'musts' and 'shoulds' individuals are likely to derive equally irrational conclusions: AWFULISING – the worse life could conceivably be; LOW FRUSTRATION TOLERANCE – e.g. 'I can't stand the circumstances in which I live my life'; DAMNATION – condemning oneself, others and/or the world. DISPUTING irrational beliefs and constructing a new rational outlook usually leads to PSYCHO-LOGICAL HEALTH (see UNHEALTHY NEGATIVE EMOTIONS).

psychological health mental attitude which promotes individual well-being. REBT asserts that a philosophy of PREFER-ENCES (including wishes, wants, hopes, desires) will usually lead to psychological health because these beliefs are flexible and adaptable, aid goal-attainment (whether it is the existing or revised one) and are therefore seen in REBT as RATIO-NAL, e.g. 'I very much want this job but I don't have to have what I want.' From these preferences individuals are likely to derive equally rational conclusions: evaluations of BADNESS, e.g. 'It's pretty bad but hardly awful'; HIGH FRUSTRATION TOLERANCE, e.g. 'I can stand it even though I don't like it and I will seek to change it if I can'. ACCEPTANCE – striving to accept oneself and others unconditionally as FALLIBLE human beings and to accept the complexity of the world. Such a viewpoint refrains from giving oneself, others or the world a single global RAT-ING. Ellis and Bernard (1985) advance 13 criteria of psychological health including ENLIGHTENED SELF-INTEREST, LONG-RANGE HEDONISM and NONUTOPIANISM (see HEALTHY NEGATIVE EMOTIONS).

psychological influences on the development of REBT views or works of psychologists which have had important effects on the evolution of this therapeutic approach. Such influences include Horney's (1950) 'tyranny of the shoulds' in emotional disturbance – ELLIS's concept of musturabation (MUSTS) plays a similarly totalitarian role in stressing the absolute and rigid nature of disturbance-producing EVALUATIVE BELIEFS. The behavioural methods used by, for example, Watson and Rayner (1920) and Dunlap (1932) not only helped Ellis to overcome some of his own problems but also to see the importance of acting against one's self-defeating beliefs and not just cognitively DISPUTING them in order to effect constructive change (see Ellis & Dryden, 1987).

psychological interactionism see INTER-ACTIONISM.

psychosis severe mental disorder that markedly alters one's personality and behaviour and results in impaired or loss of contact with reality. REBT therapists encourage clients with psychotic illnesses (e.g. schizophrenia, bipolar affective disorder) to fully accept rather than condemn themselves for having these disturbances – they assist clients to tackle their NEUROSES (e.g. anger, shame) about their psychoses and thereby help to enhance the quality of life for them during periods of remission. Clients' psychotic symptoms (e.g. delusions, paranoid thinking) can be challenged and changed but progress is much more likely if clients are taking MEDICATION as an adjunct to psychotherapy.

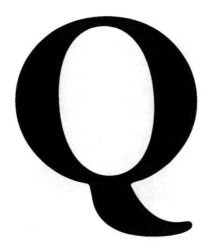

question interrogative expression used to elicit information in reply. REBT therapists use open-ended questions (ones permitting unguided and spontaneous responses) in assessing clients' IRRATIONAL BELIEFS, e.g. 'What thoughts were going through your mind when you made yourself anxious about meeting your girlfriend's parents?' Clients may not be able to uncover an irrational belief through this process and therefore may be asked a theory-driven question (one derived from REBT theory), e.g. 'What demand were you making about the possible disapproval from your girlfriend's parents in order to make yourself so anxious?' SOCRATIC questions are used in DISPUTING irrational beliefs to encourage clients to critically examine the self-defeating nature of these beliefs, e.g. 'Just because you would like the approval of your girlfriend's parents, how does it logically follow that therefore you must have it?' Walen, DiGiuseppe and Dryden (1992) suggest that 'why' questions during disputing 'may be particularly fruitful. The answer to a "why" question requires proof or justification of a belief, and since there is no proof for irrational beliefs, the patient may see the logic of giving them up' (p.159). Questions may be supplemented by DIDACTIC explanations. Too many questions may appear threatening and put clients on the defensive or simply confuse them; so therapists should be prudent in their use of them.

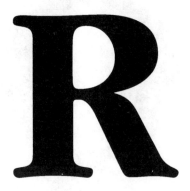

raconteur, REBT therapist as person who is skilled in telling anecdotes. REBT therapists use, among others, PARABLES, FABLES, APHORISMS, to communicate important therapeutic points to clients. Stories told should be adapted to the individual client's specific problems rather than used in an unvarying form. The therapist as raconteur may receive plaudits from her clients but it is important she also receives FEEDBACK to determine if they have understood the rational message conveyed by her stories.

rapport harmonious or sympathetic relationship. REBT therapists agree that the CORE CONDITIONS of therapy (empathy, genuineness and unconditional positive regard) help to build rapport with clients and thereby increase the chances of effecting therapeutic change. REBT therapists emphasise UNCONDITIONAL ACCEPTANCE of clients (but not always of their behaviours) rather than undue WARMTH as this can lead to reinforcing some clients' dire needs for APPROVAL and strengthening their aversion to the hard work that change usually requires. Rapport can also be established through THERAPIST SELF-DISCLOSURE.

rating classification, estimate or evaluation. Global negative ratings of self, others and the world frequently lead to emotional disturbance, e.g. depression induced by the belief, 'Because I lost my job, as I absolutely should not have done, this means I'm totally worthless'; anger created by the belief, 'How dare you let me down, as you absolutely should not have done. You are an utter bastard!' REBT therapists teach clients the futility of rating the totality and complexity of the person or world, e.g. 'Does the label "worthless" adequately sum up every aspect of your personality?' Clients are encouraged to rate only their actions or traits as 'desirable' or 'undesirable' to determine which ones help or hinder the attainment of their goals. REBT hypothesises that if people only rate their actions or traits rather than themselves they will be much less prone to emotional disturbance.

rational see RATIONAL BELIEFS.

'rational barb' self-helping and goal-oriented use of sharply critical comments. REBT therapists MODEL for the clients how to handle the barbs of others with COPING SELF-STATEMENTS and without emotional distress. The therapist then indulges in name-calling, e.g. 'No wonder they call you Marge – you spread so easily' so the client can practise a rational response, e.g. 'I do have a very active sex life which I both enjoy and can accept myself for' (see Kimmel, 1976).

rational beliefs non-absolute evaluative cognitions couched in the form of preferences, wishes, wants, hopes, likes, and usually lead to HEALTHY NEGATIVE EMOTIONS when individuals experience adverse events, e.g. a man feels sad rather than DEPRESSED because he believes 'I very much wanted her to love me but I don't have to have what I want.' From these primary preferences usually stem rational DERIVATIVES of: evaluations of BADNESS, HIGH FRUSTRATION TOLERANCE and ACCEPTANCE, e.g. 'Not having her love is certainly bad but hardly awful.' RATIONALITY in REBT is usually defined as that which helps people to reach important life goals because their belief systems underpinning their goals are seen as logical, realistic, have utility (usefulness) and therefore are adaptable when existing goals are blocked or thwarted, e.g. 'As I failed to get into medical school I can take the exams again or decide on another career to pursue.' Rationality is not defined in any absolute sense in REBT, but as relative to each individual's goal-attaining beliefs.

rational emotive behaviour reeducation teaching clients a new outlook on emotional problem-solving by internalising self-helping and goal-oriented beliefs. Such a re-education can effect a profound philosophical change in some clients by them surrendering their musturbatory (MUSTS) philosophies and replacing them with rational (PREFERENTIAL) philosophies. Techniques used to achieve this include RATIONAL ROLE REVERSAL and PROSELYTISING. For clients who are unable to achieve philosophical change because they are limited in their cognitive skills, they can learn self-helping ideas through, for example, RATIONAL INDOCTRINATION (see Grieger & Boyd, 1980).

rational emotive behaviour therapy (REBT) rational-emotive therapy's new name and reflecting the interactive role of thoughts, feelings, and actions in effecting constructive change in disturbed individuals. ELLIS (1993b) decided, almost 40 years after its inception, on the name change 'because it [RET] really has always been highly cognitive, very emotive and particularly behavioural' (p.2). Clients have to think, feel, and act against their IRRATIONAL BELIEFS if change is to occur. Ellis (*ibid.*) suggests that some practitioners will not be enthusiastic about the name change and is characteristically forthright in his reply: 'Tough – but not awful!' (see RATIONAL THERAPY).

rational-emotive education (REE) teaching the principles and practices of REBT to schoolchildren. Specifically, REE 'involves teaching children to develop perspective, build healthier self-concepts, increase frustration tolerance, and establish a realistic locus of control' (Knaus & Haberstroh, 1993, p.202). REBT principles are taught through structured lessons integrated into a school's academic curriculum to help build psychological skills the children can use to deal with daily problems or challenges. School teachers can undertake a basic training in REBT and/or use REE materials such as Ann Vernon's (1989) *Thinking, Feeling, Behaving* in order to introduce it into the classroom. The most ambitious use of REE was at the LIVING SCHOOL. REE can also be used with special needs populations such as seriously disturbed children, children with severe physical disability, student burn out.

rational-emotive hypnotherapy (REH) REBT principles coupled with hypnosis to bring about constructive change. REH 'is based on the similar assumption [to REBT] that emotional distress arises from a negative or "irrational" type of self-hypnosis' (Golden & Friedberg, 1986, p.294). Irrational ideas are challenged and changed to rational ones while a client is in a hypnotic state. Clients are also taught 'to give themselves rational suggestions during self-hypnosis'(*ibid.*). REBT hypothesizes that hypnosis has a therapeutic effect because the therapist's rational SUGGESTIONS are absorbed by clients and turned into autosuggestions which become part of their new self-helping attitudes (see RATIONAL STAGE-DIRECTED THERAPY).

rational-emotive imagery the use of one's imagination to help effect constructive change. Rational-emotive imagery has two versions: (1) ELLIS asks a client to imagine vividly a negative ACTIVATING EVENT in which an UNHEALTHY NEGATIVE EMOTION (e.g. depression) occurs. When she powerfully experiences depression, she is asked to change it to its rational alternative (sadness) while still imagining the negative event. This is achieved by replacing the irrational beliefs underpinning her depression with rational ones. (2) Maultsby (1975) asks a client to imagine vividly a negative event but this time to repeat vigorously an appropriate rational belief to bring about a HEALTHY NEGATIVE EMOTION. It is important in both versions to obtain FEEDBACK from clients that they have carried out the imagery exercises in the prescribed fashion rather than used, for example, distraction or made the negative event more pleasant in order to bring about emotional change (see IMAGERY TECHNIQUES).

rational-emotive philosophy principles and concepts underlying this therapeutic approach. A major philosophical source of REBT stems from EPICTETUS who observed that people are not disturbed by events but by the views they take of these events (see B-C CONNECTION). REBT philosophy is composed of various elements and these include: EPISTEMOLOGY – that knowledge acquired through scientific scrutiny is a more credible basis for one's beliefs than other sources such as religion or subjective impressions; DIALECTICS – that through developing logical thinking will people be more able to combat their disturbance-producing ideas; VALUES – that longer and happier lives can usually be achieved by people removing their rigid ideas about themselves, others and the world, and replacing them with flexible ones; RESPONSIBLE HEDONISM – that by establishing a balance between their short- and long-term goals, people can enjoy the present and plan constructively for the future; ETHICS – that relative concepts of good and bad or right and wrong are more helpful than absolute ones in resolving ethical dilemmas and determining goals that are both personally and socially responsible; ETHICAL HUMANISM – that human behaviour should be guided by reason rather than, for example, religion or superstition. REBT is not a form of STOICISM or RATIONALISM and views rationality as that which aids individuals to achieve important life goals.

rational-emotive problem simulation see SIMULATION.

rational-emotive theory explanation of general principles of this therapeutic approach. REBT theory posits that our emotional reactions to events are largely mediated by our EVALUATIVE BELIEFS – we feel as we think – and that emotional disturbance primarily stems from irrational ideas (rigid MUSTS and SHOULDS). In order to reduce or remove such disturbance, examining and changing one's self-defeating thinking is the most reliable way of achieving this. ELLIS (1976) hypothesises that humans have an innate ability to disturb themselves and this is reinforced by cultural factors which seem 'to furnish the specific content of these [irrational] beliefs' (Walen, DiGiuseppe & Dryden, 1992, p.16). REBT takes an AHISTORICAL approach to emotional problem-solving by focusing on how irrational thinking is being maintained in the present rather than how it was acquired in the past. In order to tackle emotional disturbance, lifelong HARD WORK AND PRACTICE is required to reduce the intensity, frequency, and duration of such disturbance (see NEGATIVE EMOTIONS).

rational-emotive therapy (RET) name of REBT between 1961–1993 which emphasised the importance of both thinking and feeling in tackling psychological disturbance. ELLIS distinguished between inappropriate negative emotions (e.g. depression, anxiety, guilt) and appropriate healthy emotions (rational alternatives to the above are, respectively, sadness, concern, remorse): the former emotions usually blocked goal-attainment and stemmed from a philosophy of DEMANDS while the latter emotions aided goal-attainment and stemmed from a philosophy of PREFERENCES. The behavioural component of RET was still vitally important in order for clients to put into practice their new RATIONAL BELIEFS. Despite the change from RATIONAL THERAPY to RET, Ellis eventually decided that the name RET did not accurately reflect its mainly trimodal approach (cognitive, emotive and behavioural) and in 1993 changed it to RATIONAL EMOTIVE BEHAVIOUR THERAPY.

rational essay self-helping and goal-oriented ideas on a particular theme or subject. In order to promote EMOTIONAL INSIGHT, clients can be asked to write an essay involving an REBT concept, e.g. 'How will unconditional self-acceptance rather than self-esteem help me achieve greater psychological health?'

rational humorous songs popular songs with rewritten lyrics in order to impart a self-helping philosophy of living or attack a self-defeating one, e.g. 'Perfect Rationality' set to the tune of Luigi Denza's *Finiculi Finicula*. The songs, like advertising jingles, are designed 'to repetitively go around and around in your patients' heads . . . and thereby to have their messages sink in and influence the person who sings them aloud or internally "hears" them' (Ellis &

Abrahms, 1978, p.147). The songs ELLIS has rewritten are of a certain vintage and therefore REBT therapists may need to use more modern songs for their younger clients.

rational indoctrination to imbue with self-helping ideas. This technique is used with clients who find it difficult, for whatever reason, to 'think about their thinking' in logical, empirical or pragmatic ways. Usually the only way to make therapeutic progress is to get clients to repeat rational ideas the therapist has presented to them, e.g. 'I can accept myself even if others don't like me'. This idea might be used by a man who lacks the ability to tease out the philosophical underpinnings of the depression he experiences whenever he is rejected. Rational indoctrination may help to modify his emotional distress (see Grieger & Boyd, 1980).

rational insight see EMOTIONAL INSIGHT; INTELLECTUAL INSIGHT.

rational recovery (RR) abstinence from alcohol abuse using the principles and practices of REBT. RR is a radically different alternative to the traditional one in this field provided by Alcoholics Anonymous (AA). Some of these important differences include: RR putting the locus of control for change within the individual rather than AA investing it in a Higher Power (e.g. God, the AA group); RR seeing alcoholism as a self-destructive personal philosophy of living as opposed to AA viewing it as a disease process; RR emphasising individuals getting over alcoholism rather than AA stressing that they are lifelong recovering alcoholics and thereby confirming their self-image. Trimpey (1989) urges his readers in *The Small Book* to 'see how quickly we can let the nation know that it's time for a Rational Recovery (RR) program everywhere an AA group is found!' (p.7). RR helps alcoholics to combat their three levels of disturbance by 'get[ting them] to their self-hatred about their alcoholism, to uproot their low frustration tolerance (LFT), that largely drives them to drink, and to tackle the original emotional problems that encouraged them to drink too much in the first place' (Ellis, 1989b, p.5).

rational stage-directed therapy (RSDT) 'is a didactic-experiential, cognitive-behavioral intervention designed to guide or direct the client through various stages', to reduce or remove 'beliefs, attitudes, and emotions that are self-defeating in nature' (Tosi & Marzella, 1977, pp. 95–96). Using the ABCDE model of self-analysis and change, the therapist guides the client through six stages: (1) the client becomes aware of her disturbance-producing ideas and the problematic situations in which they arise; she is taught how to develop self-helping rational ideas; (2) she undergoes deep relaxation or hypnosis and imagines thinking rational thoughts and engaging in constructive behaviours in these situations; (3) she makes a commitment to more rational ways of thinking and behaving; (4) she implements her new self-helping skills in the actual rather than imagined situations; (5) she internalises a rational philosophy of living; (6) she takes responsibility for continued change and the generalisability of her rational ideas to other problem areas in her life; she can be redirected through the six stages of therapy if there are other problems she wishes to work on. RSDT 'may be considered as an inclusive rubric for a rational stage directed hypnotherapy (RSDH) and a rational stage directed imagery (RSDI)' (*ibid*. p.96).

rationale statement of reasons for course of action. REBT therapists practise OPEN-NESS towards their clients and therefore present rationales for their various actions, e.g. DISPUTING, negotiating HOME-WORK assignments, the use of HUMOUR. However, there are a few occasions when presenting a rationale before an activity is carried out can undermine its therapeutic potency, e.g. problem SIMU-LATION. Generally speaking, the therapeutic ALLIANCE is strengthened when therapists explain the basis for their actions.

rationalism the philosophical view that all knowledge of the world is based on reason alone. In the debate on CONSTRUC-TIVISM as opposed to rationalism, REBT has been placed in the latter camp. ELLIS (1992), the founder of REBT, has insisted that he never was a rationalist because he believes that 'reason and the sense (as well as emotion) are the sources of human knowledge and that they had better (though do not have to) determine our opinions and actions' (p.38). REBT does not have an absolute view of RATIO-NALITY as a fixed entity, external to all humans; instead, REBT defines rationality as that which helps people to attain their goals – a relative view of each person's goal-directed beliefs. Rationalism is opposed to EMPIRICISM (the position that knowledge rests on experience) but REBT takes an explicitly empirical approach to reality-testing clients' belief systems, e.g. 'Is your belief "I must never fail" always consistent with reality?' Even though REBT is not a rationalist system of psychotherapy, critics still label it as one (see Bernard & DiGiuseppe, 1989).

'rationality isn't everything' term used by Hauck (1980b) to suggest that the principles of rational thinking can be misused when individuals who have learned REBT deliberately act in ways that cause offence to others and then absolve themselves of any responsibility for the resulting emotional reaction. For example, always being brutally honest about other people's shortcomings when asked to give an opinion and then saying such as: 'I didn't upset you. You upset yourself over my remarks.' Strictly speaking this is true, but REBT teaches individuals not only greater emotional self-control in the face of others' obnoxious behaviour and life's vicissitudes but also advocates that they act in ways that are responsible and civilised. As Hauck (*ibid*. p.44) observes: 'A person can be content to use RE[B]T as a system for self-protection only' and not as a battering ram to break down other people's defences in order to reveal their sensitivities and vulnerabilities.

rationalisation process of attributing one's behaviour to reasons that seem superficially plausible but are unrelated to the real, possibly unconscious, reasons for such behaviour. A woman who failed to get the job she desperately wanted may say 'I didn't want it anyway'. If she was to honestly admit how much she wanted the job, she might damn herself as a failure and thereby experience emotional distress. Clients frequently believe that rationalisation and rational are interchangeable terms: the former is a DEFENCE MECHANISM which helps clients to avoid painful reality; the latter is used in REBT to assist clients to confront and overcome such a reality.

rational portfolio collecting (as if to put in a case) self-helping and goal-oriented evidence in favour of one's rational beliefs, e.g. 'I would much prefer to be liked by everyone but I don't have to be.' Clients are asked to give as many detailed reasons as possible to support their rational beliefs with the therapist 'suggest[ing] others when the client has exhausted her own supply. I (WD) call this technique "Building your rational portfolio"' (Dryden, 1987a, p.128).

rational prescriptions self-helping and goal-oriented instructions as if written out by a doctor, e.g. the therapist may say to a client 'Whenever you feel really uncomfortable, apply the "I can stand it" treatment.' Dryden and Yankura (1993, p.123) hypothesise that rational prescriptions 'serve to augment clients' independent efforts at disputing their irrational beliefs in their everyday lives,

as they may prompt recall of the counsellor's "rational voice".'

rational role reversal client and therapist switch roles so that the client can strengthen her conviction in her new self-helping beliefs. The therapist voices some of the client's irrational beliefs, e.g. 'I must always be loved in order to be worthwhile' while the client plays the role of the counsellor in DISPUTING such beliefs. Such role reversal can help to identify remaining weaknesses in the client's rational arguments. Rational role reversal is best undertaken when clients understand how rational ideas will help them to be more effective problem-solvers.

rational self-statements see COPING SELF-STATEMENTS

rational therapy (RT) original name of REBT when it was founded in 1955 and emphasised the primary role of thoughts and beliefs in largely determining emotional and behavioural responses. However, ELLIS, the founder of REBT, stressed that thoughts, emotions, and behaviours were interdependent processes and therefore cognitions could not be examined in isolation from the other two processes. This observation about the real nature of RT went largely unnoticed and it was frequently confused with RATIONALISM – the major reason why Ellis in 1961 changed RT's name to RATIONAL-EMOTIVE THERAPY.

realistic thinking attitude based on adapting to what is real in the world. REBT therapists teach their clients to be realistic and not POSITIVE THINKERS: for example, that they will not always achieve their goals; bad or grim events will occur in their lives. However, if clients surrender their JEHOVIAN demands on reality, e.g. 'My life must run smoothly' and substitute a preferential and therefore realistic outlook, 'I would much prefer my life to run smoothly but it doesn't have to' they will be much more likely to adjust constructively to adverse events in their lives. To determine if clients' beliefs are realistic, they are subjected to REALITY-TESTING.

reality-testing critically examining one's thoughts and beliefs to determine if they reflect objective reality, e.g. 'I believe I am the only person in the world who is not going to grow old.' REBT therapists subject clients' IRRATIONAL BELIEFS to reality-testing to show them there is usually no evidence to support their 'musts', e.g. 'You say that your wife must not leave you under any circumstances, yet she has been gone five years now.' By teaching clients to reality-test their beliefs, therapists show them how to become PERSONAL SCIENTISTS and thereby develop flexible beliefs which are consistent with empirical reality, goal-oriented and more likely to lead to HEALTHY NEGATIVE EMOTIONS (see EMPIRICAL APPROACH).

reattribution to assign a different reason, motive or cause (e.g. for another's behaviour) than the one originally presented. Clients can make themselves emotionally distraught over attributions they make about certain facts in their lives, e.g. a male client says he is depressed because his wife must be having an affair as she gets home late on some evenings. By encouraging such a client to examine the attributions he makes about his wife's lateness may well prove his attributions to be groundless: his wife's lateness can be reattributed to, for example, staying late at the office, traffic jams, seeing friends. (If his suspicions were justified, REBT therapists would challenge his demands that such events must not occur in his life.) The process of reattribution can help to reduce clients' emotional problems and make them less prone to assume the worst about others' intentions or behaviour towards them (see Ellis & Abrahms, 1978).

rebelliousness state of resistance; refractory. ELLIS (1985a) suggests that some clients rebel against therapy 'because they see it as an impingement on their freedom, and, especially if it is active and directive, they perversely fight it even when they have voluntarily asked for it' (p.16). IRRATIONAL BELIEFS underpinning such rebelliousness might include 'I must have complete freedom to control my life without any interference or control from my therapist despite having asked for her help.' Unless such beliefs are challenged and changed, clients will not only block their progress in therapy but also fail to tackle the problems they ostensibly want help with.

recall v recognition ability to retrieve information from memory contrasted with an awareness that information has been previously presented. Clients are more likely to achieve greater retention of their self-helping rational beliefs if they are acquired through SOCRATIC DIALOGUE rather than by an overly DIDACTIC APPROACH (use of lectures) which encourages clients to recognise rather than recall which beliefs are self-helping. This difference occurs because 'the lecture format consists of unequally weighted sequential monologues, in Socratic dialogue, the client expresses the therapeutic material in his or her own words and will recall it in this modality, thus encouraging retention' (Walen, DiGiuseppe & Dryden, 1992, p.231).

recording of sessions audiocassette taping of therapy. This procedure allows clients to listen to their therapy sessions in greater detail, pick out important therapeutic points or insights and mull over the self-defeating nature of some of their beliefs. Taping sessions can accelerate the process of change for clients. However, some clients may condemn themselves for the way they sound or for 'talking such nonsense' when they listen to their tapes. Such self-downing comments can become the focus for therapeutic attention at the next session – clients can learn to accept themselves for the way they sound or for talking 'nonsense'. However, if clients believe that session recording is not helpful then it is discontinued. Recording of sessions are used by REBT therapists in SUPERVISION as an important means of determining their EFFICIENCY as psychotherapists.

reduction to absurdity proving the falsity of a client's irrational belief by demonstrating the inevitably ridiculous conclusions to which it would logically lead. For example, a client who claimed she could not bear any stress in her life was met with silence by the therapist because his questions might prove stressful but at the same time he would not be able to provide the help she was seeking. The humorous use of the reduction to absurdity technique is aimed at clients' irrational beliefs and not at clients themselves (see VIVID REBT).

referenting listing the advantages and disadvantages of particular courses of action, e.g. cessation versus continuation of illicit drug use. By frequently bringing the client's attention back to such a list (and adding to it), the therapist can concentrate on the advantages of cessation and the disadvantages of continuation thereby providing another incentive to the client's decision to become drug free.

reframing an event, situation, behaviour, etc. remains the same but its meaning is changed. A client may say she failed her HOMEWORK task of being assertive with a work colleague because he paid no attention to her when she challenged his rude comments. The therapist reframes the task by pointing out she was successful because the homework was to be assertive with her colleague, which she had failed to be in the past, and not to elicit a positive response from him (though this would have been a bonus). Reframing is a form of COGNITIVE RESTRUCTURING.

regret to feel sorry about (e.g. an act, fault, mistake). Regret is seen as a HEALTHY NEGATIVE EMOTION and a rational alternative to SHAME and EMBARRASSMENT. In regret, revealing a personal weakness or acting stupidly in public (e.g. tripping over while carrying a tray full of crockery) is evaluated in terms of PREFERENCES: 'I would greatly prefer not to have behaved stupidly in front of all those people but there is no reason why I must not behave that way. I regret my behaviour but do not see it as awful.' Behavioural responses in regret include staying in the situation rather than trying to leave it; if appropriate, looking for its humorous aspects and attempting to restore 'calm' to the situation without profuse apologies.

rehearsal the practice or trial performance of a desired behaviour before it is carried out *in vivo*. Clients can use behavioural or imaginal methods to rehearse in therapy sessions their HOMEWORK tasks, e.g. assertively tackling a work colleague's rude comments. Rehearsal can also identify clients' disturbance-producing ideas which may block them from carrying out their homework assignments.

reification regarding something abstract as a concrete thing. REBT therapists encourage clients not to reify themselves or others as gods or devils, e.g. 'His behaviour is so bad it's as if he is the devil himself.' Instead clients are taught to accept themselves and others unconditionally as complex and fallible human beings who cannot legitimately be given a single global RATING but their specific behaviours or traits can be, e.g. 'I unconditionally accept you but not your appalling behaviour' (see ETHICAL HUMANISM).

reindoctrination repeatedly imbue oneself or others with ideas, principles, opinions, etc. REBT hypothesises that individuals maintain their emotional problems because they reindoctrinate themselves (sometimes on a daily basis) with irrational ideas, e.g. 'I've been telling myself for 20 years that I'm a failure. And for 20 years I've been unable to shake off this depression.' REBT therapists teach clients how to DISPUTE such irrational ideas and thereby DEINDOCTRINATE themselves; in their place, therapists help clients to construct self-helping and goal-oriented ideas which clients can choose to accept as part of a new philosophy of living (see INDOCTRINATION; INSIGHT).

reinforcement strengthen by additional assistance or support. REBT therapists use reinforcement methods to encourage clients to carry out their HOMEWORK tasks, e.g. watching a favourite television programme after a client has tidied up his bedroom. If some clients avoid their homework tasks but still indulge in the pleasurable reinforcements therapists focus on the LOW FRUSTRATION BELIEFS (e.g. 'It's too hard to do it. I can't stand it') usually underpinning such avoidance behaviour. Reinforcements are frequently coupled with PENALTIES as a means of encouraging clients to do their homework assignments (see OPERANT CONDITIONING).

rejection refuse to accept; rebuff. Hauck (1981a) asserts that fear of rejection is one of the two most common fears (the other is fear of failure). Rejection frequently occurs at two levels: one partner is rejected by another; she then severely condemns and rejects herself, e.g. 'Because he has dumped me, as he absolutely should not have done, this means I'm completely worthless and unloveable.' Such self-downing usually leads to EMOTIONAL DISTURBANCE. REBT therapists teach clients not only to accept the sometimes grim reality of rejection in life but also to accept themselves in the face of it. With such an outlook clients can spend more time looking for new partners and much less time mired in misery.

relapse to fall or slip back into a former state or condition. This means clients who revert to irrational beliefs, feelings, and behaviours. REBT therapists certainly do not expect their clients to be perfectly rational at all times and therefore see relapse as part of human FALLIBILITY. Clients are encouraged to deal with their BACKSLIDING in the same way they did while in therapy: to look for the absolute 'musts' and 'shoulds' they have introduced into their thinking and vigorously DISPUTE them using a MULTIMODAL APPROACH in order to reinstate their rational beliefs. If clients wish to avoid relapse or greatly reduce its occurrence, they are required to engage in the HARD WORK AND PRACTICE of strengthening their rational beliefs.

relationship, therapeutic interaction between therapist and client. The ingredients involved in developing such a relationship include REBT therapists offering their clients UNCONDITIONAL ACCEPTANCE as fallible human beings who are encouraged to become collaborators in the problem-solving process; practising an ACTIVE-DIRECTIVE STYLE which quickly directs clients to the cognitive core of their emotional problems; exhibiting OPENNESS in their relationship with clients and, if clinically relevant, disclosing how they coped with similar problems to the clients'; avoiding undue WARMTH towards their clients as this may prove to have IATROGENIC potential, i.e. therapists making clients' existing problems worse. Therapeutic relationships in REBT are guided by FLEXIBILITY (see Dryden, 1990c).

relativism the position that there are no absolute truths or values. REBT theory does not absolutely insist that ABSOLUTIST THINKING is always to be found at the core of emotional disturbance but there 'is a very high correlation between their [clients'] demands, commands, insistences, necessities, and what we call emotional disturbance' (Ellis, quoted in

Dryden, 1991b, p.15). To achieve PSY-CHOLOGICAL HEALTH, clients are urged to internalise a philosophy of relativism emphasising PREFERENCES, e.g. 'I would very much like to be in love but I don't have to be in order to be happy.' REBT theory does not offer any absolute or invariant criteria of either RATIONALITY or IRRATIONALITY: both are viewed in relative terms as, respectively, that which aids individual goal-attainment and that which blocks individual goal-attainment.

relaxation calmness; relief from tense or rigid condition. Relaxation techniques are used in REBT as an adjunct to therapy, e.g. helping panic-stricken clients to feel calmer before DISPUTING their disturbance-producing ideas such as 'I must not experience panic otherwise something terrible will happen.' Clients who only use relaxation methods may FEEL BETTER but, according to REBT theory, usually do not GET BETTER because they avoid tackling the irrational ideas underpinning their emotional problems (see DISTRACTION).

religion set of beliefs and practices involving the worship of gods or the supernatural; cause, principle or interest pursued with great seriousness or zeal. REBT takes a HUMANISTIC position in emphasizing human welfare and interests guided by reason and without reference to concepts of the supernatural. Such a position does not mean that REBT therapists are disrespectful to clients' religious beliefs; indeed, REBT 'actually endorses and teaches several important religious views, especially the Christian philosophy of grace – of accepting the sinner but not his or her sins' (Ellis, 1992, p.38). ELLIS, the founder of REBT, used to believe that religion itself created emotional disturbance but later modified this view to the concept of religiosity as being the real culprit: 'religiosity to me means a devout belief in the supernatural, in faith unfounded in fact, in dogma, in absolutistic thinking' (quoted in Bernard 1986, p.260). The concept of religiosity includes a devout commitment to secular religions (e.g. fascism, communism, terrorism) and dogmatic atheism (see Hauck, 1985).

religiosity see RELIGION.

remorse deep and painful regret for wrongdoing. Remorse is seen as a HEALTHY NEGATIVE EMOTION and a rational alternative to GUILT. Remorse occurs when an individual breaks her moral code but evaluates this in terms of PREFERENCES, e.g. 'I would greatly prefer not to have smacked my child but there is no reason why I absolutely must not do so. I am a fallible human being, not a damnable one, for acting in such a way.' Behavioural responses include taking responsibility for one's actions and attempting to understand the dynamics underlying such actions. Experiencing remorse enable clients to accept responsibility for their perceived bad behaviour but avoids condemning themselves as bad.

repetition being repeated. Therapists are usually required to repeat, possibly many times, the principles and practices of REBT if clients are going to learn how successfully to challenge their irrational beliefs and construct self-helping rational ones. Repetition helps to facilitate the process of constructive change. Repeating REBT ideas does not have to be a monotonous affair but can provide the therapist with opportunities to display her CREATIVITY.

resignation submissive attitude or state; unresisting acquiescence. Some clients mistakenly believe that the REBT concept of ACCEPTANCE equals resignation, e.g. 'I suppose I'll just have to resign myself to the fact that I will always be unlucky in love.' REBT therapists do not advocate resignation in the face of adverse events but action: acceptance of oneself and empirical reality acts as a springboard to effect change in our lives; in the above example, the client would be encouraged to examine how she largely sabotages her attempts to achieve loving relationships and what steps she could take to ameliorate this problem.

resistance act of opposing or withstanding. ELLIS (1985a) states that client resistance in therapy stems from, *inter alia*, fear of discomfort – that change is too hard and uncomfortable to endure; fear of disclosure and shame – that by revealing shameful thoughts or acts clients will be condemned by their therapist; fear of success – actually, fear of subsequent failure after initial therapeutic success. Client resistance can also stem from a therapist's insistence on the cause of a client's problems, e.g. that she was sexually abused by her father. The irrational ideas underpinning clients' and therapists' self-created blocks in therapy are identified, challenged and changed in order to produce therapeutic movement (see NORMAL RESISTANCE; OBSTACLES TO CLIENT PROGRESS).

response options 'specific ways of responding that are available to the person in a given situation' (Dryden, 1987a, p.24). Response options are suggested by the ACTION TENDENCIES associated with particular emotions, e.g. looking for ways of escape or distraction as part of an overall pattern of avoidance in ANXIETY. REBT therapists help clients to find constructive response options that will act against their self-defeating action tendencies and thereby make their behaviours less maladaptive.

responsibility see EMOTIONAL RESPONSIBILITY.

responsible hedonism see LONG-RANGE HEDONISM.

rewriting the rules changing one's rigid and self-defeating ideas into flexible and self-helping ones, e.g. 'My hard work must always be appreciated' modified to 'I would prefer my hard work to be appreciated but it doesn't have to be. If it isn't, too bad!' Once clients accept that they are largely responsible for 'writing' or creating their rigid rules of living they empower themselves to 'rewrite' or construct more goal-oriented rules of living (see Burns, 1980).

rhetorical question question asked to produce an effect rather than receive an answer. Clients' rhetorical questions often imply irrational ideas, e.g. 'How could my husband treat me in such a cruel way?' might translate as 'He absolutely should not have treated me like that and is an utter bastard for doing so!' Grieger and Boyd (1980, p.102) point out that 'clients who express rhetorical questions are usually unaware of the real ideas behind them, ideas that precipitate so much of their disturbed emotional and behavioural response.' Therapists help clients to tease out these ideas in order to DISPUTE them and thereby reduce emotional distress.

risk-taking engaging in potentially threatening, dangerous or hazardous actions. Risk-taking exercises are designed to confront the fears that clients usually avoid, e.g. deliberately seeking rejection from members of the opposite sex. Such an exercise helps clients to take the 'horror' (emotional disturbance) out of rejection and thereby make a more realistic evaluation of the experience as well as learn to accept themselves when others reject them. Risk-taking exercises need to be CHALLENGING, BUT NOT OVERWHELMING. Risk-taking helps clients to develop more ambitious life goals, make their lives less self-restricting and indicates PSYCHOLOGICAL HEALTH.

roadblocks obstacles which prevent or make difficult some clients' ability to strengthen their conviction in their rational beliefs and weaken or remove their adherence to their irrational beliefs. Grieger and Boyd (1980) list a number of client roadblocks which include: the 'I won't be me' syndrome – thinking, feeling, and acting in new ways is for some clients alien to their character and therefore unnatural (see COGNITIVE-EMOTIVE DISSONANCE); self-hate – clients who believe they are worthless will have their beliefs confirmed when they change into a 'worthless person' or their worthlessness merits continual punishment, not attempts to overcome it; paying lip service – learning by rote rational concepts without making much effort to think through these ideas or act on them. Therapist roadblocks include too much LECTURING which can turn clients into passive rather than active participants in the DISPUTATION process and failing to note clients' progress can lead to their disillusionment with therapy.

role playing recreating in the consulting room situations in which clients experience emotional and behavioural problems. For example, a client who says he is unable to be assertive with a noisy neighbour is encouraged to re-enact the scene in therapy with the therapist taking the role of the noisy neighbour. Such a re-enactment enables the therapist to pinpoint the irrational beliefs largely responsible for the client's unassertiveness (e.g. 'I couldn't stand his disapproval. He might not ever talk to me again') and to challenge and change them to rational and self-helping beliefs. The client rehearses the new beliefs and constructive behaviour he wishes to adopt in the real-life situation. Another form of role playing is RATIONAL ROLE REVERSAL.

sadness state of grief or unhappiness; sorrowful or mournful. Sadness is seen as a HEALTHY NEGATIVE EMOTION and a rational alternative to DEPRESSION. Sadness occurs when an individual evaluates a loss in terms of PREFERENCES, e.g. 'I would greatly prefer not to have lost my job but there is no reason why it must not happen. It is bad that this happened, but not awful.' Behavioural responses include remaining in contact with reality rather than withdrawing from it and being able to talk to others about one's feelings of loss.

scepticism attitude which takes no knowledge for granted. REBT is sceptical that there is any logical or empirical evidence for absolute musts and shoulds or dire necessities in the universe, e.g. 'I absolutely must be loved in order to accept myself.' Scepticism denotes an enquiring mind rather than the closed one usually associated with rigidly held IRRATIONAL BELIEFS and REBT therapists encourage clients to introduce doubt into such beliefs, e.g. 'Is it really true that you can't accept yourself unless you are loved? Let's see if we can test this idea in some way.' Even when clients are able to falsify their irrational beliefs and construct self-helping rational ones, they are urged not to abandon their scepticism towards these new beliefs or anything else in life. ELLIS (1983c) has stated that scepticism (along with certain other

characteristics) is synonymous with mental health.

scientific thinking an approach to problem-solving which emphasises setting up, testing and evaluating hypotheses in order to determine if changes are required in existing theories or explanations accounting for the problem. REBT follows the scientific method in viewing clients' beliefs (e.g. 'I must always be loved in order to be happy') as hypotheses not facts and therefore are subjected to (1) empirical testing, e.g. 'Is it consistent with reality that you have never been happy without love?' Such questions attempt to FALSIFY clients hypotheses; (2) logical scrutiny, e.g. 'Does it follow that you must have love, just because you want it?' Clients usually explain why it would be highly desirable to be loved, but are unable to marshal proof why they must be loved. Such replies are inconsistent and contradictory and therefore reveal the illogical nature of their beliefs. Scientific thinking is, ideally, open, flexible and 'never dogmatic, doesn't' claim that any theory is perfectly true under all conditions and at all times, and happily seeks for better, more workable, alternative theories' (Ellis, 1993a, p.10). REBT hypothesises that much emotional disturbance stems from anti-scientific and inflexible thinking and if clients take on the role of PERSONAL SCIENTIST they will be able to reduce or minimise such disturbance.

secondary disturbances see SECONDARY EMOTIONAL PROBLEMS.

secondary emotional problems disturbed feelings derived from primary disturbances, e.g. ashamed about feeling anxious; angry about feeling hurt. One of the DISTINCTIVE FEATURES OF REBT 'is emphasis[ing] the human disposition first to disturb oneself over some failure or frustration and secondarily to disturb oneself over one's disturbances' (Ellis & Bernard, 1985, p.18). Dryden (1990c) suggests that therapists should tackle the secondary emotional problem first if: (1) the secondary emotional problem blocks or interferes with working on the primary one; (2) the secondary problem is more clinically significant than the primary one; (3) the client can understand the rationale for working on his secondary problem first. However, if clients wish to work on the primary problem first rather than follow the therapist's advice, this request should be accepted by the therapist in order to avoid disrupting the therapeutic ALLIANCE (see PERPETUATION OF PSYCHOLOGICAL DISTURBANCE).

secondary gains advantages derived from original problems. Clients who receive benefits from their primary disturbances are usually very reluctant to give them up and therefore are likely to resist therapy, e.g. a woman with agoraphobia sabotages her attempts to overcome her problems because she believes her husband will leave her if he sees her improve. REBT therapists identify, challenge and change the irrational beliefs underpinning the secondary gains (e.g. 'My husband must never leave me otherwise I'll never have any happiness again') in order to help the client determine if her secondary gains really are more important than her primary goal of overcoming her agoraphobia (see PAYOFFS FROM PROBLEMS).

selective abstraction choosing one aspect of a situation or event and interpreting the whole situation on the basis of this one aspect or detail. Selective abstraction is seen as an inferential distortion stemming from underlying MUSTS, e.g. 'My workshop presentation was ruined because someone in the audience yawned, as they absolutely should not have done.'

self, complexity of the the view that individuals consist of many complicated and interrelated parts or aspects. Teaching clients about the complexity of the self encourages them to avoid RATING themselves but not their particular actions or traits, e.g. 'I dislike my unassertiveness but I am too complex to be rated in any way.' If clients accept the concept of the complexity of the self they will usually make themselves less prone to emotional distress and more likely to consider SELF-ACCEPTANCE.

self-acceptance see ACCEPTANCE.

self-actualisation realising one's potential. REBT therapists teach their clients how to overcome their emotional and behavioural problems in order to help them 'actively to seek and arrange for a fuller, happier, and more self-actualising existence' (Ellis, 1993a, p.25). Clients are encouraged to individually choose goals which emphasise self-actualisation (e.g. becoming self-employed) and are taught how to tackle the various blocks standing in the way of such goals. Self-actualisation is more likely to occur if clients develop flexible beliefs in the form of PREFERENCES rather than rigid beliefs in the form of DEMANDS.

self-defeating thoughts, feelings and behaviours beliefs, emotions and actions which create and maintain psychological disturbance and block individual goal-attainment, e.g. a woman who believes 'I can't stand rejection' experiences anxiety and avoids social situations where she might find suitable partners. REBT therapists teach their clients how to construct SELF-HELPING THOUGHTS, FEELINGS AND BEHAVIOURS.

self-denigration see SELF-DOWNING.

self-dialogues (forceful) teaching clients to have vehement arguments between their irrational and rational voices. For example, Irrational Voice: I'll have a few more hits [of heroin] then I'll stop for good; Rational Voice: Don't talk crap! How many times have you said that in the past? You know it's going to end in grief; Irrational Voice: Not this time. As I'm going to quit I might as well have a final treat; Rational Voice: Garbage! All your treats ever do are to prolong your self-destructive behaviour. Yet again you're putting off the day when you have to face your problems; Irrational Voice: You might just have a point there; Rational Voice: It's a damn good point and you know it. The hard work of abstinence has to start sometime, so let it be now. Such dialogues can be tape-recorded by clients to determine '. . . not only . . . if they have rational content but if their rational arguments are vigorously and convincingly presented' (Ellis *et al.* 1988, p. 86).

self-direction guiding one's own conduct without being impelled by external forces. Self-direction means individuals taking responsibility for their own lives 'while simultaneously preferring to cooperate with others. They do not need or demand considerable support or succoring from others' (Ellis & Bernard, 1985, p.7). Self-direction is seen in REBT as a criterion of PSYCHOLOGICAL HEALTH.

self-discipline control and training of oneself usually for improvement. Problems of self-discipline (e.g. procrastination, drug abuse) are usually viewed in REBT as underpinned by LOW FRUSTRATION TOLERANCE beliefs, e.g. 'I can't stand being deprived of alcohol when I'm so tense.'

Such SHORT-RANGE HEDONISM usually leads to adverse long-term consequences, e.g. perpetuating rather than overcoming her anxiety. REBT therapists show clients how to achieve self-discipline by learning HIGH FRUSTRATION TOLERANCE (see Dryden, 1987a).

self-disclosure talking about oneself often in an intimate and revealing way. Therapy cannot usually begin or be sustained without client self-disclosure but many clients may come from backgrounds or cultures which discourage such disclosure (e.g. 'real' men do not talk intimately about themselves) or it is a practice they are not accustomed to. Walen, DiGiuseppe and Dryden (1992) suggest that failure to self-disclose is not necessarily a sign of RESISTANCE but may be due to other reasons such as fear. Clients can be encouraged to talk about themselves through such methods as THERAPIST SELF-DISCLOSURE.

self-downing condemning or disparaging oneself. This usually occurs when individuals not only condemn an action or trait as horrible or rotten but also condemn themselves as rotten on the basis of these actions or traits, e.g. 'I did a terrible thing by smacking my daughter and this makes me a horrible person who deserves bad things to happen to her.' Such beliefs frequently lead to GUILT and DEPRESSION. REBT therapists teach clients how to overcome their self-downing and learn SELF-ACCEPTANCE thereby constructively tackling their perceived bad actions or traits.

self-efficacy belief that one can develop a sense of mastery over problems or difficulties. A client who believes he has low self-efficacy i.e. he will have little chance of achieving a desired outcome such as cessation of heroin use, may not make much effort in therapy as he experiences a sense of helplessness over his inability to change, e.g. 'I just can't control my smack [heroin] habit'. REBT therapists would DISPUTE the client's belief of help-lessness in order to effect a cognitive shift, e.g. 'I can have some control over my habit but it's difficult to maintain' coupled with behavioural strategies such as STIMULUS CONTROL. Such methods can reinforce the client's growing sense of self-efficacy. Walen, DiGiuseppe and Dryden (1992, p.145) suggest that a 'patient's belief in self-efficacy may be one of the most important prerequisites for success in therapy. . .'

self-esteem confidence and satisfaction in oneself; self-respect. REBT views self-esteem as a trap that clients unwittingly set for themselves because they measure themselves on the basis of their acts or traits, e.g. 'Because my life is so success-ful at the moment, this proves that I am worthwhile after all.' However, when things go wrong in life, individuals can disesteem themselves on the basis of their acts or traits, e.g. 'Because I've experienced so many failures recently, this means I'm not worthwhile any longer and am a total failure.' Therefore self-esteem usually works only tem-porarily and carries the potential for emotional disturbance. REBT urges indi-viduals to avoid self-esteem and strive for UNCONDITIONAL SELF-ACCEPTANCE which implies no measurement of any kind of themselves, no matter how well or badly they do in life.

self-fulfilling prophecy realisation of an outcome (e.g. rejection) that one had predicted. Such an outcome is not usual-ly due to foresight but to an individual acting in such a way as to maximise the chances of a predicted outcome occur-ring, e.g. a woman who says she will not enjoy going to a party because she is an unlikeable person behaves in ways at the party which greatly reduce her chances of social interaction thereby confirming her self-image. REBT therapists show clients the self-defeating ideas and actions underpinning their prophecies and how they perpetuate their psycho-logical problems.

self-helping thoughts, feelings and behaviours beliefs, emotions and actions which tackle and reduce psycho-logical disturbance and aid individual goal-attainment, e.g. a woman who believes 'I can stand rejection but I don't like it' experiences only concern when she enters social situations where she might find suitable partners. REBT thera-pists teach clients how to identify, chal-lenge and change SELF-DEFEATING THOUGHTS, FEELINGS AND BEHAVIOURS.

self-help material resources for improv-ing or assisting oneself without depen-dence on others. Between REBT therapy sessions clients can listen to audiocas-settes, watch videos or read self-help books which will assist them to deepen their understanding of REBT concepts. Such self-help material is widely avail-able to the general public as REBT advo-cates a policy of PSYCHOEDUCATION on the causation, maintenance and ameliora-tion of emotional problems. Self-help material can help individuals to achieve INTELLECTUAL INSIGHT into their problems but is usually insufficient to effect EMO-TIONAL INSIGHT

self-instructions orders or directions one gives to oneself. Clients feel frequently overwhelmed by their emotional prob-lems and thereby paralysed to tackle them. REBT therapists teach clients to stand back from the onrush of their dis-turbance-producing ideas and for the 'detached self' to give constructive instructions to the 'involved self', e.g. 'You can put up with this highly anxious situation. If you stay rather than leave you will make considerable progress; so sit tight.'

self-interest see ENLIGHTENED SELF-INTEREST.

self-management success in handling one's own affairs. Clients can learn self-management techniques as part of their

HOMEWORK assignments, e.g. rewarding themselves with pleasurable activities only after they have carried out a usually avoided task such as exercising. For clients who continue to engage in self-defeating habits, penalties rather than rewards might prove more effective, e.g. burning a £5 note every time a client has a cigarette. Self-management procedures can teach clients how to gain control over their problems (see Ellis & Abrahms, 1978).

self-rating see RATING.

self-responsibility see EMOTIONAL RESPONSIBILITY.

self-sabotage clients who destroy or obstruct their attempts to effect constructive change in their lives. Self-sabotage may occur because of, for example, LOW FRUSTRATION TOLERANCE beliefs, e.g. 'I really want to overcome my anxiety but I can't bear the thought of all that fear, discomfort and hard work that I will have to go through' and SELF-DOWNING, e.g. 'No romantic relationship I enter into will succeed because I am completely worthless and therefore I don't deserve any happiness.' REBT therapists help clients to identify, challenge and change such self-sabotaging beliefs in order to encourage them to strive for SELF-ACTUALISATION. Some clients may not be aware of the role of self-sabotage in their thwarted attempts to overcome their problems. Therapists would need to bring these goal-blocking beliefs to clients' conscious attention by retrieving them from their PRECONSCIOUS through such methods as INFERENCE CHAINING.

self-statements declarations or assertions that individuals make to themselves. REBT therapists help clients to construct rational or coping self-statements to tackle or tolerate their problems. Such self-statements can be: (1) realistic, e.g. 'Just because I've had some failures doesn't mean I'll always fail'; (2) philo-sophical and anti-musturbatory (usually advocated in REBT), e.g. 'I would strongly prefer not to fail but there is no reason why I must not fail'; (3) encouraging, e.g. 'I'm sure if I try harder I'll experience less failure'; (4) unrealistic (not usually recommended for use in REBT), e.g. 'Failure now means success in the future.' Self-statements are used by clients when they are unable to, for whatever reason, dispute their disturbance-creating ideas.

self-talk usually internal dialogues that individuals have with themselves. Clients are frequently unaware that their self-talk is largely responsible for their emotional and behavioural reactions to life events because they do not stop to think about the consequences of their thinking in any detailed way. Such self-talk is often outside of clients' conscious attention (e.g. 'I just don't know why I get so anxious around my friends') and is usually found in their PRECONSCIOUS. REBT therapists help clients to discover and verbalise their self-talk through such methods as INFERENCE CHAINING in order to challenge and change their irrational beliefs, e.g. 'Why must you have the approval of your friends?' Through such DISPUTING clients learn to develop realistic rather than positive self-talk.

self-therapy being one's own counsellor. The aim of REBT therapy is for the therapist to become redundant and for the client to become her own therapist. When she has shown sufficient proficiency in using the ABCDE model to conceptualise and tackle her emotional problems, therapist and client move towards TERMINATION. REBT therapists encourage their clients to be life-long self-therapists in order to maintain their gains from therapy and tackle future problems. Clients who develop difficulties as self-therapists or who just want to report on their progress in their new role are offered FOLLOW-UP or BOOSTER SESSIONS.

semantic precision exactness or accuracy in the use of words and their meanings. Clients' emotional difficulties frequently stem from their CROOKED THINKING which is reflected in their imprecise use of language, e.g. a man who is depressed believes 'I am a failure because nothing ever goes right for me.' Such OVERGENERALISATION prevents a realistic assessment of how many times he has actually failed in his life. By teaching clients semantic precision, they can develop clear and rational thinking in order to overcome their problems and reduce emotional distress, e.g. 'I am a fallible human being who has had a number of failures in his life but who can learn from them to improve my chances of more things going right for me. This can be achieved without putting myself down.' Correcting distorted thinking requires clients to monitor continually their use of language (see E-PRIME; GENERAL SEMANTICS).

serenity prayer philosophical position expounded by Reinhold Niebuhr: 'God grant me the serenity to accept the things I cannot change, the courage to change the things I can, and the wisdom to know the difference.' Such an outlook is endorsed by REBT as it teaches individuals ACCEPTANCE of themselves and others as fallible human beings as well as of empirical reality (what actually exists in the world). However, acceptance in REBT does not mean PASSIVITY and clients are urged to tackle adverse events in their lives which are capable of being changed. Internalising the serenity prayer helps clients to achieve HIGH FRUSTRATION TOLERANCE.

sex therapy the therapeutic arena in which individuals with sexual problems are counselled. REBT therapists teach their clients how to undisturb themselves emotionally about their sexual problems, e.g. a man who is anxious because he experiences rapid ejaculation; a woman who feels ashamed because she is unable to achieve orgasm, before looking for specific practical techniques which will help clients to achieve greater sexual success. Indeed, ELLIS, the founder of REBT and a pioneering sex therapist, states that 'almost more than any other human psychological problem sexual malfunctioning practically requires . . . the effective use of direct teaching, training, and homework assigning methods by an effective therapist' (Ellis & Dryden, 1987, p.193).

shame painful feeling arising from consciousness of something dishonourable, improper, ridiculous, etc. done by oneself or another; ignominy. Shame is seen as an UNHEALTHY NEGATIVE EMOTION and a more powerful (and painful) form of EMBARRASSMENT. Shame occurs when an individual reveals a personal weakness in public (e.g. incontinence) and evaluates this in terms of DEMANDS, e.g. 'I absolutely should not have wet myself in public and am completely worthless for doing so.' Individuals who experience shame often predict that others watching them will also agree with their self-denigration thereby depriving them of the approval they believe they need. Behavioural responses include trying to remove oneself from the centre of attention by leaving the situation if possible or avoiding the gaze of others; if individuals are unable to leave the situation they often draw attention back to themselves because of their acute discomfort, e.g. blushing and/or stammering. *Shame-attacking exercises* teach clients to act in a 'shameful' way in order to attract public ridicule or disapproval (e.g. taking an imaginary dog for a walk) and at the same time vigorously dispute their shame-producing beliefs, e.g. 'Just because I am acting stupidly does not make me a stupid or worthless person. I can accept myself no matter what others think of me.' Such exercises can teach clients that they frequently overestimate the degree of opprobrium they believe they will incur and that it is not AWFUL to behave stupidly or reveal a weakness.

Shame-attacking exercises are not designed to bring harm to oneself or others or to break the law (see REGRET).

shame-attacking exercises see SHAME.

short-term hedonism seeking immediate fulfilment of one's pleasures. Individuals who pursue excessive short-term hedonism often sabotage their longer-term goals, e.g. someone who wants to become physically fitter is reluctant to give up his present existence as a 'couch potato' (watches too much television). REBT therapists target for challenge and change the LOW FRUSTRATION TOLERANCE beliefs underpinning short-term hedonism, e.g. 'It's much too hard to change. I can't stand it' in order to help clients achieve a balance between their short- and long-term goals in the form of LONG-RANGE HEDONISM.

'shithood' seeing oneself as completely worthless, incompetent, inadequate. Individuals who fail to live up to their perfectionistic DEMANDS often severely condemn themselves, e.g. 'I shouldn't have made so many blasted mistakes. I'm a useless shit!' Such conditional self-acceptance is based on SELF-ESTEEM which 'depends on your doing the right thing, and when you do the wrong thing, back to shithood you go' (Ellis, quoted in Bernard, 1986, p.52). Individuals may try to mollify their self-denigration by pleasing others or carrying out 'good' acts – ELLIS calls this 'perfuming your shit-hood'. All attempts to disguise one's self-downing are usually self-defeating because Ellis asks: 'How can a shit ever be deshittified?' The REBT solution to this problem is to encourage individuals to strive for UNCONDITIONAL SELF-ACCEP-TANCE and give up their dogmatic demands on themselves and others: 'Shouldhood equals shithood. Instead of trying to prove yourself, you'd better try to be yourself and enjoy yourself' (*ibid.* p.53).

should verb expressing duty, propriety or expediency, e.g. 'You should not do that.' REBT hypothesises that absolute shoulds, among others, lie at the core of emotional disturbance, e.g. the anger-producing belief 'You should not treat me like that. I hate your guts!' Clients are taught how they make their lives more difficult than is necessary by subjecting themselves to the 'tyranny of the shoulds' (Horney, 1950). However, it is important for REBT therapists to distinguish between disturbance-producing shoulds and other non-pathological forms, e.g. what REBT therapists preferably should do to improve their clinical skills; 'You should watch that television programme, it's so funny' – recommended should; 'Once I've mended this plug, the light should work' – empirical should (see Dryden, 1986). If all shoulds, like MUSTS, are disputed clients can develop an IATROGENIC irrational belief ('I should not use the word "should"') rather than follow the REBT tenet on absolute shoulds: 'I will not should on myself today.'

skill-training teaching individuals how to acquire particular abilities or techniques. As REBT is a DOUBLE SYSTEMS THERAPY, it first helps clients to undisturb themselves emotionally about their practical problems, e.g. anxiety about approaching women; angry about not being listened to, and then looks at clients' skill deficits in order to determine what remedial steps need to be taken, e.g. interpersonal and assertion skills training. Emotional and practical-problem solving frequently go hand in hand in REBT.

simulation attempting to reproduce in therapy the conditions or circumstances which engender client problems. Examples of simulation may include a woman who is afraid of eye contact is asked to maintain eye contact with the therapist; a man who continually interrupts is asked to wait until the therapist has finished speaking. Such simulation assists the therapist to develop hypotheses about clients' presenting problems and enable clients to become more aware of the beliefs and emotions underlying their AVOIDANCE BEHAVIOUR.

slogan brief and often catchy phrase used to express an idea or aim. Slogans devised by ELLIS, the founder of REBT, are all intended to make important therapeutic points, e.g. 'All neurosis is simply a high class name for whining' – endless whinging and whining usually derives from clients' LOW FRUSTRATION TOLERANCE beliefs; 'Cherchez le should, cherchez le must: look for the should, look for the must' – when clients are emotionally upset they are urged to search for the rigid demands they are making upon themselves or others. Slogans are often used as part of REBT's HUMOROUS approach to psychotherapy (see Yankura & Dryden, 1990).

social interest term used by Adler (1964) to take into account the concerns and needs of the wider community when helping an individual to think about his goals. Individuals who incorporate social interest into their thoughts and actions are considered in REBT to meet a criterion of PSYCHOLOGICAL HEALTH. Individuals who believe that exploiting others is the way to achieving their goals are shown by REBT therapists how such goals will probably backfire and create more emotional problems. Clients are encouraged to avoid selfishness and pursue ENLIGHTENED SELF-INTEREST (see HEDONISM).

social learning theory study of the environmental determinants on human behaviour particularly observational learning and role modelling. Some REBT therapists (e.g. Grieger & Boyd, 1980) take a social learning approach to the development of IRRATIONAL BELIEFS but ELLIS 'clearly distinguishes between the standards, goals and values which peo-ple largely learn and their irrational beliefs about these standards which they largely invent or construct' (quoted in Dryden, 1991b, p.25). REBT hypothesises that human irrationality is a BIOLOGICALLY-BASED TENDENCY reinforced by environmental conditions, e.g. an individual's innate ability to disturb herself is manifested in her absolute demand that she must be slim in order to be worthwhile and happy; such an attitude finds ready encouragement in the prevailing culture of Western society.

socialisation of clients into REBT process whereby clients learn what is expected of them in order to participate effectively in this therapeutic approach. Such socialisation includes an early problem focus (e.g. 'What problem(s) would you like to work on?') and goal setting, encouraging clients to COLLABORATE with the therapist in overcoming their problems, accepting RESPONSIBILITY for their emotional disturbance, understanding the crucial role of EVALUATIVE BELIEFS in their emotional reactions to life events, learning how to identify and DISPUTE their irrational ideas and carrying out HOMEWORK tasks. REBT therapists present clear RATIONALES for every aspect of the socialisation process and are alert to client RESISTANCE to this process.

Socratic disputing asking thought-provoking questions which guide clients towards understanding the ultimately self-defeating nature of their irrational ideas, e.g. 'Where's the evidence that just because you've had some recent failures in your life these make you a failure as a person?' Socratic disputing encourages clients to think for themselves thereby promoting greater RECALL of REBT material than if a DIDACTIC format is used. The use of brief lectures by REBT therapists is usually required if clients find Socratic disputing unhelpful in their attempts to understand REBT concepts (e.g. the emotional pitfalls of SELF-ESTEEM). Socratic disputing is also used to help clients see the self-helping nature of their newly acquired RATIONAL BELIEFS, e.g. 'If you believe "I would prefer to succeed but I don't have to", how will this prevent you from becoming depressed next time you experience failure?'

songs see RATIONAL HUMOROUS SONGS.

sorrow see REMORSE.

specificity in problem assessment eliciting from clients precise and explicit details regarding their emotional and behavioural difficulties. REBT therapists want to know which specific disturbed negative emotions (e.g. guilt, depression) are involved rather than relying on clients' descriptions of them such as 'I feel bad'; the particular situations in which these emotions occur (e.g. 'I feel guilty every time my father telephones me') in order to discover the clients' disturbance-producing beliefs (e.g. 'I'm a bad person because I never telephone my father'). Specificity enables REBT therapists to formulate clients' problems within the ABC model and thereby teach clients a concrete way of understanding and tackling their problems.

'stay-in-there' assignments behavioural tasks designed to increase clients' ability to tolerate usually avoided uncomfortable or unpleasant situations. Clients are encouraged to stay in such situations (e.g. going to parties on one's own, driving through tunnels, mixing with boring colleagues) in order to challenge and change their disturbed feelings and ideas about these situations (e.g. the anger-producing belief 'I can't stand having to make conversation with these people when they are so bloody boring!'). Grieger and Boyd (1980) suggest that stay-in-there tasks are one of the most widely applied behavioural techniques in REBT.

'step-out-of-character' exercises clients who enact a desired behaviour not presently in their behavioural repertoire, e.g. to talk in a slower and more measured way rather than in a manic gush. Clients are encouraged to tolerate the 'unnatural feelings' of this new behaviour until such behaviour becomes customary.

stimulus control learning to reduce or avoid exposure to conditions or situations which reinforce maladaptive behaviour. Stimulus control for illicit drug users would include identifying high-risk situations (e.g. visiting certain pubs or friends, particular areas of a town or city) and devising ways of avoiding them or quickly removing themselves from such situations. Greenwood (1985) suggests that such methods are a 'quick way for people to gain some control over substance abuse behaviour . . .' (p.224). However, REBT generally views stimulus control as an important behavioural adjunct to the DISPUTATION process but simply changing ACTIVATING EVENTS is not seen as the ELEGANT SOLUTION to problematic behaviour.

Stoicism school of philosophy founded by Zeno (c.336–c.264 BC) who taught that men should be free from passion, unmoved by joy or grief, and that wisdom consists in self-mastery and submission to natural law. The PHILOSOPHICAL INFLUENCES ON THE DEVELOPMENT OF REBT can be traced to the Stoic philosophers, particularly EPICTETUS and Marcus Aurelius who both emphasised that it is our views of events rather than the events themselves which cause our distress – this viewpoint is the cornerstone of cognitive psychotherapy including REBT. However, REBT is not a stoical form of therapy: it does not expect clients to be indifferent to or detached from adverse life events. ELLIS, the founder of REBT, has stated that REBT is opposed to many Stoic views: 'Epictetus . . . believed in inalterable fate; he did not usually advocate changing obnoxious conditions that can be changed; he was utopian, he downplayed human emotion and pleasure; he advocated calmness, serenity, and detachment; and he had many other ideas which are quite antithetical to RE[B]T' (quoted in Bernard & DiGiuseppe, 1989, p.215). Indeed, as REBT advocates LONG-RANGE HEDONISM, Ellis has suggested that it is 'in many ways more Epicurean [the philosophy which emphasises, *inter alia*, attaining moderate but enduring pleasures rather than intense transient ones which often bring more pain than pleasure] than Stoic' (*ibid*. p.211).

stories narrative designed to interest, amuse or instruct the reader or listener. Stories, such as FABLES or PARABLES, are used in REBT to convey a therapeutic point that is pertinent to the client's problems. The therapist obtains FEEDBACK from the client to ascertain if she has understood the point of the story. Stories are used as an adjunct to cognitive DISPUTING.

stress 'is a demand made upon the adaptive capacities of the mind and body' (Fontana, 1989, p.3). When the mind and body are not able to adapt constructively to the demands made upon them, individuals often say they are 'stressed out' or 'burnt out' with accompanying symptoms of fatigue, irritability, sleep difficulties, anxiety, depression, etc. This kind of debilitating stress is, from the REBT viewpoint, largely self-created: individuals appraise pressure in an absolute and rigid way, e.g. 'My work must always be perfect otherwise I'm a failure'; 'I shouldn't be given so much work. I can't stand it'; 'My colleagues should pull their weight but instead are a lazy bunch of bastards!' 'Stress is a natural and unavoidable feature of life' (*ibid*. p.4) but REBT therapists teach individuals how to remove their self-imposed pressures by surrendering their musturbatory (MUSTS) thinking and replacing it with flexible and goal-oriented thinking (PREFERENCES). When individuals have

undisturbed themselves then they can look at practical ways of dealing with stress, e.g. relaxation, time management methods, assertiveness training.

structure of sessions how formal meetings between therapist and client are organised. Some REBT therapists prefer to set an agenda which will incorporate a review of the last session's HOMEWORK, which clients' problems will be discussed in the present session including issues the therapist wants to focus on, setting more homework and obtaining FEEDBACK from the client as to what was helpful or unhelpful about the session. The highly structured form of the session is intended to maximize therapy time but flexibility not rigidity is the guiding principle, e.g. the format would be temporarily shelved if the client said she was feeling suicidal.

suggestion mention as a possibility; put forward for consideration (e.g. an idea). Clients who find cognitive introspection difficult to grasp and thereby do not succeed in achieving an ELEGANT SOLUTION to their problems, can still be considerably helped by using therapist suggestion in the form of POSITIVE THINKING, e.g. 'Do you really think that just because you have been rejected, no one else is going to want you?' Ellis and Abrahms (1978) point out that therapist suggestion can be beneficial because clients turn it into autosuggestion which then becomes part of their new self-helping outlook. However, suggestion and autosuggestion usually help clients to FEEL BETTER but not to GET BETTER because they have not dealt with their underlying irrational ideas, e.g. 'I must be loved in order to be worthwhile.' Ellis and Abrahms assert 'that all psychotherapy tends to include a great deal of suggestion' (*ibid*. p.126).

suicidal clients individuals attending therapy who are contemplating killing themselves. Suicidal clients are usually severely DEPRESSED with accompanying

IRRATIONAL BELIEFS of hopelessness and helplessness, e.g. 'My life is always going to be miserable and there is nothing I can do about it.' ELLIS (1987a, p.135) emphasises that during 'this critical period . . . I do strongly and concretely dispute their suicidal ideation in most instances' while remaining supportive in tone and agreeing that their ACTIVATING EVENTS (e.g. end of a relationship; death of a partner) are very bad but not AWFUL. In addition to vigorous DISPUTING, Ellis may make contracts with some clients to contact him before they kill themselves or that therapy will continue only after they have been admitted to hospital. By following these and other procedures Ellis claims 'I have done very well with literally hundreds of suicidal clients during the last thirty years. So far, I have not heard that any of them actually committed suicide while seeing me' (*ibid.* pp.135–136).

supervision work of practising counsellors is overseen by an experienced and suitably qualified counsellor. Supervision is largely concerned with critiquing supervisees' video- or audiotapes in order for them to enhance and develop their clinical skills as well as examining their own problems or blocks in relation to their professional practice. Supervisees' anxieties about presenting tapes for supervision have been well documented (see Dryden, 1987b) and such emotional problems would be subjected to an analysis to determine the cognitive dynamics involved – another opportunity for learning. Supervision does not always have to be carried out face-to-face: AUDIOTAPE SUPERVISION BY MAIL is a common practice in REBT. REBT counsellors can also use inventories for self-supervision (see Wessler & Wessler, 1980) and/or clients' questionnaires on their progress in therapy. Ellis (1985a) has identified five therapist IRRATIONAL BELIEFS (e.g. 'I have to be successful with all my clients practically all the time') which usually block client progress and may not be uncovered unless therapists have regular supervision.

syllogism form of reasoning involving three propositions of which the first two, the premises, entail the third, the conclusion, e.g. 'All men are mortal; Socrates is a man; therefore Socrates is mortal.' Such deductive reasoning is frequently used by clients to denigrate themselves, e.g. 'People have to have a relationship to be worthwhile; I am without a relationship; therefore I am completely unloveable and worthless.' REBT therapists would challenge the veracity of the first proposition, acknowledge the accuracy of the second and demonstrate how such illogical and distorted thinking leads to a disturbance-producing conclusion. Sometimes clients offer only a major premise (e.g. 'All my friends are successful and happy') and the therapist completes the syllogism ('I am unsuccessful; therefore I am a complete failure') in order to uncover the self-defeating thinking. Walen, DiGiuseppe & Dryden (1992, p.5) state that clients 'are rarely aware of the major premises in their thinking or the syllogistic flow of their thoughts. More commonly, they focus only on the conclusion which, if it is distorted, is likely to produce emotional problems.' In order to combat this tendency, clients are taught how to develop LOGICAL THINKING (see Cohen, 1992).

symptom stress additional emotional problems that clients experience in relation to their primary emotional problems, e.g. ashamed about feeling anxious. Symptom stress is an old-fashioned term for SECONDARY DISTURBANCES.

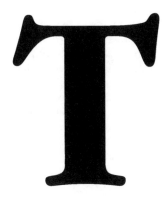

tape-recorded disputing clients who reproduce on audiocassette their attempts to challenge their irrational ideas, e.g. 'It is awful if I do not have a relationship.' Clients are encouraged to play both the rational and irrational parts of themselves particularly using FORCE AND ENERGY in attacking their irrational beliefs. REBT therapists listen to the tapes to ascertain if clients have been forceful in their disputation and to discover the reasons if they have not been; and to tease out any remaining or potential weaknesses in their RATIONAL BELIEFS. Tape-recorded disputing is a cognitive technique designed to promote EMOTIONAL INSIGHT.

tape-recording of sessions see RECORDING OF SESSIONS.

target problem the aspect of a client's presenting problem(s) which becomes the focus for clinical assessment and intervention. For example, a client may say she avoids meeting her husband's friends because she feels uncomfortable in their presence. The REBT therapist would focus on the uncomfortable feelings as the target problem as they help to maintain her avoidance and may indicate the presence of an UNHEALTHY NEGATIVE EMOTION (e.g. anxiety). Client-therapist agreement on the target problem helps to strengthen the therapeutic ALLIANCE and create the impression of clinical competence (see Dryden, 1990c).

tasks assigned activities or work an individual is expected to carry out. Tasks in REBT are considered to be one of the most important domains within the therapeutic ALLIANCE (see BONDS; GOALS). Tasks are undertaken by both the therapist and client in order to realise the latter's goals for change. Therapist tasks include structuring the counselling process so both participants understand and agree to carry out their respective tasks; arriving at a shared understanding of the client's problems and what accounts for them; selecting suitable MULTIMODAL techniques and strategies to achieve an amelioration of the client's problems. Clients' tasks include understanding the crucial role of EVALUATIVE BELIEFS in their emotional reactions to events, executing HOMEWORK assignments and working towards assuming more responsibility for the progress of therapy. Client RESISTANCE in the task domain includes reluctance to undertake homework assignments and refusal to accept EMOTIONAL RESPONSIBILITY for one's problems (see Dryden & Yankura, 1993).

taxonomy of negative emotions see NEGATIVE EMOTIONS..

termination end or conclusion. Termination occurs in REBT when clients have made considerable progress in tackling their emotional problems so as to be able to practise, ideally, SELF-THERAPY on an enduring basis. However, some clients will prematurely terminate counselling thereby leaving intact the self-defeating philosophical ideas underlying their current problems. Working towards an agreed termination includes the therapist 'smoking out' and disputing any lingering irrational beliefs (e.g. 'I can't face my problems on my own') and usually decreasing the frequency of sessions. Some clients may express SADNESS at the loss of an important relationship in their lives. Termination in REBT does not imply an irrevocable end but leaves the door open for BOOSTER or FOLLOW-UP SESSIONS.

'terriblising' assuming that an event is the worst it could conceivably be. Terriblising is a form of AWFULISING and stems from primary MUSTS, e.g. 'I must not be rejected by the person I love and it is terrible to have to experience such an ordeal.' Clients can further disturb themselves by demanding that terrible events (like rejection) must not exist. Once therapists have determined that clients are using the word 'terrible' in the REBT sense, then they can dispute clients' terriblising and encourage them to construct a realistic assessment of the BADNESS of particular events, e.g. 'Rejection is a very unpleasant experience but hardly a terrible one' and ACCEPT the empirical reality that bad or unpleasant events do occur.

'terrorist dispute' a technique to show clients that under extreme circumstances they are capable of carrying out tasks they would usually fearfully avoid, e.g. a woman with agoraphobia is told by terrorists to go out on her own otherwise they will kill her family. Clients usually agree that under such circumstances they would undertake the task in order to save their loved ones. Dryden (1990c) suggests a suitable reply: 'Yes, but will you do it [the task] for your own mental health?' (p.54). The terrorist dispute can give offence to some clients and indicate a certain callousness on the counsellor's part; therefore the dispute is best employed with clients after RAPPORT has been established.

themes in emotional problems central ideas which recur in clients' emotional difficulties. For example, loss or failure in DEPRESSION; breaking one's own moral code in GUILT; fear of a dreaded event occurring in ANXIETY. Such themes usually emerge during the assessment phase of REBT and thereby act as a guide to the UNHEALTHY NEGATIVE EMOTIONS which may be involved; alternatively, clients say how they are feeling (e.g. anxious) and the theme of fear directs the therapist's questions to discover what the clients are most fearful about. Thematic ideas are usually expressed by clients either in absolute terms, e.g. the depression-inducing belief 'I absolutely should not have experienced this loss and it is awful to endure' or relative terms, e.g. the sadness-producing believe 'I would greatly prefer not to have experienced this loss but there is no reason why it absolutely should not have happened' (see Dryden & DiGiuseppe, 1990).

'then what?' questions a form of questioning used to uncover a series of client cognitions. 'Then what?' questions are used in INFERENCE CHAINING to pinpoint the client's most clinically relevant part of the ACTIVATING EVENT, e.g Client: If I get to the meeting late everyone will look at me; Therapist: Let's assume they do, then what? Client: They might ignore me; Therapist: Okay, they do ignore you. Then what? Client: They might not like me. 'Then what?' questioning has located the client's most relevant inference (the last one) which triggers his anxiety-producing IRRATIONAL BELIEF, e.g. 'I must have their approval in order to accept myself.' The uncontrolled use of 'then what?' questions can lead to the BAG LADY/TRAMP SCENARIO: inferences that could theoretically occur but are not actually linked to the client's presenting problems (see Moore, 1983).

theoretically consistent eclecticism borrowing of techniques from other therapies but these are used in a manner consistent with the principles of one particular approach (e.g. REBT). Examples in REBT of theoretically consistent eclecticism include using the EMPTY CHAIR EXERCISE from Gestalt therapy and DREAM interpretation from PSYCHOANALYSIS to facilitate the process of uncovering clients' disturbed thoughts and feelings when other more traditional REBT assessment methods have proved ineffective. REBT therapists are wary of borrowing techniques that may have IATROGENIC potential, i.e. reinforcing a client's existing problems, e.g. giving undue WARMTH may actually strengthen some clients dire NEEDS for love and approval.

theory-driven question question derived from a set of principles or assumptions. This would involve asking a question based on the crucial role of musturbatory (MUSTS) thinking in largely creating emotional disturbance, e.g. 'What demand were you making about your boyfriend's lateness in order to make yourself so angry about it?' Theory-driven questions can be used when clients find open-ended SOCRATIC dialogue unhelpful in uncovering their IRRATIONAL BELIEFS; such questions literally direct the client towards her irrational ideas in the above example. However, theory-driven questions can induce some clients to offer irrational beliefs they do not actually subscribe to. Persistent theory-driven questioning can force the pace of therapy without a corresponding understanding from the client of the centrality of DEMANDS in her emotional problems.

theory of REBT particular conception of unhealthy and healthy psychological functioning including the methods required to reduce the former and increase the latter. REBT theory asserts that at the core of emotional disturbance lies the BIOLOGICALLY-BASED TENDENCY of humans to TRANSMUTE their desires, wishes and wants into rigid, absolute and dogmatic musts, shoulds, oughts, have to's, got to's, e.g. the anger-producing belief 'Because I want you to obey me therefore you must!' REBT theory views thoughts, feelings and behaviours as interdependent processes but does emphasize the role of thoughts, specifically EVALUATIVE BELIEFS, in largely creating emotional health and disturbance – the ABC model demonstrates this causal relationship between thoughts and emotional and behavioural consequences. REBT hypothesises that most human distress can be divided into two but not usually discrete categories: EGO and DISCOMFORT DISTURBANCE. Ego disturbance involves self-denigration while discomfort disturbance reveals an inability to tolerate frustrating conditions in one's life. Disturbance-producing ideas are DISPUTED in order to achieve PSYCHOLOGICAL HEALTH, which includes SELF-ACCEPTANCE and HIGH FRUSTRATION TOLERANCE (see Ellis & Dryden, 1987).

therapeutic alliance see ALLIANCE.

therapeutic change, theory of principles underlying constructive change. REBT's theory of therapeutic change includes clients accepting EMOTIONAL RESPONSIBILITY for their problems; identifying, challenging and changing their IRRATIONAL BELIEFS through SCIENTIFIC THINKING; internalising their new RATIONAL BELIEFS through the use of MULTIMODAL tasks; committing themselves to the lifelong process of HARD WORK AND PRACTICE not only to maintain their therapeutic gains but also to tackle future emotional problems. Therapeutic change in REBT can provide an ELEGANT or INELEGANT SOLUTION to clients' problems.

'therapeutic markers' means of drawing clients' attention to important points that are going to be or have been made. Dryden (1990b) gives several examples of therapeutic markers including 'chang[ing] one's body position. For example, by moving their torsos forward towards clients, therapists can indicate the importance of their following statements' (p.64); and therapists' exclamations of surprise followed by requests for reiteration when clients have made rational statements. Therapeutic markers are a form of VIVID REBT.

therapeutic modalities specific arenas in which counselling is practised, e.g. individual, couples, group, family. Choice of a specific arena can be influenced by practical considerations (e.g. cramped offices would be unsuitable for group therapy); a therapist's demands for COMFORT may limit him to just one arena such as individual counselling; clients' preferences for a specific modality (e.g. couples counselling). As INDIVIDUAL THERAPY is the most widely practised form of therapy (see Ellis & Dryden, 1987), these authors suggest indications and contraindications for its use particularly by REBT therapists. These indications include: when clients will only disclose personal information in an individual setting; the client's pace of LEARNING requires the therapist's undivided attention; clients' emotional problems involve just themselves rather than their relationships with others. Contraindications for its use include when clients are likely to become dependent upon the therapist thereby making their original problems worse; clients who find individual counselling too comfortable which thereby militates against creating a therapeutic milieu sufficiently stimulating to promote constructive change. Clients can be switched between therapeutic modalities depending on the prevailing circumstances, e.g. to enhance a client's progress; when no apparent progress is made. Ellis and Dryden advise REBT therapists (in the absence of any firm criteria) to 'work with clients in the modality that seems to be the most productive for them but regard such decisions as tentative and to a large degree experimental' (*ibid.* p.80). Therapeutic modalities (see Lazarus, 1981) also refers to the various sensory systems – cognitive (verbal and imaginal), emotive and behavioural – which therapists may select from as the most productive in effecting client change, e.g. emotive techniques for clients who are overly cerebral; and behavioural tasks for clients who find it difficult to express themselves verbally. Therapists may need to experiment before discovering which modality provides the best clinical focus for intervention.

therapeutic relationship see RELATIONSHIP, THERAPEUTIC.

therapeutic responsibility the concept that clients are primarily responsible for executing their goal-directed tasks. Some clients who come to therapy believe their role is just to listen to the therapist's 'wisdom' and constructive change will naturally occur. REBT therapists quickly disabuse such clients of this idea and explain to them the highly active role that is expected of them, e.g. 'I can teach you to play chess but I can't play the game for you. Similarly with your problems, I can teach you what largely causes and maintains them but you have to undertake the hard work in order to overcome them.' Clients' self-defeating ideas underpinning their reluctance or refusal to accept therapeutic responsibility, e.g. 'I'm not here to help you. You're supposed to be helping me!' are disputed by the therapist (see EMOTIONAL RESPONSIBILITY).

therapeutic style distinctive manner or approach which will help to facilitate client change. The predominant therapeutic style of REBT therapists is an ACTIVE-DIRECTIVE one which quickly directs clients to the cognitive core of their emotional problems. Such a 'forceful intervention on the part of therapist [sic] is more likely to help them [clients] change themselves than is a more nondirective methodology' (Ellis, 1980a, p.21). REBT therapists do not practise an unvarying style but take account of clients' preferences in forging a therapeutic BOND, e.g. a forthright approach for clients who want to 'get on with it' and a formal one for clients who rely on the therapist's expertise to guide the course of therapy. Therapeutic styles may need to be tempered in the light of some clients' personal characteristics, e.g. a less directive approach for passive clients. Flexibility guides the choice of therapeutic styles during the course of therapy particularly 'easing off' the active-directive approach as clients learn to practise SELF-THERAPY (see 'AUTHENTIC CHAMELEON').

therapist errors mistakes made by counsellors. Walen, DiGiuseppe and Dryden (1992, pp.250–252) list 'Ten Common Errors to Avoid' in REBT. These include failing to obtain clients' explicit goals for change rather than assuming they are self-evident; failing to be assertive by letting clients talk too much or being too assertive by brusquely interrupting them; using too many 'why' questions which can put clients on the defensive; and presenting oneself as a wiseacre – the therapist as a know-all who 'hands' clients their insights into their problems rather than letting them discover these insights through their own efforts. Therapist errors, particularly if they are repeatedly made, can lead to a disruption of the therapeutic ALLIANCE and/or early TERMINATION of therapy.

therapist self-disclosure personal information revealed by counsellors to their clients. Therapist self-disclosure is used if it is deemed to be clinically relevant: the therapist says she experienced a problem and accompanying irrational ideas similar to those of the client's and how she eventually overcame her problem through a variety of DISPUTING methods. REBT therapists are encouraged to use a coping model of self-disclosure rather than a mastery one: the former model suggests how the therapist managed her problem while the latter model boasts a perfect outcome to it. Therapist self-disclosure can teach clients to accept themselves as FALLIBLE human beings and thereby help them to remove the SHAME they may experience as a result of their problems (see Dryden, 1990b).

thinking using the mind to form ideas, opinions, judgements, etc. REBT hypothesises that emotional disturbance is largely created by CROOKED THINKING, i.e. absolute and devout demands that individuals make on themselves, others and the world, e.g. the anxiety-producing belief 'I must be certain that all the important things in my life turn out successfully.' ELLIS (1976) asserts that crooked thinking is biologically-based and therefore requires a lifelong commitment to moderate its frequently destructive influence. This can be achieved by helping individuals to think rationally, also biologically-based, using the LOGICO-EMPIRICAL METHODS of science, i.e. subjecting individuals' self-defeating ideas to logical and realistic scrutiny, e.g. 'If the world reflected your demands then you would be absolutely certain of things turning out successfully. Is this the case?' By developing SCIENTIFIC THINKING, individuals can minimise the frequency, intensity and duration of their emotional disturbances.

thinking, brain v. gut styles of thinking in which individuals believe that feelings are created by ideas against individuals who believe that feelings are created by events or are just natural occurrences. According to Grieger and Boyd (1980, p.84) individuals who employ gut thinking 'are people so enamored by their feelings that they tend to define reality with their feelings', e.g. 'I feel so depressed this must mean I'm a failure.' REBT therapists would point out to clients who use gut thinking that their feelings are not facts about themselves and orientate them to their disturbance-producing ideas as the real mediator of their self-image, e.g. the depression-inducing belief 'As I have failed at several important things, as I must not, this means I am a failure.' When gut thinking clients understand the B-C CONNECTION of emotional causation – have adopted brain thinking – they empower themselves to tackle constructively their emotional problems. REBT emphasises that clients who use brain thinking are not emotionless robots but individuals who think, feel and act in self-helping and goal-directed ways.

thirteen step counselling sequence a systematic approach to emotional problem-solving. The counselling sequence quickly SOCIALISES clients into REBT's early problem-focus (step one: Ask For A Problem) in order to pinpoint the TARGET PROBLEM (step two) and elicit the client's UNHEALTHY NEGATIVE EMOTION(S) about it (step three). Once the therapist has discovered what the client is most disturbed about in relation to his presenting problem (step four), and probed to determine whether or not he has a SECONDARY EMOTIONAL PROBLEM about it (step five), she then digresses from the client's problem to teach the B-C CONNECTION of emotional causation (step six). When the client has understood this connection, and the therapist has assessed his IRRATIONAL BELIEFS (step seven), she returns to his problem to help him connect his irrational beliefs to his unhealthy negative emotion (step eight). Once this has been achieved, his irrational beliefs are DISPUTED and rational alternatives are constructed (step nine). The client is taught what will be required to deepen his conviction in his new rational beliefs (step ten) before HOMEWORK tasks are negotiated (step eleven) and reviewed at the next session (step twelve). To internalise his new rational outlook, the client is encouraged to challenge his irrational beliefs in a variety of problematic situations (step thirteen). The treatment sequence is, in essence, the ABCDE model of emotional disturbance: its causation, maintenance and eventual amelioration. As one of his biggest contributions to REBT, Dryden (Dryden, Neenan & Doggart, 1993, p.10) selects 'the development of the counselling sequence (with Ray DiGiuseppe) that appears in several of my books. This makes clear the 13 steps that comprise the effective and efficient practice of RE[B]T' (see Dryden 1990c).

thoroughgoingness working methodically and leaving nothing incomplete. Thoroughgoingness is a form of EFFICIENCY in REBT whereby therapists use a variety of MULTIMODAL techniques to help clients detect and dispute their IRRATIONAL BELIEFS, e.g. using in-session SIMULATION to discover why a client is so anxious about speaking on the telephone.

thought-monitoring listening in to one's ideas. Thought-monitoring encourages clients to look for their MUSTS and SHOULDS when they are upset, e.g. 'I must not get upset' in order to move on to the next step of DISPUTING. Clients frequently report that they are unaware of any irrational ideas in their thinking but REBT therapists show clients that their DEMANDS are often implicit in their statements, e.g. a woman says she is anxious because 'I don't like going to the supermarket on my own', but the therapist points out that the probable belief is: 'I must not go to the supermarket on my own.' Thought-monitoring is a standard HOMEWORK task in REBT.

thought-stopping technique used to halt one's train of thought. Clients who experience self-defeating obsessive thoughts are instructed to say 'Stop!' whenever these thoughts intrude into their thinking (this is one form of the technique). REBT generally views thought-stopping as a form of DISTRACTION as it only brings short-term relief from obsessional thinking but does not tackle the musturbatory (MUSTS) ideas that maintain it (see Ellis, 1985a).

thoughts and feelings, differences between the distinctions between one's ideas and emotions. Clients frequently state that they feel 'worthless', 'inadequate' or 'a failure'. Such 'feelings' are not found in REBT's lexicon of NEGATIVE EMOTIONS; instead they are considered to be EVALUATIVE BELIEFS which produce disturbed negative emotions (e.g. guilt, shame, depression). REBT therapists would restructure clients' statements in order to emphasise this difference, e.g. 'How do you feel when you hold your belief that you are a failure?' The client may reply: 'Depressed'. When clients pinpoint what REBT considers to be a genuine disturbed negative emotion, then the focus of therapy can switch to the irrational ideas underlying the emotion in order to change it. By correcting clients use of thinking and feeling language, therapists can teach them how to quickly zero in on their disturbance-producing ideas.

three major REBT insights see INSIGHT.

time-limited irrationalities disturbance-producing ideas that are of relatively short duration because individuals are able eventually to reappraise more rationally their initial reactions. For example, flying into a rage for thirty minutes over being stuck in a traffic jam, then calming down because of the realisation of the futility of such an outburst – it will not move the traffic any faster. REBT does not usually tackle such time-limited irrationalities or view them as pathological; instead it focuses on those irrationalities which clients have 'for an extended period of time and cannot do anything constructive about shifting them [depressed

for several months about the end of a relationship]' (Dryden, 1994c, p.56).

time projection visualising the future impact of present events. Time projection is an IMAGERY TECHNIQUE used to dispute indirectly clients' irrational beliefs, e.g. a woman says it would be AWFUL if her marriage ended and therefore avoids thinking about it; the therapist encourages her to imagine the relationship failing and seeing herself over time adapting constructively to it. The therapist has not challenged directly the client's irrational beliefs (e.g. 'A breakup must not occur') but helped her to reappraise the breakup and its consequences in order to DE-AWFULISE them.

tolerance, statements of see HIGH FRUSTRATION TOLERANCE.

tough customers see DIFFICULT CUSTOMERS.

'tough shit' philosophy a hard-headed attitude which accepts without despair or resignation human fallibility and the grim reality of adverse events while still able to enjoy a reasonably happy life. According to Ellis (1972), 'If you really believe these words [tough shit], and the basic philosophy for which they stand, you will instantly start to lose your extreme feelings of anxiety, depression, and shame and become emotionally unblocked' (pp. 154–155). A 'tough shit' philosophy can teach clients how to develop a resilient temperament to withstand the vicissitudes of life (see COPING SELF-STATEMENTS).

tragedy disastrous often fatal event; a calamity. A client's tragedy (e.g. the death of a family member) is not considered to be AWFUL in the sense that this tragic event must not be as bad as it is or must not have occurred. It takes a skilled and sensitive REBT therapist to make this distinction between tragedy and awfulising about it. As in dealing with CATASTROPHISING, therapists can appear insensitive and even callous and this impression can disrupt or destroy the therapeutic ALLIANCE.

training obtaining a desired degree of proficiency in this therapeutic approach. Opportunities for REBT training in Britain are very limited: the main centre is in London. Training at the London centre offers a primary certificate, diploma, advanced diploma and a training and supervision course. All courses are recognised by the Association For Rational Emotive Behaviour Therapists (AREBT). The world centre for REBT is located at the Institute for RET in New York and, among other activities, offers training programmes for mental health professionals and FRIDAY NIGHT WORKSHOPS for the general public. The addresses of both centres can be found at the front of this book.

transcript, REBT verbatim record of a counselling session. Transcripts of TAPE-RECORDED SESSIONS and accompanying commentaries of counsellors' interventions are frequently presented in REBT textbooks (for a transcript of an entire course of therapy, see Dryden & Yankura, 1992). Transcripts and commentaries are also used in REBT TRAINING where students are expected to demonstrate the application of theory to practice. Transcripts are a highly detailed method of assessing the EFFICIENCY of REBT therapists.

transference the process whereby clients unconsciously displace on to the therapist emotions and attitudes towards significant others in their lives. REBT therapists would tackle the disturbance-producing ideas or attitudes of the transference relationship once these have been brought to the client's conscious attention (see PRECONSCIOUS). A common transferential attitude might be 'I must have your approval and if I don't I'm worthless.' By DISPUTING such an irrational belief, clients can acquire a ratio-

nal outlook which will help them to develop healthier and more balanced relationships in their lives (see COUNTER-TRANSFERENCE).

transmutation act of changing from one form or state to another. Ellis has frequently used the word 'ESCALATION' to describe the process whereby individuals convert their PREFERENCES (rational beliefs) into DEMANDS (irrational beliefs), e.g. 'Because I want your love therefore I must have it.' However, as Gilmore (1986) has shown, escalation implies a quantitative change rather than a qualitative one, i.e. one based on increasing and intensifying an individual's desires until they become demands rather than a transformation of desires into demands. Ellis (1987b) has argued that when he used the quantitative 'escalation' he meant it in the qualitative sense of a fundamental change in one's thinking to produce EMOTIONAL DISTURBANCE; therefore it 'would have been much better had I said "look for the transmutation or metamorphosis of a desire into a must and a bad into an awful"' (p.195). Ellis hopes that such clarification will result in less confusion over this issue for REBT practitioners.

transpersonal therapy counselling approach which stresses, among other things, spiritual values, mysticism, the search for a higher consciousness outside of the realm of rational thought. Ellis is generally dismissive towards transpersonal therapy and sees it 'as a poor kind of therapy' (quoted in Dryden, 1991b, p.116). Some of his criticisms include that it is unscientific because its hypotheses (e.g. the belief in clairvoyance) are not FALSIFIABLE; that it passively tolerates rather than tries to change adverse life events because it is our karma to experience these events; advocates conditional self-acceptance because individuals have to accept a higher power or truth before they can accept themselves. One of Ellis's critics has suggested that his 'comments often seem to refer to his own caricature of transpersonal psychology . . .' (Edwards, 1992, p.220) rather than to a balanced view of it. Ellis does acknowledge some advantages of transpersonal therapy including, like REBT, a belief in creating and changing our emotional destinies (see Ellis & Yeager, 1989).

treatment plan therapeutic strategy agreed by the therapist and client to tackle the latter's emotional and behavioural problems. A treatment plan is usually developed after an initial ASSESSMENT has been carried out and is used, among other things, to prioritise a client's PROBLEM LIST; to draw up multimodal strategies to tackle each problem within the ABCDE model of emotional disturbance and its remediation; to provide an overview of the course of therapy and, along with a session AGENDA, to keep it on track; to determine when COPING CRITERION has been established with each problem and to TROUBLESHOOT when obstacles to client progress occur. Treatment plans are not rigid protocols but flexible procedures which are able to deal with immediate or urgent clients' problems which may supervene, e.g. suicidal thoughts (see Walen, DiGiuseppe & Dryden, 1992).

treatment techniques methods chosen to tackle a particular problem. REBT uses a MULTIMODAL APPROACH to combat emotional disturbance and selects techniques on the basis of their long-term efficacy and not on their short-term relief (e.g. confronting one's fears rather than being distracted from them). Major treatment techniques include: cognitive, e.g. disputing irrational beliefs such as 'Where is the evidence that you can't stand being in a lift?'; emotive, e.g. shame-attacking exercises which encourage clients to solicit public ridicule or criticism in order to accept themselves and tolerate the subsequent discomfort; behavioural, e.g. FLOODING

assignments which help clients to face their problems immediately rather than gradually and thereby rapidly overcome their LOW FRUSTRATION TOLERANCE. All treatment techniques are employed to challenge and change clients' disturbance-producing ideas (see APPROACHES AVOIDED IN REBT).

trial counselling sessions encouraging hesitant clients to try out several therapy sessions to determine if this psychotherapeutic approach will be helpful to them. The OPENNESS of such an offer frequently results in clients agreeing to a full course of therapy once the trial sessions have finished. Trial counselling sessions can be used as part of clients' INDUCTION into REBT.

troubleshooting identifying and removing the causes of problems. REBT therapists troubleshoot to help clients remove the potential or actual blocks to their progress, e.g. a client says he might not be able to carry out his HOMEWORK tasks because of lack of time; another client makes little therapeutic advance because her 'I-CAN'T-STAND-IT-ITIS' prevents her from undertaking the hard work required to effect constructive change in her life. In these examples, and on other occasions, REBT therapists identify and DISPUTE the disturbance-producing and self-blocking ideas in order to reduce or remove the obstacles in the path of clients' progress.

trust confident belief in or reliance on someone or something. Trust enables clients to disclose often intimate personal problems to therapists secure in the knowledge that they will not be humiliated or ridiculed or their problems trivialised. Trust, along with other qualities such as GENUINENESS and EMPATHY, helps to build a productive therapeutic ALLIANCE. Trust in the therapist may be the key reason for some clients why they are prepared to undertake risks (e.g. actively seek rejection) to bring about therapeutic change in their lives and thereby achieve PSYCHOLOGICAL HEALTH. REBT therapists are alert to the dysfunctional aspects of some clients difficulties in developing trust with them, e.g.

'Because I've been hurt badly in the past, I absolutely must be sure that you won't let me down. I couldn't stand it if this happened again.'

unassertiveness not standing up respectfully and positively for one's rights; not communicating one's positive feelings to someone. Unassertive behaviour often means that individuals let themselves be pushed around or taken advantage of. REBT therapists assist clients to locate the blocks to acting assertively, e.g. a client says she is fearful of being assertive with her husband because he might withdraw his love and this would be AWFUL to bear. By DISPUTING and thereby removing the 'horror' (emotional disturbance) of being unloved, the client is able to make a rational assessment of the short- and long-term advantages and disadvantages of being assertive with her husband. Clients can practise acting assertively through in-session behavioural REHEARSAL.

uncertainty, acceptance of ability to adapt or reconcile oneself to an unpredictable and unstable world. Individuals frequently disturb themselves and thereby block their goals by demanding certainty in their lives, e.g. 'I want to overcome this problem but I must be certain of success before embarking on therapy.' REBT therapists teach individuals that there are in all probability no absolute certainties in life but the probability exists that they will be able to realise some of their important life goals through hard work and determination.

Therefore uncertainty can be seen as a challenge not to be deflected from striving to achieve one's goals because there is no certainty of success rather than as a deterrent blocking any kind of goal-directed action. Acceptance of uncertainty in REBT is seen as a criterion of PSYCHOLOGICAL HEALTH.

unconditional acceptance an unqualified and nonjudgemental attitude towards individuals. By offering unconditional acceptance to their clients, REBT therapists encourage clients to accept themselves unconditionally as FALLIBLE human beings who can never be legitimately given a single global RATING though their individual performances or traits can be (e.g. 'I did a bad thing but that doesn't make me a bad person'). Unconditional acceptance does not mean that therapists shrink from confronting clients' obnoxious or self-defeating actions (e.g. 'I accept you but not your drunken behaviour. Please turn up sober at the next appointment'). Unconditional acceptance can lead to the development of a productive BOND between the therapist and client. REBT views unconditional acceptance as more beneficial for therapeutic change than WARMTH – too much therapist warmth can actually reinforce clients' existing problems such as dire NEEDS for love or approval (see IATROGENIC TECHNIQUES).

unconditional self-acceptance an un-qualified and nonjudgmental attitude towards oneself. Much emotional distur-bance derives from negative self-rating, e.g. 'Because you no longer love me therefore I'm worthless.' REBT argues that such self-rating is arbitrary and therefore is not an accurate evaluation of the complexity of the SELF. REBT advo-cates giving 'up all self-rating in favour of self-acceptance, which means, "I don't rate my self, my being, or my essence at all – only my traits, deeds and acts. I accept myself because I choose to do so – whether or not I do well, whether or not people love me"' (Ellis, quoted in Dry-den, 1991b, p.27). Unconditional self-acceptance is part of the ELEGANT SOLUTION in REBT and is more likely to produce enduring emotional stability than SELF-ESTEEM; it also encourages indi-viduals to pursue SELF-ACTUALISATION as they are now less inhibited in their atti-tudes and behaviour, e.g. no longer dread failure (see CONDITIONAL SELF-ACCEPTANCE).

unconscious part of the mind that does not ordinarily enter a person's aware-ness but in Freudian psychology is held to influence significantly conscious processes and behaviour. REBT rejects the Freudian concept of the unconscious as the repository of our deeply-embed-ded disturbance-producing ideas and feelings and asserts that such ideas and feelings can be readily retrieved from our PRECONSCIOUS (just outside of our con-scious awareness). ELLIS discounts the idea of unconscious motivation, derived from early childhood experiences, as the determinant of individuals' present behaviour and states that such behaviour is largely created by individuals' current and relatively conscious EVALUATIVE BELIEFS, e.g. 'Because my parents didn't love me when I was a child, as they absolutely should have done, I am still unable today to accept myself and I can't see how it's ever going to change.' REBT rapidly uncovers and DISPUTES such self-

defeating beliefs in stark contrast to the often inordinate amount of time needed (e.g. several years) in psychoanalysis to work through clients' unconscious con-flicts. Such a length of time is anathema to Ellis who claims to have 'a gene for efficiency. My goal in about everything that I do is to be efficient . . . Time is of the essence . . . Therefore, I wouldn't toler-ate the Freudian practice, which is very inefficient' (quoted in Bernard, 1986, p.15).

unconstructive negative emotions see UNHEALTHY NEGATIVE EMOTIONS.

understanding to grasp the meaning, sig-nificance, nature or explanation of. REBT therapists strive to understand not only the nature of clients' presenting problems but also what accounts for them, e.g. 'It sounds like guilt because you're telling yourself "I should not have done such a bad thing and this makes me a bad person."' Such affective and philo-sophical understanding of clients' prob-lems is REBT's conception of EMPATHY. Therapists obtain FEEDBACK from clients to ascertain if they have accurately understood clients' difficulties. Thera-pists seek clarification from clients that they have understood REBT concepts, e.g. 'Can you put into your own words the differences between preferences and demands?' Client-therapist understand-ing throughout the course of therapy will enhance the working ALLIANCE and more likely lead to a successful outcome.

unevocative questions 'asking questions which do not promote client thought' (Grieger and Boyd, 1980, p.174). Exam-ples of unevocative questions include asking too many questions which can put clients on the defensive and impa-tient therapists answering their own questions. Unevocative questioning can maroon clients at the level of INTELLECTU-AL INSIGHT, i.e. they lightly understand how their rational beliefs will help them to overcome their problems. However, if

REBT therapists avoid unevocative questions and replace them with stimulating, open-ended and thought-provoking questions (e.g. 'In what ways will these new rational beliefs help you to overcome your anxiety?') clients are more likely to reach EMOTIONAL INSIGHT and thereby achieve a philosophical change in their belief systems.

unfairness lack of honesty or justness; not conforming to approved standards. Unfairness is a major theme in HURT, e.g. 'I should not have been treated in such an unfair way especially since I've been so hard working'. REBT therapists point out to clients that life is frequently unfair but retreating into self-pity and sulking is hardly a constructive way to fight back. Accepting the empirical reality of unfairness is the first step towards encouraging others to act in fairer ways and thereby make life a little more equitable (see DISAPPOINTMENT).

unhealthy negative emotions these are emotions underpinned by irrational beliefs (absolute musts and shoulds) and which block goal-attainment, decrease one's ability to enjoy life and lead to self-defeating behaviours. Such emotions include GUILT, DEPRESSION and SHAME. By challenging and changing their irrational beliefs, clients can experience HEALTHY NEGATIVE EMOTIONS (see EMOTIONAL DISTURBANCE; NEGATIVE EMOTIONS).

upbringing rearing and training received during childhood. Clients frequently blame their present problems on their upbringing, e.g. 'My parents treated me abysmally, they never praised me. They have made my life a mess.' While acknowledging and without minimizing the harsh treatment some clients received from their parents, REBT therapists show clients that their present problems largely result from the absolute DEMANDS they made in their childhood and have carried with them ever since, e.g. 'As my parents didn't love

me, as they absolutely should have done, this means I am totally worthless and can never expect any happiness in life.' Clients can also reconstruct in the present what they believe may have happened to them in the past, e.g. 'Thinking back on it, what my father did to me, as he absolutely shouldn't have done, was tantamount to sexual abuse. He's ruined me and my life.' Therapists teach clients to undisturb themselves about their upbringing and thereby demonstrate that they, not the past, control their emotional destiny, e.g. 'I would have greatly preferred my parents to love me but there is no reason why they must have done. I can totally accept myself without their love and get on happily with my life.' Clients can be shown that their parents' behaviour may have resulted from their own disturbances and one way to reconcile the past with the present is to see them as FALLIBLE human beings who behaved badly. In the final analysis, our innate ability to disturb ourselves will largely determine our reaction to whatever kind of upbringing we experience (see BIOLOGICALLY-BASED TENDENCIES).

upsetness state of disorder or disturbance. ELLIS (1976) asserts that individuals have a strong innate tendency to upset themselves about the conditions in or state of their lives and frequently blame others or their circumstances for this disturbance, e.g. 'Because my parents were poor, as they absolutely should not have been, they didn't give me a good start in life and I'll never be able to overcome this disadvantage.' If individuals accept EMOTIONAL RESPONSIBILITY for their upsetness, they will be more able to counteract or minimise the harmful effects of their CROOKED THINKING. *Upsetness about upsetness* occurs when individuals frequently exacerbate their existing problems (e.g. rejection) by demanding of themselves, for example, 'I must not be depressed about being rejected' which, in turn, encourages even greater crooked thinking. So clients can end up more disturbed or upset about their depression than the original rejection. ELLIS hypothesises that upsetness about upsetness is largely self-constructed because it would be difficult to observe this process in others so 'most of the time . . . feelings of anxiety and depression are internal, so that other people don't observe these feelings and don't tell them [individuals] that they must not have them' (quoted in Dryden, 1991b, p.26).

upsetness about upsetness see UPSETNESS.

utopianism the view that human perfection and an ideal society are achievable. REBT is not necessarily against the pursuit of perfection in oneself or society but does challenge individuals who demand that self-perfection is a condition of their worth or they cannot experience any or much happiness while imperfect LIFE CONDITIONS exist. Given the probability that utopias are unachievable, clients can learn to ACCEPT the empirical reality of life conditions and their own FALLIBILITY while striving to improve those conditions as well as to attain SELF-ACTUALISATION (see NONUTOPIANISM).

values ideals, goals or standards upon which actions or beliefs are based. 'RE[B]T does not pretend to be objective and value free. Quite the contrary. It is a system of psychotherapy designed to help people live longer, minimize their emotional disturbances and self-defeating behaviours, and actualize themselves so that they live a more fulfilling, happier existence' (Ellis & Bernard, 1985, p.5). If clients wish to subscribe to these values then it would be prudent for them to select individual goals for change that reflect these values, e.g. learning to overcome one's social anxiety in order to increase one's range of potential friends and partners. Such goals can be realised by clients through learning rational and SELF-HELPING THOUGHTS, FEELINGS AND BEHAVIOURS. REBT values are underpinned by the concept of psychological health which includes HIGH FRUSTRATION TOLERANCE and SELF-DIRECTION – clients are encouraged to develop these and other characteristics as the most effective way of achieving a happier and more satisfying life.

ventilation of feelings often forceful expression of one's emotions. REBT therapists usually avoid encouraging excessive ventilation of clients' feelings (e.g. anger, anxiety) as the irrational ideas underlying these feelings are the real focus of clinical intervention (e.g. 'I shouldn't have to put up with all this crap in my life!'). However, it can be used briefly to encourage clients to identify disturbed emotions when other assessment methods have proved unhelpful. Ventilation of feelings can bring temporary relief from emotional distress because clients may FEEL BETTER but at the expense of actually GETTING BETTER as the disturbance-producing ideas not only remain intact but may also be strengthened through frequent ventilation (see CATHARSIS).

verifiability the condition which allows procedures to be carried out which check whether a statement is true. Clients' EVALUATIVE BELIEFS (e.g. 'I want a new car therefore I must have one') are subjected to verification procedures in order to provide solid evidence supporting an individual's rational PREFERENCE for a new car but no empirical evidence for his irrational DEMAND that he must have what he wants. Verification does not establish that clients' RATIONAL BELIEFS are absolutely true but continual and successful checking of them points to their probable truth. ELLIS, greatly influenced by Popper, eventually abandoned the LOGICAL POSITIVIST position of seeking verification of client statements in favour of trying to prove their FALSIFIABILITY.

victimization state or condition where an individual finds herself adversely affected by the actions of others. REBT therapists show clients how they either encourage others, wittingly or unwittingly, to victimize them or how they prevent themselves from breaking out of this position, e.g. 'I have to let him treat me badly because if I fight back he'll stop loving me. Without his love I am nothing. Living on my own would be terrible.' Therapists dispute vigorously such victim-producing thoughts in order to construct rational alternatives which will help clients to achieve autonomy and self-acceptance. Crawford and Ellis (1989) suggest that victimization 'may be summed up as, "Ain't it awful this bad thing happened to me. It shouldn't have happened to poor helpless me"' (p.25).

vignette any brief story, excerpt or self-contained passage. REBT therapists use vignettes to illustrate to clients important therapeutic points, e.g. the MONEY EXAMPLE describes how beliefs largely create emotions. Case vignettes can be found in REBT textbooks to illustrate, for example, the cognitive dynamics involved in ANGER (see Dryden, 1990a).

visual aids in disputing instructional devices (e.g. diagram) depending on the sense of sight as a means of challenging clients' irrational ideas. Visual aids can be used to dispute clients' negative GLOBAL EVALUATIONS, e.g. 'Because I failed to get the job, as I absolutely should have done, I'm a complete failure.' By drawing and filling in three circles (see Figure 3) representing a person who is a 'complete failure', a person who is a 'complete success' and a person who is a 'fallible human being', therapists can teach clients the inaccuracy and disturbance-producing potential of such global evaluations; instead they encourage them to understand the complexity of the SELF as well as to accept their own FALLIBILITY.

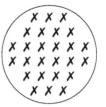

A complete failure

A complete success

A fallible human being

Figure 3 Diagrams showing the futility and inaccuracy of rating oneself on the basis of global evaluations. (see entry: Visual aids in disputing)

visual cues hints or guiding suggestions which involve the sense of sight. Cues can be used by clients to remind them to carry out their HOMEWORK tasks (e.g. leaving messages on the fridge door) or to DISPUTE their irrational beliefs (e.g. a client imagining his former army sergeant yelling at him to 'dispute those bloody beliefs!'). Such visual cues can help clients to start the process that will eventually bring them EMOTIONAL INSIGHT into their problems.

visual models imagining or observing specifically designed situations or illustrations in order to teach clients rational ideas. For examples of visual models see 'LFT SPLASH' and 'BIG I/LITTLE I' DIAGRAM.

vivid language striking, lively, vigorous use of words, expressions, phrases, etc. Dryden (1987a, p.139) has 'found that one of the major benefits of vivid nonprofane language is that clients remember these vivid expressions, or catchphrases, and can use them as shorthand ways of disputing irrational beliefs in their everyday lives'. Examples of vivid language used in disputing might include 'delay now, suffer later' for overcoming PROCRASTINATION and 'Robert the Rule Maker' (Wessler & Wessler, 1980, p.147) to remind a client to give up his anger-producing demands on others.

vivid REBT practising this therapeutic approach in a striking, lively, fresh and memorable way. Examples of vivid REBT include SIMULATION, FLAMBOYANT THERAPIST ACTIONS and THERAPIST SELF-DISCLOSURE. Vivid REBT is one way of fully engaging clients' attention and making therapy a stimulating and entertaining experience for them as well as the likelihood of producing a successful therapeutic outcome. However, the indiscriminate use of vivid REBT can lead to some clients feeling overwhelmed by such a 'dazzling' display and thereby have little or no therapeutic impact upon them. Also some therapists might forget that their primary purpose is to help clients and not to entertain themselves. Whenever vivid REBT is practised, it is important for therapists to obtain FEEDBACK from their clients on the effectiveness of such an approach (see Dryden, 1990b).

want flexible and goal-oriented evaluative belief, see PREFERENCE.

'warm cognitions' these are evaluative rational beliefs in the form of preferences and wishes and usually lead to emotional and behavioural stability, e.g. 'I would prefer you not to behave like that but there is no reason why you must not do so. I deplore your behaviour but not you' – such a view is likely to produce annoyance followed by assertion. Individuals can 'increase the temperature' of their warm cognitions by TRANSMUTING their preferences into demands and thereby creating 'HOT COGNITIONS' which have the potential for emotional disturbance (see 'COLD COGNITIONS').

warmth displaying attachment, intimacy, affection to others. REBT therapists generally refrain from showing clients undue warmth. This occurs for two major reasons. First, therapists may unwittingly reinforce some clients' dire NEEDS for love and approval and thereby help them to FEEL BETTER but not to GET BETTER, i.e. their underlying disturbance-producing ideas remain intact. Second, therapists may unwittingly strengthen some clients' LOW FRUSTRATION TOLERANCE beliefs that they need lots of support in tackling their problems and thereby avoid the hard work necessary to take responsibility for their own problems. REBT therapists are not absolutely against showing undue warmth and may consider it appropriate with certain clients, e.g. suicidal ones (see Dryden & Ellis, 1985).

'what if' thinking clients who are afraid of a feared outcome occurring. 'What if' thinking is usually associated with ANXIETY, e.g. 'What if I do lose control of myself during the meeting, as I must not do. It would be awful'. REBT therapists encourage clients to ASSUME THE WORST has happened and see themselves coping with the situation by replacing their musturbatory (MUSTS) thinking with PREFERENCES, e.g. 'I would strongly prefer not to lose control during the meeting but there is no reason why it must not happen. It would be an unpleasant experience but not a terrible one.' By seeing himself coping with the feared event, the client has removed the 'horror' (emotional disturbance) from it. The client can also consider whether the effects of such an event would be time-limited or lifelong thereby introducing a realistic appraisal of the event's consequences. 'What if' thinking eventually teaches clients how to ANTI-AWFULISE.

what is going on (WIGO) accepting the world as it actually is rather than demanding how it should be. Accepting empirical reality does not mean resignation or passivity in the face of it, nor does it mean condoning it if it is negative. Clients are encouraged to become PERSONAL SCIENTISTS and seek evidence that their beliefs are empirically consistent with reality, e.g. 'I must not make mistakes'. Through such checking, clients can construct realistic and goal-oriented beliefs which will help to make them less prone to emotional upsets (see SCIENTIFIC THINKING).

'why?' questions questions which attempt to discover causes, reasons, purposes, etc., e.g. 'Why do you never speak up in groups?' The judicious use of 'why' questions during DISPUTING. 'may be particularly fruitful. The answer to a 'why' question requires proof or justification of a belief, and since there is no proof for irrational beliefs, the patient may see the logic for giving them up' (Walen, DiGiuseppe & Dryden, 1992, p.159). 'Why' questions can be used to facilitate the process of INFERENCE CHAINING when 'THEN WHAT?' QUESTIONS have proved unhelpful, e.g. Client: He might ignore me; Therapist: Let's assume that he does. Then what? Client: I'd get angry; Therapist: Then what?; Client: I'd just get angry. That's all; Therapist: Why would you get angry?; Client: Because it means he doesn't love me any more. The 'why' question has provided the therapist with further inferences in his search for the client's most clinically relevant one. Too many 'why' questions can put clients on the defensive, turn the therapist into a prosecutor and transform the counselling setting into a courtroom.

wilfully resistant clients clients who deliberately and obstinately fight against therapy and frequently attempt to initiate and win power struggles with the therapist. To gain such clients' cooperation, ELLIS (1985a) suggests several approaches including: the therapist showing her clients that her own ego is not involved in the struggle and therefore she will not be unduly upset if the clients win; the therapist informing her

clients that they can play such games if they wish but it is they not her who will suffer because they will remain emotionally disturbed. Once clients' cooperation has been gained, therapists can DISPUTE the irrational ideas underlying their wilful resistance, e.g. 'I must win every argument otherwise this will prove I'm weak and spineless' (see ARGUING).

willpower mental strength or control over one's wishes, actions, etc., e.g. 'You must have great willpower to be able to train every day'. Clients who complain that they lack the willpower to achieve their goals in life can be shown to have, among others, beliefs of helplessness (e.g. 'Nothing I do will make the slightest difference'), immutability (e.g. 'I was born unhappy. You can't fight nature') and LOW FRUSTRATION TOLERANCE (e.g. 'It's so hard to change. I just haven't got the strength for it'). By disputing these irrational ideas and following a rational philosophy of living, clients can develop considerable willpower not only to overcome their present problems but also to achieve SELF-ACTUALIZATION.

'wise rabbi' story the tale of a sage religious teacher who taught others that things in life can always be worse. The point of the story is to encourage clients to stop AWFULISING about their life conditions and thereby make a nondisturbed realistic appraisal of them. It is important for therapists to obtain FEEDBACK from clients to discover if they have understood the moral of the story. The story of the wise rabbi is an example of the REBT therapist as RACONTEUR (see Dryden & Yankura, 1993).

wish flexible and goal-oriented evaluative belief (see PREFERENCE).

witticism cleverly witty remark. Witticisms are aimed at clients' irrational ideas and not at the clients themselves, e.g. a man who is relentlessly self-denigratory can be asked if he lives in self-Downing

Street. Some clients may interpret a therapist's witticisms as insults so therapists should ascertain if clients find these remarks both funny and therapeutically relevant to their problems. Witticisms are used as an adjunct to cognitive DISPUTING techniques.

workaholism compulsion to work excessively or unrelentingly. REBT views workaholics as individuals who are driven by the rigid DEMANDS that they place on themselves, e.g. 'I have to work this hard to prove I'm not a failure'; 'I must work all the time. I can't stand boredom'. Such demands can lead to some workaholics finding little real pleasure in their work (e.g. 'It's never good enough, as it should be'), developing problems in their interpersonal relationships both at home and work, increasing their chances of emotional disturbance (e.g. anxiety, anger, depression) and of physical problems (e.g. a heart attack). By challenging and changing these rigid ideas, the workaholic can learn how to become a non-compulsive workaphile who 'works because he or she actively enjoys working and the results that come from it ... [and] strongly prefers effort to idleness or relaxation, but can be quite happy without it, though less happy than when actively engaged in meaningful work' (Dryden & Gordon, 1993, p.123). By demonstrating to themselves that their personal worth is not contingent upon their work (or anything else), workaphiles introduce flexibility and self-acceptance into their lives.

working alliance see ALLIANCE.

working hypothesis the therapist's assumption(s) about a client's disturbance-producing ideas which serve as a basis for further exploration, e.g. 'I think at the root of her anxiety is a demand for certainty'. The therapist seeks logical and empirical evidence to support, reject or modify his working hypothesis – DISPUTING is usually only effective when the therapist is challenging the correct irrational belief. Therapists should be wary of only selecting evidence that they believe supports their hypothesis: this not only undermines the SCIENTIFIC approach of REBT but also indicates the presence of irrational beliefs in the therapist, e.g. 'My hypothesis must be right otherwise this proves how incompetent and useless I am both as a therapist and as a person' (see HYPOTHESIS TESTING).

working-through the process whereby clients repeatedly and forcefully challenge their irrational beliefs in a variety of problematic situations in order to internalise a rational philosophy of living which will effect lasting therapeutic change. Working through enables clients to strengthen their conviction in their RATIONAL BELIEFS and weaken or extinguish their conviction in their IRRATIONAL BELIEFS; in other words, working through is the bridge from INTELLECTUAL INSIGHT to EMOTIONAL INSIGHT. Multimodal HOMEWORK tasks can provide clients with increasing opportunities and confidence to practise SELF-THERAPY and thereby set the stage for TERMINATION. Working through also involves the therapist explaining to clients the NON-LINEAR MODEL OF CHANGE, i.e. the path of continuing progress is not a straight or smooth one and the need for lifelong hard work to maintain their therapeutic gains and thereby avoid or minimise BACKSLIDING.

workplace setting for paid/unpaid employment. Introducing REBT concepts into the workplace started as early as 1967 when Ellis and Blum recommended 'Rational Training' to improve management-labour relations; Ellis's 1972 book *Executive Leadership* looked at how business executives could increase their personal efficiency and effectiveness. Eventually, during the 1970s, the Institute for RET in New York set up its own corporate services division to take REBT into the workplace for management training and, more ambitiously, to influence corporate cultures. REBT is a DOUBLE SYSTEMS THERAPY which first looks at how employees can undisturb themselves emotionally over workplace problems (e.g. anxiety about new responsibilities) before looking at practical ways of tackling the problems (e.g. prioritising the new responsibilities rather than being overwhelmed by them all at once). When REBT is used in the workplace, the word 'therapy' is removed and the 'focus in training is always on the relation of self-defeating beliefs to low productivity, not on irrationality and emotional consequences' (DiMattia, 1991, p.309). Therefore REBT becomes Rational Effectiveness Training or Rational-Emotive Training. Organisations using REBT can expect to have 'a more efficient and lasting method of dealing with motivating workers and establishing a flexible work force able to problem-solve rather than react to daily crises' (*ibid.* p.316).

workshop in problems of daily living SEE FRIDAY NIGHT WORKSHOP.

'worst bet' hypothesis clients who make the most adverse inference(s) about themselves, others or the world based on the immediately available information, e.g. a wife who sees her husband talking to another woman assumes 'He no longer loves me. Our marriage is finished.' REBT views 'worst bet' hypotheses or inferences as not directly causing emotional problems but stemming from underlying disturbance-producing MUSTS, e.g. 'He must love me. It would be awful if our marriage was finished.' Clients can be shown that the musts and their DERIVATIVES are the real target for therapeutic intervention (see 'BEST BET' HYPOTHESIS).

'worst case' scenario see ASSUMING THE WORST.

world view general attitude towards life and one's relationship with it; global outlook. Some clients may not be con-

sciously aware of the self-defeating ideas contained within their world view (e.g. 'Life should be easy and straightforward. I can't stand hassle') and REBT therapists retrieve such ideas from clients' PRECONSCIOUS in order to subject them to logical and empirical scrutiny and examine their usefulness. For some clients, therapy may be the first occasion in their lives when the EPISTEMOLOGICAL basis for their world view is rigorously tested. By making modifications in their world view, clients can find it is now more self-helping than self-defeating.

worthlessness state or condition of viewing oneself or others as having no use, value, importance, etc. Clients frequently damn themselves on the basis of certain actions or traits, e.g. 'Because I lost my job, as I absolutely shouldn't have done, this proves I'm worthless.' Such self-RATING can frequently lead to emotional disturbances such as DEPRESSION and SHAME. Clients are encouraged to rate only their actions or traits insofar as they help or hinder the attainment of their goals, e.g. the client might label his poor time-keeping as a 'worthless' or 'unhelpful' attribute. Clients are taught that the SELF is far too complex to be given a single global rating such as 'worthless' no matter how many times, for example, a person loses her job; and such self-denigration does not help clients to tackle their problems constructively. REBT therapists refrain from statements of 'worth' as these imply a measurement of the self, e.g. 'You are worth a great deal because you have a family and friends'; instead they encourage clients to ACCEPT themselves unconditionally as FALLIBLE human beings.

written essays prose compositions on particular subjects written by clients to help them strengthen their rational beliefs and weaken their irrational ones. For example, clients may write down challenges to an irrational belief such as 'I must always succeed otherwise this proves I am a failure' or increase their understanding of human FALLIBILITY by describing 'Why my boss should be a person who is lazy' rather than usually raging against why he should not be. Written essays are given as part of cognitive HOMEWORK assignments (see Walen, DiGiuseppe & Dryden, 1992).

written self-help forms forms which act as guides to the ABCDE model of emotional and behavioural disturbance and their remediation. After being taught how to use them, clients fill in the forms between therapy sessions (usually as part of cognitive HOMEWORK assignments) in order to develop their skills at identifying, challenging and changing their irrational beliefs to rational beliefs. These forms can be lifelong tools for clients to use when they are emotionally upset.

'yes, but' statements clients who seemingly accept their own or the therapist's rationale for constructive change yet express doubt or ambivalence about it. REBT therapists can use the BUT-REBUTTAL METHOD to 'wear down' clients' 'yes, but' statements, e.g. Client: Yes I want to engage in public speaking but I must have the confidence first; Therapist: You're putting the cart before the horse. Confidence usually comes after you've undertaken some public speaking engagements; Client: Yes, that's probably true, but what happens if I make a fool of myself? I could never do another one; Therapist: If you're prepared to learn by trial and error, accept yourself for making mistakes, it's more likely that your skill at public speaking will increase along with your enthusiasm for doing them. The therapist rebuts clients' 'buts' until they are exhausted. Such a method encourages them to make a commitment to change and the hard work usually associated with it. Clients can learn to challenge their 'yes, but' statements as part of their cognitive HOMEWORK assignments.

'you are what you do' thinking clients who believe that their actions equal their character, e.g. 'I failed to accomplish an important task so this means I'm a failure'. Such thinking can lead to emotional upsets such as DEPRESSION or SHAME. The task of the therapist is to convince clients that their actions can never adequately sum up or equal the totality and complexity of the SELF and therefore their self-downing is neither legitimate nor helpful. ANALOGIES can be used to illustrate this point, e.g. Young (1988) suggests asking clients if they would get rid of their cars on the basis of a flat tyre. Most clients agree this would be ridiculous, but Young points out this is what they are doing to themselves on the basis of a particular action: they have consigned themselves to the dustbin. Clients can learn SEMANTIC PRECISION in order to describe more accurately their disappointments in life, e.g. 'I failed to accomplish an important task but this certainly does not mean I'm a failure as a person.'

zeal, therapeutic therapist eagerness and ardent interest in helping clients overcome their problems. REBT takes an ACTIVE-DIRECTIVE approach to uncovering clients' musturbatory (MUSTS) thinking and using FORCE AND ENERGY to surrender it and replace it with a rational philosophy of living. Therapeutic zeal helps clients to achieve, ideally, an ELEGANT SOLUTION to their problems in a relatively short period and thereby reduce the time spent emotionally distressed. Such zeal should be tempered by the clients' LEARNING and INTERACTIVE STYLES so that counsellor and client keep in therapeutic step. Therapists whose zeal drives therapy to the detriment of the working ALLIANCE may have LOW FRUSTRATION TOLERANCE beliefs, e.g. 'I can't stand the slow pace of therapy. Why the hell don't these clients buck themselves up!' REBT therapists see responsible zeal as an effective means of PERSUASION: encouraging, pushing, urging clients to bring about change in their lives (see EFFICIENCY).

References

Adler, A. (1964). *Social Interest: A Challenge to Mankind*. New York: Capricorn.

Bard, J.A. (1980). *Rational-Emotive Therapy in Practice*. Champaign, IL: Research Press.

Barlow, D.H., & Craske, M.G. (1989). *Mastery of Your Anxiety and Panic*. Albany, N.Y: Graywind Publications; Center for Stress and Anxiety Disorders, State University of New York at Albany.

Beck, A.T., Rush, A.J., Shaw, B.F. and Emery, G. (1979). *Cognitive Therapy of Depression*. New York: Guilford.

Bernard, M.E. (1986). *Staying Rational in an Irrational World: Albert Ellis and Rational-Emotive Therapy*. Carlton, Australia: McCulloch.

Bernard, M.E. & DiGiuseppe, R. (Eds) (1989). *Inside Rational-Emotive Therapy*. San Diego, CA: Academic Press.

Bernard, M.E. & Joyce, M.R. (1991). RET with children and adolescents. In: Bernard, M.E. (Ed.), *Using Rational-Emotive Therapy Effectively: A Practitioner's Guide*, pp. 319–347. New York: Plenum Press.

Bessai, J.L. (1977, June). A factored measure of irrational beliefs. Paper presented at the Second National Conference on Rational-Emotive Therapy, Chicago.

Bordin, E.S. (1979). The generalizability of the psychoanalytic concept of the working alliance. *Psychotherapy: Theory, Research and Practice* 16, 252–60.

Burns, D.D. (1980). *Feeling Good: The New Mood Therapy*. New York: William Morrow.

Burns, D.D. (1989). *The Feeling Good Handbook*. New York: William Morrow.

Cohen, E.D. (1992). Syllogizing RET: applying formal logic in rational-emotive therapy. *Journal of Rational-Emotive and Cognitive-Behavior Therapy* 10(4), 235–252.

Crawford, T. & Ellis, A. (1989). A dictionary of rational-emotive feelings and behaviors. *Journal of Rational-Emotive and Cognitive-Behavior Therapy* 7(1), 3–28.

DiGiuseppe, R. (1988). Thinking what to feel. In: Dryden, W. & Trower, P. (Eds), *Developments in Rational-Emotive Therapy*, pp 22–29. Milton Keynes: Open University Press.

DiGiuseppe, R. (1991a). Comprehensive cognitive disputing in RET. In: Bernard, M.E. (Ed.), *Using Rational-Emotive Therapy Effectively: A Practitioner's Guide*, pp. 173–195. New York: Plenum.

DiGiuseppe, R. (1991b). A rational-emotive model of assessment. In: Bernard, M.E. (Ed.), *Using Rational-Emotive Therapy Effectively: A Practitioner's Guide*, pp. 151–172. New York: Plenum.

DiGiuseppe, R. & Zeeve, C. (1985). Marriage: rational-emotive couples counseling. In: Ellis, A. & Bernard, M.E. (Eds), *Clinical Applications of Rational-Emotive Therapy*, pp. 55–80. New York: Plenum.

DiMattia, D.J. (1991). Using RET effectively in the workplace. In: Bernard, M.E. (Ed.), *Using Rational-Emotive Therapy: A Practitioner's Guide*, pp. 303–317. New York: Plenum.

Dryden, W. (1980, June 7). Nightmares and fun. Paper presented at the Third National Conference on Rational-Emotive Therapy, New York.

Dryden, W. (1984a). *Rational-Emotive Therapy: Fundamentals and Innovations*. Beckenham, Kent: Croom Helm.

Dryden, W. (Ed.) (1984b). *Individual Therapy in Britain*. London: Harper & Row.

Dryden, W. (1986). Language and meaning in rational-emotive therapy. In: Dryden, W. & Trower, P. (Eds), *Rational-Emotive Therapy: Recent Developments in Theory and Practice*. Bristol: Institute for RET (UK).

Dryden, W. (1987a). *Counselling Individuals: The Rational-Emotive Approach*. London: Taylor & Francis.

Dryden, W. (1987b). *Current Issues in Rational-Emotive Therapy*. Beckenham, Kent: Croom Helm.

Dryden, W. (1989). The use of chaining in rational-emotive therapy. *Journal of Rational-Emotive and Cognitive-Behavior Therapy* 7(2), 59–66.

Dryden, W. (1990a). *Dealing With Anger Problems: Rational-Emotive Therapeutic Interventions*. Sarasota, FL: Professional Resource Exchange.

Dryden, W. (1990b). *Creativity in Rational-Emotive Therapy*. Loughton, Essex: Gale Centre Publications.

Dryden, W. (1990c). *Rational-Emotive Counselling in Action*. London: Sage.

Dryden, W. (1991a). *Reason and Therapeutic Change*. London: Whurr.

Dryden, W. (1991b). *A Dialogue With Albert Ellis: Against Dogma*. Buckingham: Open University Press.

Dryden, W. (1992). *The Incredible Sulk*. London: Sheldon Press.

Dryden, W. (1993). *Reflections on Counselling*. London: Whurr.

Dryden, W. (1994a). *Overcoming Guilt*. London: Sheldon Press.

Dryden, W. (1994b). *Invitation to Rational-Emotive Psychology*. London: Whurr.

Dryden, W. (1994c). *Progress in Rational Emotive Behaviour Therapy*. London: Whurr.

Dryden, W. & Backx, W. (1987). Problems in living: the friday night workshop. In: Dryden, W., (Ed.), *Current Issues in Rational-Emotive Therapy*, pp. 154–170. Beckenham, Kent: Croom Helm.

Dryden, W. & DiGiuseppe, R. (1990). *A Primer on Rational-Emotive Therapy*. Champaign, IL: Research Press.

Dryden, W. & Ellis, A. (1985). Dilemmas in giving warmth or love to clients (Interview). In: Dryden, W. (Ed.), *Therapists' Dilemmas*, pp. 5–16. London: Harper & Row.

Dryden, W. & Gordon, J. (1990). *What is Rational-Emotive Therapy? A Personal and Practical Guide*. Loughton, Essex: Gale Centre Publications.

Dryden, W. & Gordon, J. (1993a). *Beating the Comfort Trap*. London: Sheldon Press.

Dryden, W. & Gordon, J. (1993b). *Peak Performance: Become More Effective at Work*. Didcot, Oxfordshire: Mercury Business Books.

Dryden, W., Neenan, M. & Doggart, L. (1993). Professorial rationality: An interview with Windy Dryden. *The Rational-Emotive Therapist: Journal of the Association for Rational-Emotive Therapists* 1(1), 5–11.

Dryden, W. & Yankura, J. (1992). *Daring To Be Myself: A Case Study in Rational-Emotive Therapy*. Buckingham: Open University Press.

Dryden, W. & Yankura, J. (1993). *Counselling Individuals: A Rational-Emotive Handbook*, 2nd edition. London: Whurr.

Dunlap, K. (1932). *Habits: Their Making and Unmaking*. New York: Liveright.

Edwards, G. (1992). Rebuttal to Albert Ellis. In: Dryden, W. & Feltham, C. (Eds), *Psychotherapy and its Discontents*, pp. 220–224. Buckingham: Open University Press.

Ellis, A. (1962). *Reason and Emotion in Psychotherapy*. Secaucus, NJ: Lyle Stuart.

Ellis, A. (1963). Toward a more precise definition of 'emotional' and 'intellectual' insight. *Psychological Reports* 13, 125–126.

Ellis, A. (1965). *Homosexuality*. Secaucus, NJ: Lyle Stuart.

Ellis, A. (1972). *Executive Leadership: A Rational Approach*. New York: Institute for Rational Living.

Ellis, A. (1973a). Emotional education at the living school. In: Ohlsen, M. M. (Ed.), *Counseling Children in Groups*. New York: Holt, Rinehart & Winston.

Ellis, A. (1973b). The no cop-out therapy. *Psychology Today* 7(2), 56–62.

Ellis, A. (1976). The biological basis of human irrationality. *Journal of Individual Psychology* 32, 145–168.

Ellis, A. (1977a). *Anger – How to Live With and Without it*. Secaucus, NJ: Citadel Press.

Ellis, A. (1977b). Fun as psychotherapy. *Rational Living* 12(1), 2–6.

Ellis, A. (singer) (1977c). *A Garland of Rational Songs* (cassette recording). New York: Institute for Rational-Emotive Therapy.

Ellis, A. (1980a). An overview of the clinical theory of rational-emotive therapy. In: Grieger, R. & Boyd, J. (Eds), *Rational-Emotive Therapy: A Skills-Based Approach*. New York: Van Nostrand Reinhold.

Ellis, E. (1980b). Rational-emotive therapy and cognitive-behavior therapy: similarities and differences. *Cognitive Therapy and Research* 4 (4), 325–340.

Ellis, A. (1982). Must most psychotherapists remain as incompetent as they now are? *Journal of Contemporary Psychotherapy* 13 (1), 17–28.

Ellis, A. (1983a). The philosophic implications and dangers of some popular behavior therapy techniques. In: Rosenbaum, M., Franks, C.M. & Jaffe, Y. (Eds), *Perspectives on Behavior Therapy in the Eighties*, pp. 138–151. New York: Springer.

Ellis, A. (1983b). Failures in rational-emotive therapy. In: Foa, E.B. & Emmelkamp, P.M.G. (Eds), *Failures in Behavior Therapy*, pp. 159–171. New York: Wiley.

Ellis, A. (1983c). *The Case Against Religiosity*. New York: Institute for Rational-Emotive Therapy.

Ellis, A. (1984a). *How to Maintain and Enhance Your Rational-Emotive Therapy Gains*. New York: Institute for Rational-Emotive Therapy.

Ellis, A. (1984b). *Intellectual Fascism*. New York: Institute for Rational-Emotive Therapy.

Ellis, A. (1985a). *Overcoming Resistance: Rational-Emotive Therapy with Difficult Clients*. New York: Springer.

Ellis, A. (1985b). Love and its problems. In: Ellis, A. & Bernard, M.E. (Eds), *Clinical Applications of Rational-Emotive Therapy*, pp. 31–53. New York: Plenum.

Ellis, A. (1985c). Expanding the ABC's of rational-emotive therapy. In: Mahoney, M.J. & Freeman, A. (Eds), *Cognition and Psychotherapy*, pp. 313–323. New York: Plenum.

Ellis, A. (1987a). Ask Dr. Ellis. *Journal of Rational-Emotive Therapy* 5(2), 135–137.

Ellis, A. (1987b). Ask Dr. Ellis. *Journal of Rational-Emotive Therapy* 5(3), 194–196 and 197–199.

Ellis, A. (1988). *How to Stubbornly Refuse to Make Yourself Miserable About Anything – Yes, Anything!* Secaucus, NJ: Lyle Stuart.

Ellis, A. (1989a). Ineffective consumerism in the cognitive-behavioural therapies and in general psychotherapy. In: Dryden, W. & Trower, P. (Eds), *Cognitive Psychotherapy: Stasis and Change*, pp. 159–174, London: Cassell.

Ellis, A. (1989b). Introduction. In: Trimpey, J. (Ed.), *Rational Recovery from Alcoholism: The Small Book*, 2nd edition, pp. 5–6. Lotus, CA: Lotus Press.

Ellis, A. (1990). Is rational-emotive therapy (RET) 'rationalist' or 'constructivist'? *Journal of Rational-Emotive and Cognitive-Behavior Therapy*, 8(3), 169–193.

Ellis, A. (1991). The revised ABC's of rational-emotive therapy (RET). *Journal of Rational-Emotive and Cognitive-Behavior Therapy* 9(3), 139–172.

Ellis, A. (1992). My current views on rational-emotive therapy (RET) and religiousness. *Journal of Rational-Emotive and Cognitive-Behavior Therapy* 10(1), 37–40.

Ellis, A. (1993a). Fundamentals of rational-emotive therapy for the 1990s. In: Dryden, W. & Hill, L.K. (Eds), *Innovations in Rational-Emotive Therapy*, pp. 1–32. London: Sage.

Ellis, A. (1993b). Letter to mental health professionals. *Catalogue of Institute for Rational-Emotive Therapy*, 1993–1994, p.2.

Ellis, A. & Abrahms, E. (1978). *Brief Psychotherapy in Medical and Health Practice*. New York: Springer.

Ellis, A. & Bernard, M.E. (Eds) (1985). *Clinical Applications of Rational-Emotive Therapy*. New York: Plenum.

Ellis, A. & Blum, M.L. (1967). Rational training: a new method of facilitating management and labor relations. *Psychological Reports* 20, 1267–84.

Ellis, A. & Dames, J. (1991). Counseling in the classroom: interview with Albert Ellis *Journal of Rational-Emotive and Cognitive-Behavior Therapy* 9(4), 247–263.

Ellis, A. & Dryden, W. (1987). *The Practice of Rational-Emotive Therapy*. New York: Springer.

Ellis, A. & Knaus, W. (1977). *Overcoming Procrastination*. New York: Institute for Rational Living.

Ellis, A., McInerney, J.F., DiGiuseppe, R. & Yeager, R.J. (1988). *Rational-Emotive Therapy with Alcoholics and Substance Abusers*. New York: Pergamon Press.

Ellis, A., Sichel, J.L., Yeager, R.J., DiMattia, D.J. & DiGiuseppe, R. (1989). *Rational-Emotive Couples Therapy*. New York: Pergamon Press.

Ellis, A. & Yeager, R.J. (1989). *Why Some Therapies Don't Work: The Dangers of Transpersonal Psychology*. Buffalo, NY: Prometheus.

Epictetus. (1948). *Enchiridion*. Indianapolis, IN: Bobbs-Merrill.

Festinger, L. (1957). *A Theory of Cognitive Dissonance*. Evanston, IL: Row, Peterson.

Fontana, D. (1989). *Managing Stress*. London: Routledge.

Gilmore, I. (1986). An exposition and development of the debate on the nature of the distinction between appropriate and inappropriate beliefs in rational-emotive therapy. *Journal of Rational-Emotive Therapy* 4, 155–168.

Golden, W.L. & Dryden, W. (1986). Cognitive-behavioural therapies: commonalities, divergences and future developments. In: Dryden, W. & Golden, W. (Eds), *Cognitive-Behavioural Approaches to Psychotherapy*, pp. 356–378. London: Harper & Row.

Golden, W.L. & Friedberg, F. (1986). Cognitive-behavioural hypnotherapy. In: Dryden, W. & Golden, W. (Eds), *Cognitive-Behavioural Approaches to Psychotherapy*, pp. 290–319. London: Harper & Row.

Goncalves, O.F. & Craine, M.H. (1990). The use of metaphors in cognitive therapy. *Journal of Cognitive Psychotherapy* 4(2), 135–149.

Greenwood, V. (1985). RET and substance abuse. In: Ellis, A. & Bernard, M.E. (Eds), *Clinical Applications of Rational-Emotive Therapy*, pp. 209–235. New York: Plenum Press.

Grieger, R.M. (1991). Keys to effective RET. In: Bernard, M.E. (Ed.), *Using Rational-Emotive Therapy Effectively: A Practitioner's Guide*, pp. 35-67. New York: Plenum Press.

Grieger, R. & Boyd, J. (1980). *Rational-Emotive Therapy: A Skills-Based Approach*. New York: Van Nostrand Reinhold.

Guidano, V.F. (1988). A systems, process-oriented approach to cognitive therapy. In: Dobson, K.S. (Ed.), *Handbook of Cognitive-Behavioral Therapies*, pp. 307–356. New York: Guilford.

Haaga, D.A.F., Dryden, W. & Dancey, C.P. (1991). Measurement of rational-emotive therapy in outcome studies. *Journal of Rational-Emotive and Cognitive-Behavior Therapy* 9(2), 73–93.

Harrell, T.H., Chambless, D.L. & Calhoun, J.F. (1981). Correlational relationships between self-statements and affective states. *Cognitive Therapy and Research* 5, 159–173.

Hauck, P, (1966). The neurotic agreement in psychotherapy. *Rational Living* 1(1), 31–34.

Hauck, P. (1974). *Depression: Why it Happens and How to Overcome It*. London: Sheldon Press.

Hauck, P. (1980a). *Calm Down: How to Cope with Frustration and Anger*. London: Sheldon Press.

Hauck, P. (1980b). *Brief Counseling with RET*. Philadelphia, PA: Westminster Press.

Hauck, P. (1981a). *Why Be Afraid?* London: Sheldon Press.

Hauck, P. (1981b). *Making Marriage Work*. London: Sheldon Press.

Hauck, P. (1982). *Jealousy: Why it Happens and How to Overcome It*. London: Sheldon Press.

Hauck, P. (1983). *How to Love and be Loved*. London: Sheldon Press.

Hauck, P. (1985). Religion and RET: friends or foes? In: Ellis, A. & Bernard, M.E. (Eds), *Clinical Applications of Rational-Emotive Therapy*, pp. 237–255. New York: Plenum Press.

Hauck, P. (1991). RET and the assertive process. In: Bernard, M.E., (Ed.), *Using Rational-Emotive Therapy Effectively: A Practitioner's Guide*, pp. 197–218. New York: Plenum Press.

Heidegger, M. (1949). *Existence and Being*. Chicago: Henry Regnery.

Horney, K. (1950). *Neurosis and Human Growth*. New York: Norton.

Jacobs, S. (1989). Karl Popper and Albert Ellis: their ideas on psychology and rationality compared. *Journal of Rational-Emotive and Cognitive-Behavior Therapy* 7(3), 173–185.

Jones, R. (1968). A factored measure of Ellis' irrational belief sytem with personality and maladjustment correlates. Unpublished doctoral dissertation. Texas Technological University, Lubbock.

Kelly, G.A. (1955). *The Psychology of Personal Constructs*. New York: Norton.

Kimmel, J. (1976). The rational barb in the treatment of social rejection. *Rational Living* 11, 23–25.

Knaus, W.J. & Haberstroh, N. (1993). A rational-emotive education program to help disruptive mentally retarded clients develop self-control. In: Dryden, W. & Hill, L.K. (Eds), *Innovations in Rational-Emotive Therapy*, pp. 201–217. London: Sage.

Kwee, M.G.T. & Lazarus, A.A. (1986). Multimodal therapy: the cognitive-behavioural tradition and beyond. In: Dryden, W. & Golden, W. (Eds), *Cognitive-Behavioural Approaches to Psychotherapy*, pp. 320–355. London: Harper & Row.

Lazarus, A.A. (1977). Toward an egoless state of being. In: Ellis, A. & Grieger, R. (Eds), *Handbook of Rational-Emotive Therapy*. New York: Springer.

Lazarus, A.A. (1981). *The Practice of Multimodal Therapy*. New York: McGraw-Hill.

Lazarus, A.A. & Lazarus, C.N. (1991). *Multimodal Life History Inventory*. Champaign, IL: Research Press.

Macaskill, N.D. (1989). Educating clients about rational-emotive therapy. In: Dryden, W. & Trower, P. (Eds), *Cognitive Psychotherapy: Stasis and Change*, pp. 87–98. London: Cassell.

Mahoney, M.J. (1988). The cognitive sciences and psychotherapy: patterns in a developing relationship. In: Dobson, K.S. (Ed.), *Handbook of Cognitive-Behavioral Therapies*, pp. 357–386. New York: Guilford.

Malouff, J. & Schutte, N. (1986). Development and validation of a measure of irrational belief. *Journal of Consulting and Clinical Psychology* 54, 860–862.

Maultsby, M.C. Jr. (1975). *Help Yourself to Happiness: Through Rational Self-Counseling*. New York: Institute for RET.

Meichenbaum, D. (1985). *Stress Inoculation Training*. New York: Pergamon Press.

Moore, R.H. (1983). Inference as 'A' in RET. *British Journal of Cognitive Psychotherapy* 1(2), 17–23.

Palmer, S., Dryden, W. & Ellis, A. (1993). Ellis on REBT (Interview). *The Rational-Emotive Therapist: Journal of the Association for Rational Emotive Behaviour Therapists* 1(2), 44–52.

Palmer, S. & Ellis, A. (1993). In the counsellor's chair: interview with Albert Ellis. *Journal of the British Association for Counselling* 4(3), 171–174.

Popper, K.R. (1959). *The Logic of Scientific Discovery*. New York: Harper & Bros.

Popper, K.R. (1963). *Conjectures and Refutations*. New York: Harper & Bros.

Popper, K.R. (1966). *The Open Society and its Enemies*, vol. 2, 5th edition. London: Routledge & Kegan Paul.

Robb, H.B. & Warren, R. (1990). Irrational belief tests: new insights, new directions. *Journal of Cognitive Psychotherapy* 4(3), 303–311.

Shorkey, C.T. & Whiteman, V.L. (1977). Development of the rational behavior inventory: initial validity and reliability. *Educational and Psychological Measurement* 37, 527–534.

Silverman, M.S., McCarthy, M. & McGovern, T. (1992). A review of outcome studies of rational-emotive therapy from 1982–1989.

Journal of Rational-Emotive & Cognitive-Behavior Therapy **10**(3), 111–186.

Thorpe, G.L., Parker, J.D. & Barnes, G.S. (1992). The common beliefs survey III and its subscales: discriminant validity in clinical and nonclinical subjects. *Journal of Rational-Emotive and Cognitive-Behavior Therapy* **10**(2), 95–104.

Tosi, D.J. & Marzella, J.N. (1977). Rational stage directed therapy. In: Wolfe, J.L. & Brand, E. (Eds), *Twenty Years of Rational Therapy*, pp. 95–114. New York: Institute for Rational Living.

Trimpey, J. (1989). *Rational Recovery from Alcoholism: The Small Book*, 2nd edition. Lotus, CA: Lotus Press.

Vernon, A. (1989). *Thinking, Feeling, Behaving. An Emotional Education Curriculum for Children Grades 7–12*. Champaign, IL: Research Press.

Vesey, G. & Foulkes, P. (1990). *Dictionary of Philosophy*. London: Collins.

Walen, S.R., DiGiuseppe, R. & Dryden, W. (1992). *A Practitioner's Guide to Rational-Emotive Therapy*, 2nd edition. New York: Oxford University Press.

Warren, R. & Zgourides, G. (1989). Further validity and normative data for the Malouff and Schutte belief scale. *Journal of Rational-Emotive and Cognitive-Behavior Therapy* **7**(3), 167–172.

Watson, J.B. & Rayner, R. (1920). Conditioned emotional reactions. *Journal of Experimental Psychology* **3**, 1–14.

Weinrach, S.G. & Ellis, A. (1980). Unconventional therapist: Albert Ellis (Interview). *Personnel and Guidance Journal* **59**, 152–160.

Wessler, R.A. & Wessler, R.L. (1980). *The Principles and Practice of Rational-Emotive Therapy*. San Francisco, CA: Jossey-Bass.

Wolfe, J.L. (1985). Women. In: Ellis, A. & Bernard, M.E. (Eds), *Clinical Applications of Rational-Emotive Therapy*, pp. 101–127. New York: Plenum Press.

Woods, P.J. (1991). Orthodox RET taught effectively with graphics, feedback on irrational beliefs, a structured homework series, and models of disputation. In: Bernard, M.E. (Ed.), *Using Rational-Emotive Therapy Effectively: A Practitioner's Guide*, pp. 69–109. New York: Plenum Press.

Yankura, J. & Dryden, W. (1990). *Doing RET: Albert Ellis in Action*. New York: Springer.

Young, H.S. (1988). Teaching rational self-value concepts to tough customers. In: Dryden, W. & Trower, P. (Eds), *Developments in Rational-Emotive Therapy*, pp. 132–158. Milton Keynes: Open University Press.

Ziegler, D.J. (1989). A critique of rational-emotive theory of personality. In: Bernard, M.E. & DiGiuseppe, R. (Eds), *Inside Rational-Emotive Therapy*, pp. 27–45. San Diego, CA: Academic Press.